D0948895

EXPLORING EPHESIANS

EXPLORING EPHESIANS

JOHN PHILLIPS

LOIZEAUX BROTHERS
Neptune, New Jersey

A Publication of Loizeaux Brothers, Inc.
*A Nonprofit Organization Devoted to the Lord's Work
and to the Spread of His Truth*

Unless otherwise indicated, Scripture quotations in this book
are from the King James version of the Bible.

Quotations from THE NEW TESTAMENT IN MODERN ENGLISH,
Revised Edition by J. B. Phillips are reprinted with the permission of
Macmillan Publishing Company and HarperCollins Publishers Limited.
Copyright © 1958, 1959, 1960, 1972 by J. B. Phillips.

Library of Congress Cataloging-in-Publication Data

Phillips, John, 1927 –
Exploring Ephesians / John Phillips.
Includes bibliographical references.
ISBN 0-87213-650-7 (hard)
1. Bible.   N.T.   Ephesians—Commentaries.   I. Title.
BS2695.3.P48   1993
227'.5077—dc20   93-6579

Printed in the United States of America.
10 9 8 7 6 5 4 3 2 1

CONTENTS

CONTENTS

PREFACE

In some ways the city of Ephesus is unique in the New Testament. It was not a religious center like Jerusalem, a cultural center like Athens, or a political center like Rome. It was a Christian center. Pagans knew the city as a center of heathen activities. Its famous temple of Diana (Artemis) was one of the seven wonders of the ancient world and a source of terrible moral and spiritual pollution. But Ephesus is known around the world today not because of the temple that attracted thousands to its courts and courtesans, not because of its trade, but because of the Biblical truth that was taught there. Ephesus is known to all who know the Bible.

Paul spent several years in Ephesus and a truly great church resulted from his ministry. Paul's final farewell words to the Ephesian elders reveal how diligently he had preached and pastored there (Acts 20). Mark and the apostle John also ministered in Ephesus. Timothy is believed to have been martyred there for denouncing the licentiousness of a feast of Diana.

It was from Ephesus that John was exiled to the offshore island of Patmos. During that exile he wrote to Ephesus one of the letters to the seven churches. In that letter, dictated personally by the ascended Lord, he exposed the church's lack of love for the Lord Jesus (Revelation 2:1-7). Their labors were commended, their loyalty was praised, but their lack of love was lamented. The Lord took this lack of love for Himself so seriously that He warned that if there were no repentance and revival, He would remove the lampstand. Light without love is a barren thing. The Lord has no use for a church that no longer loves Him.

When Paul wrote his Ephesian letter, the events foreseen by John were still over the horizon. Yet the warnings Paul had issued several years before in his farewell to the Ephesian elders at Miletus show that he had his own private fears. The onslaught of a cult at nearby Colossae alerted Paul to growing dangers, but what destroyed the Ephesian church in the end was not falsehood, but formality. It became, so to speak, a cold, fundamental, orthodox, evangelical,

Bible-believing church that lacked even a spark of its original love for Christ.

⦶As we read this Ephesian letter, what impresses us is <u>Paul's</u> <u>emphasis on love</u>. He told us about our blessings, he talked about our behavior, and he warned us about our battles. But it is our Beloved—Christ—who dominates it all.

Come, then; join me in a tour of this letter, perhaps the grandest of all Paul's Epistles. Doctrine will thrill us in the book of Romans and discipline will confront us in Corinthians. We will read of deliverance in Galatians, deception in Colossians, discord in Philippians, duty in Philemon, and discovery in Thessalonians. But <u>in Ephesians devotion is the theme.</u> There Paul was saying, "<u>Take</u> <u>another look at the Beloved. Fall in love with Him afresh. He is the</u> <u>chiefest among ten thousand, the altogether lovely One, fairer than</u> <u>the fair, the glorious Bridegroom of our hearts.</u>"

In His matchless love,
John Phillips

COMPLETE OUTLINE
OF THE EPISTLE TO THE EPHESIANS

I. Introduction (1:1-2)

A. Greetings from Paul (1:1)
    1. The Author (1:1a)
    2. The Audience (1:1b-c)
       a. The Local Church (1:1b)
       b. The Larger Church (1:1c)
B. Grace for All (1:2)

II. The Christian and His Blessings (1:3–3:21)

A. The Realities of the Christian Life (1:3-23)
    1. Where We Stand: Basic Principles (1:3-14)
       a. The Will of the Father (1:3-6)
          (1) The Source of Our Blessings (1:3a)
          (2) The Sphere of Our Blessings (1:3b)
          (3) The Scope of Our Blessings (1:4-5)
             (a) We Have Been Chosen (1:4a)
             (b) We Have Been Changed (1:4b-5)
                i. God Has Removed All Our Sins (1:4b)
                ii. God Has Remade Us As Sons (1:5)
          (4) The Significance of Our Blessings (1:6)
             (a) The Father's Benevolence
             (b) The Father's Beloved
       b. The Work of the Son (1:7-12)
          (1) Redemption (1:7)
             (a) The Person Involved (1:7a)
             (b) The Price Involved (1:7b)
             (c) The Pardon Involved (1:7c)
          (2) Revelation (1:8-9)
             (a) The Divine Perception (1:8)
             (b) The Divine Purpose (1:9)
          (3) Royalty (1:10-11)
             (a) For the Christ (1:10)
             (b) For the Christian (1:11)
          (4) Rejoicing (1:12)
       c. The Witness of the Spirit (1:13-14)

(1) His Word: A Witness to the Christ (1:13a)
(2) His Work: A Witness to the Christian (1:13b-14)
  (a) The Proof of Our Faith (1:13b)
  (b) The Pledge of Our Future (1:14)
2. Why We Stand: Believing Prayer (1:15-23)
  a. A Church-centered Prayer (1:15-16)
  (1) The Cause of It (1:15)
  Paul had heard how they:
  (a) Trusted the Savior (1:15a)
  (b) Treated the Saints (1:15b)
  (2) The Constancy of It (1:16)
  b. A Christ-centered Prayer (1:17-23)
  Paul wanted them to know more of:
  (1) The Person of Christ (1:17)
  (2) The Portion of Christ (1:18)
  (a) Our Hope Is in Him (1:18a)
  (b) His Heritage Is in Us (1:18b)
    i. The Fact of It
    ii. The Fame of It
    iii. The Fullness of It
  (3) The Power of Christ (1:19-21)
  (a) The Direction of It (1:19a)
  (b) The Dimensions of It (1:19b)
  (c) The Demonstration of It (1:20a)
  (d) The Distinction of It (1:20b-21)
    i. All Seats of Power Are Beneath Him (1:20b-21b)
     a. Where He Is Seated (1:20b)
     b. What He Has Subdued (1:21a-b)
      1. All Spiritual Seats of Power (1:21a)
      2. All Secular Seats of Power (1:21b)
    ii. All Spheres of Power Are Before Him (1:21c)
  (4) The Position of Christ (1:22-23)
  Paul wanted us to consider:
  (a) The Lord's Feet (1:22a)
  (b) The Lord's Fullness (1:22b-23)
    i. The Church Finds All Its Fullness in Him,
    the Head (1:22b)
    ii. The Christ Finds All His Fullness in Us,
    the Body (1:23)

B. The Revolution of the Christian Life (2:1-22)
  1. The Great Dispositional Change (2:1-10)
    a. The Past (2:1-3)
    We were:
    (1) Dead (2:1)
    (2) Deluded (2:2a)
    (3) Disobedient (2:2b)

a. Its Uniqueness (4:1-3)
  (1) It Is Undaunted (4:1a)
  (2) It Is Undivided (4:1b-3)
    (a) Its Character (4:1b-2)
    (b) Its Curriculum (4:3)
b. Its Unity (4:4-6)
  (1) Its Functional Unity (4:4a-b)
    (a) The Diverse Life It Shows (4:4a) (One Body)
    (b) The Divine Life It Shares (4:4b) (One Spirit)
  (2) Its Fundamental Unity (4:4c-5)
    (a) Of Calling (4:4c)
    (b) Of Confession (4:5)
      i. "One Lord" (I am saved)
      ii. "One Faith" (I am sure)
      iii. "One Baptism" (I am separated)
  (3) Its Family Unity (4:6)
    One God and Father of us all:
    (a) Absolute in His Power (Over All)
    (b) Absorbed in His Purpose (Through All)
    (c) Abiding in His Presence (In All)
2. The Gifts of the Mystical Body (4:7-13)
  a. Grace to Accompany Gifts (4:7)
  b. Gifts to Accompany Grace (4:8-13)
    (1) The Gifts Assured (4:8-10)
      (a) The Old Testament Promise (4:8)
      (b) The New Testament Proof (4:9-10)
    (2) The Gifts Assigned (4:11-13)
      (a) The Nature of Them (4:11)
      (b) The Need for Them (4:12-13)
        i. The Purpose Involved (4:12)
        ii. The Period Involved (4:13)
3. The Growth of the Mystical Body (4:14-16)
  a. Growth Diabolically Inhibited (4:14)
    (1) Pictures of Their Instability
    (2) Perils of Their Instability
  b. Growth Divinely Inherent (4:15-16)
    (1) The Law of Love (4:15a)
    (2) The Law of Life (4:15b-16)
      (a) The Head Controls (4:15b-16a)
      (b) The Heart Consoles (4:16b)

B. In His Moral Relationships (4:17–5:21)
1. A Complete Deliverance (4:17-24)
  a. A New Life (4:17-21)
    (1) The Sinner's Condition (4:17-19)
      (a) His Intellect Darkened (4:17-18)
      (b) His Inclinations Depraved (4:19)

  (2) The Saint's Conversion (4:20-21)
   (a) The Change (4:20)
   (b) The Challenge (4:21)
 b. A New Look (4:22-24)
  (1) What Must Be Put Off (4:22-23)
   (a) The Old Disposition (4:22a)
   (b) The Old Desires (4:22b)
   (c) The Old Direction (4:23)
  (2) What Must Be Put On (4:24)
2. A Converted Disposition (4:25-26)
 a. A Transformed Tongue (4:25)
 b. A Transformed Temper (4:26)
3. A Conquered Devil (4:27)
4. A Conspicuous Difference (4:28-29)
 a. In Conduct (4:28)
 b. In Conversation (4:29)
5. A Christlike Demeanor (4:30-32)
 a. An Ungrieved Holy Spirit (4:30)
  (1) Who He Is (4:30a)
  (2) What He Does (4:30b)
 b. An Ungrudging Human Spirit (4:31-32)
  (1) Things to Be Discarded (4:31)
  (2) Things to Be Displayed (4:32)
6. A Categorical Demand (5:1-7)
 a. Love Is to Be Enthroned (5:1-2)
  (1) The Exhortation (5:1)
  (2) The Example (5:2)
 b. Lust Is to Be Dethroned (5:3-7)
  (1) God's Demands Are Not to Be Underestimated (5:3-5)
   (a) The Principle Is Underlined (5:3-4)
    The Holy Spirit states:
    i. His Antipathy to Lust (5:3-4a)
     Whether:
     a. Immorality in Our Walk (5:3)
     b. Impurity in Our Talk (5:4a)
    ii. His Antidote to Lust (5:4b)
   (b) The Penalty Is Underlined (5:5)
  (2) God's Demands Are Not to Be Undermined (5:6-7)
   We are to:
   (a) Recognize Deception (5:6)
   (b) Repudiate Deception (5:7)
7. A Convicting Distinction (5:8-14)
 a. Where Light Radiates (5:8-10)
  It brings:
  (1) A Change of Character (5:8)
  (2) A Change of Conduct (5:9)
  (3) A Change of Criterion (5:10)

   b. What Light Repudiates (5:11-12)
      What is done in darkness is not:
      (1) Something with Which We Can Compromise (5:11)
      (2) Something about Which We Can Converse (5:12)
   c. Why Light Regenerates (5:13-14)
      It has to do with:
      (1) The Work of the Spirit (5:13)
      (2) The Work of the Savior (5:14)
8. A Conscious Decision (5:15-17)
   a. Concerning Time (5:15-16)
      We are to be:
      (1) Wise concerning Our Ways (5:15)
      (2) Wise concerning Our Days (5:16)
   b. Concerning Truth (5:17)
9. A Captivating Discovery (5:18-21)
   a. How to Be Filled with the Spirit (5:18)
   b. How to Be Thrilled in the Spirit (5:19-20)
      (1) Joyful Acclamation in Song (5:19)
      (2) Joyful Acceptance of Wrong (5:20)
   c. How to Be Drilled by the Spirit (5:21)

C. In His Marital Relationships (5:22–6:4)

1. As a Partner (5:22-33)
   a. Some Priorities of the Marriage Relationship (5:22-29)
      (1) The Wife: Loyalty Revealed in Surrender (5:22-24)
          (a) The Exhortation (5:22)
          (b) The Example (5:23)
          (c) The Expectation (5:24)
      (2) The Husband: Love Revealed in Sacrifice (5:25-29)
          (a) The Exhortation (5:25a)
          (b) The Example (5:25b-27)
              i. Love That Travails (5:25b)
              ii. Love That Transforms (5:26-27)
          (c) The Expectation (5:28-29)
              i. The Self Motive (5:28-29a)
              ii. The Supreme Motive (5:29b)
   b. Some Principles of the Marriage Relationship (5:30-33)
      (1) The Concept (5:30-32)
          (a) A Man and Christ's Body (5:30)
          (b) A Man and Christ's Bride (5:31-32)
      (2) The Conclusion (5:33)
2. As a Parent (6:1-4)
   a. The Child's Simple Task (6:1-3)
      (1) The Principle (6:1)
      (2) The Precept (6:2)
      (3) The Promise (6:3)
   b. The Father's Sublime Trust (6:4)

B. Assailing the Enemy (6:18-20)
   1. Warring (6:18a)
   2. Watching (6:18b)
   3. Witnessing (6:19-20)
      Sharing in:
      a. A Brother's Opportunity (6:19)
      b. A Brother's Opposition (6:20)
         (1) His Bonds (6:20a)
         (2) His Boldness (6:20b)

V. Conclusion (6:21-24)

A. Paul's Fellow Worker (6:21-22)
   1. His Titles (6:21a)
   2. His Task (6:21b-22)
      a. To Minister Tidings to Them (6:21b-22a)
      b. To Minister Tenderness to Them (6:22b)
B. Paul's Final Word (6:23-24)

PART I

Introduction
Ephesians 1:1-2

INTRODUCTION

The city of Ephesus was large and important in Paul's day. It had a population of some 350,000 people. Centrally located on the western coast of Asia Minor, Ephesus was positioned midway between two continents. Here east met west. Here oriental luxury, extravagance, and sensuality met occidental enterprise, discipline, and ambition. Here sensual oriental religion blended with lofty and progressive Greek culture and firm, but on the whole fair, Roman government. Here crowds of government officials, Roman soldiers, and Jewish businessmen rubbed shoulders with Eastern pilgrims flocking into Ephesus to worship at the notorious temple of Artemis.

The city was famous for the great arterial Roman road that linked it with the world, for its markets and warehouses, and for its administrative buildings and schools. But above all Ephesus was famous for its temple of Diana (Artemis). Heralded as one of the wonders of the world, it was the sacred shrine of the repulsively ugly image of the mother goddess Artemis—an image reputed to have descended from the sky. In that temple worshipers enacted the licentious rites characteristic of many Eastern religions.

Ephesus was Paul's headquarters during his third missionary journey. He stayed in the city for nearly three years and established a large, influential church. His colleagues and converts fanned out from Ephesus to evangelize the hinterland. They planted churches in city after city, including Smyrna, Pergamos, Thyatira, Sardis, Philadelphia, Laodicea, Colossae, and Hierapolis. Names associated with the church at Ephesus include Paul, Aquila, Priscilla, Apollos, Tychicus, Timothy, and the apostle John. The church there enjoyed the prolonged ministries of two apostles and was the only church in the New Testament to receive letters from two apostles.

The letters to the Ephesians and the Colossians are complementary Epistles, written to address a heresy that had raised its head in the churches of the Lycus valley. Paul seems to have written the

Epistle to the Colossians first, to emphasize the deity of Christ and His *headship* over the church, His body. In Colossians he set forth a cosmic Christ, the Creator of Heaven and earth. In Ephesians, on the other hand, he emphasized the church as the *body* of Christ. The mystical relationship between Christ and His church—between the head and the body—is so real, however, that the church shares in Christ's exalted position on high.

It is not surprising, therefore, that Ephesians introduces us to the most sublime themes that have ever occupied the human mind. Expositors have likened the Ephesian letter to the Grand Canyon and the European Alps. Vista after vista appears. In Ephesians we get the eagle's view of things. We see the eagle rising and wheeling, then soaring off into the high vault of Heaven. We trace the apostle Paul's thoughts as they wheel and as they soar above the confines of time and space beyond the mundane thoughts of ordinary men. We marvel at Paul's command of language, only to discover that even his eloquence is inadequate to convey the concepts of eternity completely.

I. INTRODUCTION (1:1-2)

A. Greetings from Paul (1:1)

1. The Author (1:1a) "Paul, an apostle of Jesus Christ by the will of God."

The name *Paul* at the head of this letter commanded immediate attention. Paul's name had power in Ephesus. He had won large numbers of people there to Christ. As he reminded the Corinthians, a person might have ten thousand teachers in Christ, but he does not have many fathers. So a letter from the one who led them to Christ would always be cherished.

At the end of his second missionary journey, on his way to Jerusalem, Paul paid a brief visit to Ephesus. He stopped at the local synagogue and made a friendly contact with the Jews and rabbis. He declined an invitation to stay in Ephesus because of his desire to be at Jerusalem for the feast. However, he left Aquila and Priscilla in Ephesus to cultivate the spiritual ground there in preparation for his return.

During Paul's third missionary journey, Ephesus became the center of a spiritual awakening that embraced the whole area. The Jews as usual soon turned hostile but Paul, undaunted, turned to the Gentiles and the revival thrived. Miracles were performed. Paul's converts built a public bonfire to destroy their books of magic—books that were worth a small fortune⤬The Holy Spirit's power was poured out in ways that put the fear of God into those who tried to counterfeit His work. Describing this revival Luke wrote, "So mightily grew the word of God and prevailed" (Acts 19:20).

Possibly it was at Ephesus that Paul suffered one of his many imprisonments, for this spectacular spread of the gospel did not go unhindered (2 Corinthians 11:23). In 1 Corinthians 15:32 he spoke of fighting with wild beasts at Ephesus. In the end Paul was forced out of the city by a riot instigated by Demetrius the silversmith. When the mob seized Gaius and Aristarchus, Paul would have rushed to the support of his companions since he was well used to hazarding his life for the gospel. But he was restrained by believers who were concerned for their beloved apostle's safety.

⤬After he left Ephesus, Paul went to Europe. Then he made his last, fatal visit to Jerusalem. On the way to Jerusalem he stopped at Miletus, a city close to Ephesus. The elders of the Ephesian church met Paul at Miletus where he gave them his last charge and warned them of doctrinal heresies he could foresee.

2.   The Audience (1:1b-c)

a.   The Local Church (1:1b) "To the saints which are at Ephesus."

The local church in this case was probably not just the church in Ephesus itself, but all the local churches in the area.

To be a saint at Ephesus was to be like a lovely lily in a stagnant pond.⤬Ephesus rivaled Corinth as the "filth capital" of the Roman world. People from all over the world came to Ephesus to see the temple of Artemis and to patronize the sacred prostitutes whose services were offered as the consummation of worship.⤬Sin was at the very heart of religion in Ephesus, as it is to this day in Hinduism and other Eastern religions.

⤬In contrast, God's people were to be saints—called-out ones—cleansed and made holy, separated unto the true and living God and His Son by the power of the indwelling Spirit of God⤬The true temple of God at Ephesus was to be found in the bodies of the believers where Jesus was enshrined as Lord. It was to these people—God's people—that Paul addressed his letter.

b.   The Larger Church (1:1c) "And to the faithful in Christ Jesus."

In some original manuscripts the words "at Ephesus" are not found in Ephesians 1:1. The writings of such early fathers as Origen and Basil intimate that their copies of the Epistle also omit these words. The usual explanation is that this Epistle was a circular letter; the words *en Epheso* were omitted so that the names of the various churches to which it was sent could be written in the blank space. In Colossians 4:16 Paul asked the Colossians to share their letter with other churches. He also told the Colossians to read the letter from Laodicea (some think he was referring to the letter to the Ephesians).

If the letter to the Ephesians was encyclical and the actual name of the church was left blank, we can write the name of our church in the blank and read the letter as if Paul addressed it to us. This is true of course of all the Epistles, but especially the encyclical ones. The salutation encourages us to adopt such an attitude even if we reject the idea of a blank space since the letter is addressed to "the faithful in Christ."

The Ephesian saints were to be faithful amid much temptation, and so are we. Pollution, perversion, and pornography were accepted norms in their world and in ours. Our calling is to be "faithful in Christ Jesus" in our corrupted world. How did Jesus react to the corruption of human life and society? He loved the sinner and hated the sin. So must we.

B. Grace for All (1:2) "Grace be to you, and peace, from God our Father, and from the Lord Jesus Christ."

The word "grace" occurs a dozen times in this letter. Paul customarily replaced the regular Greek salutation "Rejoice" (*chiare*) with the phonetically similar word "Grace" (*charis*). The regular Jewish salutation was "Peace" (*shalom*). Paul joined Jews and Gentiles in the bond of love in his greetings.

But he did more. He customarily lifted the salutation even higher. It came from "God *our* Father" (italics added), indicating that Jews and Gentiles in the church are members of a common family—children of the same Father.

And then Paul added, "From the Lord Jesus Christ," equating the Lord Jesus to the Father. Thus Paul emphasized the deity of Christ. Jesus is coequal, coeternal, and coexistent with the Father. The greeting comes from "God our Father" *and* from "the Lord Jesus Christ." Thus "Grace and peace" is elevated from a marketplace salutation to a benediction and an affirmation of faith.

PART II

The Christian
and His Blessings

Ephesians 1:3–3:21

II. THE CHRISTIAN AND HIS BLESSINGS (1:3–3:21)

This section of the book of Ephesians introduces us to the unscalable heights and unfathomable depths of the Christian life. The Bible contains no greater truths than those written here. As we examine this great segment we will look at the realities, the revolution, and the revelations of the Christian life.

A. The Realities of the Christian Life (1:3-23)

1. Where We Stand: Basic Principles (1:3-14)

a. The Will of the Father (1:3-6)

(1) The Source of Our Blessings (1:3a) "Blessed be the God and Father of our Lord Jesus Christ."

The paragraph opening up before us is probably the longest single sentence of unbroken discourse in ancient literature. Ephesians 1:3-14 is really one long sentence. It winds around and about, here and there, climbing higher and higher. In some ways it baffles analysis because its thoughts are complex and interwoven. We have to read it over and over before we can grasp the overall significance of its complex themes. Before going a step farther, let's look at it in its entirety:

> Blessed be the God and Father of our Lord Jesus Christ, who hath blessed us with all spiritual blessings in heavenly places in Christ: According as he hath chosen us in him before the foundation of the world, that we should be holy and without blame before him in love: Having predestinated us unto the adoption of children by Jesus Christ to himself, according to the good pleasure of his will, To the praise of the glory of his grace, wherein he hath made us accepted in the beloved. In whom we have redemption through his blood, the forgiveness of sins, according to the riches of his grace; Wherein he hath abounded toward us in all wisdom and prudence; Having made known unto us the mystery of his will, according to his

good pleasure which he hath purposed in himself: That in the dispensation of the fulness of times he might gather together in one all things in Christ, both which are in heaven, and which are on earth; even in him: In whom also we have obtained an inheritance, being predestinated according to the purpose of him who worketh all things after the counsel of his own will: That we should be to the praise of his glory, who first trusted in Christ. In whom ye also trusted, after that ye heard the word of truth, the gospel of your salvation: in whom also after that ye believed, ye were sealed with that holy Spirit of promise, Which is the earnest of our inheritance until the redemption of the purchased possession, unto the praise of his glory.

Now let's read it in modern English, in J. B. Phillips's translation:

Praised be the God and Father of our Lord Jesus Christ for giving us through Christ every spiritual benefit as citizens of Heaven! For consider what he has done—before the foundation of the world he chose us to be, in Christ, his children, holy and blameless in his sight. He planned, in his love, that we should be adopted as his own children through Jesus Christ—this was his will and pleasure that we might praise that glorious generosity of his which he granted to us in his Beloved. It is through him, at the cost of his own blood, that we are redeemed, freely forgiven through that free and generous grace which has overflowed into our lives and given us wisdom and insight. For God has allowed us to know the secret of his plan, and it is this: he purposed long ago in his sovereign will that all human history should be consummated in Christ, that everything that exists in Heaven or earth should find its perfection and fulfillment in him. In Christ we have been given an inheritance, since we were destined for this, by the One who works out all his purposes according to the design of his own will. So that we, in due time, as the first to put our hope in Christ, may bring praise to his glory! And you too trusted him, when you had heard the message of truth, the gospel of your salvation. And after you gave your confidence to him you were, so to speak, stamped with the promised Holy Spirit as a pledge of our inheritance, until the day when God completes the redemption of what is his own; and that will again be to the praise of his glory.

When I was a little boy, my aunt and uncle took me to see Hampton Court, a famous palace built on the outskirts of London by Cardinal Wolsey in the days of Henry VIII. When the palace was finished, Wolsey made the mistake of inviting Henry to come and see his magnificent new home. The king cast covetous eyes upon it. "This," he said, "is a palace fit for a king." Ever jealous of any rivals to his power and glory he added, "I think you'd better give it to me." Valuing his head more than his home, the cardinal did just that, but he lost his head a few years later anyway.

On the grounds of Hampton Court is a maze of hedges and for a penny or two, visitors could have the privilege of getting lost in that maze. My uncle and I went in. The paths were narrow and the hedges high. All the paths looked the same and after a few turns we were lost. Eventually we wandered into the middle of the maze where the authorities had thoughtfully provided a seat so that one could sit and think things over and try to unravel the maze's mystery before setting out again. But the maze simply defied analysis. I don't know how long we wandered around in there before an attendant took pity on us and showed us the way out.

Although the maze defied all our attempts at analysis, it is not merely a jumble of hedges; it has been laid out according to an orderly plan. For those who know its secret, for those who have seen the blueprint, the maze is no mystery. It is only puzzling to those who are content with casually attempting to find a way through it.

It is the same with Ephesians 1:1-14. This passage is not just a jumble of words. It is laid out according to a definite plan: verses 3-6 describe *the will of the Father*; verses 7-12 describe *the work of the Son*; and verses 13-14 describe *the witness of the Spirit*. These three main divisions can be separated phrase by phrase into their component parts to display the intricate mosaic of Paul's thoughts.

It is the will of the Father to bless us and that is where Paul begins. He directs our attention to the source of our blessings.

The supreme revelation of God in the Bible is that He is the *Father* and that He is the God and Father of our Lord Jesus Christ. The concept of God as Father scarcely appears in the Old Testament. God is revealed there as the creator, *Elohim*; as the God of covenant, *Jehovah*; and as the Lord, *Adonai*. He is *El*, the almighty; *El Shaddai*, the gracious giver; *Jehovah Jireh*, the Lord who provides; *Jehovah Nissi*, the Lord our banner; *Jehovah Shalom*, the Lord of all peace; *Jehovah Sabaoth*, the Lord of hosts; *Jehovah Tsidkenu*, the Lord our righteousness; and *Jehovah Shammah*, the Lord who is there.

Not until Jesus came was God fully revealed as the Father. Jesus' first recorded words enshrine this truth: "Wist ye not that I must be about my Father's business?" (Luke 2:49) In the greatest of Christ's parables—the parable of the prodigal (Luke 15:11-32)—the word *father* occurs a dozen times. That name was on the Lord's lips as He prayed in dark Gethsemane, as He hung on the cross, as He greeted His loved ones on the resurrection morning, and as He walked on the road to Olivet on the day of His ascension.

God is the Father. What a wonderful truth! He is the God and Father of our Lord Jesus Christ. What a blessed fact! He is just like Jesus, who could say as He walked among us, "He that hath seen me hath seen the Father" (John 14:9). Jesus was "the visible expression of the invisible God" (Colossians 1:15, J. B. PHILLIPS). And together the Father and the Son (along with the Holy Spirit) are the source of all the abundant blessings mentioned in this opening statement of Ephesians 1.

(2) The Sphere of Our Blessings (1:3b) "Who hath blessed us with all spiritual blessings in heavenly places in Christ."

There are two spheres of blessing. Our blessings (and our battles) are *"in heavenly places"* and also *"in Christ,"* in whom "we live, and move, and have our being" (Acts 17:28). We meet these two expressions repeatedly in this Epistle.

The heavenlies (heavenly places) at the present time are Satan's sphere of operations. He holds them as "the prince of the power of the air" (Ephesians 2:2) and he is aided by countless hosts of spirit beings who accept his lordship and follow his lead. So we have to take the heavenlies by storm. Later chapters in the Epistle tell us how to arm ourselves and how to fight victoriously against these entrenched foes who try to deny us our inheritance and keep us out of our rightful sphere.

Ephesians is the New Testament counterpart of the book of Joshua. Just as Israel's blessings were found *in Canaan,* so ours are found *in the heavenlies.* Just as the Israelites had to battle many enemies in Canaan in order to possess all that God had promised them, so we have to battle Satan and his army in order to enter into all that is ours in heavenly places. Just as Israel's inheritance in Canaan was fiercely contested by the foe, so our inheritance in the heavenlies is also strongly contested. Just as Joshua led God's chosen people into victory, so Jesus leads us.

If our blessings are in heavenly places, they are also in Christ. Satan and his evil hosts may haunt the heavenlies, but Christ has conquered them.

The Israelites only had to trust and obey in order to enter into all the blessings God had in store for them in Canaan. The Canaanites, despite their formidable appearance, were already defeated. Yet

the Israelites did not believe God's promises. We recall how ten of
the twelve spies discouraged the people:

> The people is greater and taller than we; the cities are great
> and walled up to heaven; and moreover we have seen the sons
> of the Anakims there (Deuteronomy 1:28).
>   And they brought up an evil report of the land which they
> had searched unto the children of Israel, saying, The land,
> through which we have gone to search it, is a land that eateth
> up the inhabitants thereof; and all the people that we saw in it
> are men of a great stature. And there we saw the giants, the sons
> of Anak, which come of the giants: and we were in our own
> sight as grasshoppers, and so we were in their sight (Numbers
> 13:32-33).

How different was the minority report of Joshua and Caleb in
Numbers 14:7-9:

> And they spake unto all the company of the children of Israel,
> saying, The land, which we passed through to search it, is an
> exceeding good land. If the Lord delight in us, then he will
> bring us into this land, and give it us; a land which floweth with
> milk and honey. Only rebel not ye against the Lord, neither
> fear ye the people of the land; for they are bread for us: their
> defence is departed from them, and the Lord is with us: fear
> them not.

Their report was confirmed later by Rahab's testimony: "I know
that the Lord hath given you the land, and that your terror is fallen
upon us, and that all the inhabitants of the land faint because of
you" (Joshua 2:9). All the Israelites had to do was enter the land and
possess their possessions. The Canaanites were already thoroughly
demoralized.

All Israel had to do was go forward in faith and obedience, and
the same is true of us. The heavenlies are occupied by the foe and
there can be no blessings without battles, but the foe is already
defeated. Christ, our heavenly Joshua, leads us into victory and into
the actual possession of all that has been promised to us in Him.

(3) The Scope of Our Blessings (1:4-5)

(a) We Have Been Chosen (1:4a) "According as he hath chosen us
      in him before the foundation of the world."

There is a mystery here that centers in the fact that we are finite and God is infinite. We are creatures of time; God inhabits eternity. We express our mode of being in three tenses of time—I was, I am, I will be. God expresses His mode of being in the eternal present—I am, I am, I am. Thus Jesus did not say, "Before Abraham was, I was" (which in itself would have been an astonishing statement expressing a longevity of life His enemies would have found bewildering). Jesus said, "Before Abraham was, I am" (John 8:58). He was claiming eternity of being and coexistence with the Father, and His enemies considered His statement blasphemous.

We are hindered in experience and understanding by the limited nature of our being. As finite creatures we live in the here and now and can deal with only one thing at a time. Life is presented to us, so to speak, in tiny little packages. We live it moment by moment. The future lies before us, but we cannot experience it until it touches us in a fleeting moment of the present before it recedes instantly into the past. We can anticipate the future and recall the past, but we live in the flickering moment we call the present. In God's mind, however, the past, present, and future are swallowed up in the all-embracing present.

Thus when we read that we were chosen in Him "before the foundation of the world," we must realize that the Holy Spirit has stated the issue from our perspective. Since God lives in the present tense, there is to Him no time difference between the moment He chose me and the moment I chose Him. The perception of time difference is ours alone. From the standpoint of God's eternal present tense, both acts are simultaneous. That explanation does not, however, lessen the mystery of God's grace. With the chorus writer we still wonder:

> Why did He love me? I never can tell;
> Why did He suffer to save me from Hell?
> Nothing but infinite grace from above
> Could have conceived such a story of love.
>
> (G. R. Harding)

Spurgeon said, "If God hadn't chosen me before the foundation of the world, He wouldn't choose me now!"

(b) We Have Been Changed (1:4b-5)

i.   God Has Removed All Our Sins (1:4b) "That we should be holy and without blame before him in love."

God saves us, sanctifies us, and sees no blemish in us. His love can be content with nothing less than our complete Christlikeness. This is the practical purpose of His grace. The full realization of Christlikeness awaits a coming day when "we shall be like him; for we shall see him as he is" (1 John 3:2). Meanwhile the indwelling Holy Spirit is at work in our hearts to produce in us—here and now—the same quality of unblemished holiness that characterized the Lord Jesus when He lived on earth. God already sees us positionally as holy and without blemish because He sees us in Christ. That is, when He looks at us, He sees Christ. The work of the Holy Spirit is to make us holy and without blame in the everyday aspects of life. Because God is so pleased with Jesus, He wants everyone to be like His Son. The Holy Spirit is here to begin the process of bringing my imperfect state into line with my position, which is perfect. As the apostle John stated in nine apt monosyllables, "As he is, so are we in this world" (1 John 4:17). Christlikeness is our goal, and the driving force is love—His infinite love for us and our increasing love for Him.

ii.   God Has Remade Us As Sons (1:5) "Having predestinated us unto the adoption of children by Jesus Christ to himself, according to the good pleasure of his will."

Some have rephrased Ephesians 1:5 as "Having fore-ordained us unto adoption as sons through Jesus Christ unto himself." That is an important change. There is all the difference in the world between *children* and *sons*. The word *children* has to do with our membership in God's family. For example, I became a member of that family by virtue of the new birth, by being born into it. The word *sons*, on the other hand, has to do with maturity in the family. It refers to the position we occupy in God's family as adult sons.

If we see a sign on a business that reads Henry Brown and Sons, we know that Henry Brown's sons are partners in their father's business. They have grown up and assumed positions of authority and responsibility in their father's business. We never see a sign that reads Henry Brown and Children!

God has predestinated us to maturity. Those who are saved are predestinated. The word *predestinated* is not used in connection with the lost. God does not predestinate certain people to go to Hell and others to go to Heaven. The concept of predestination is reserved in Scripture for those who are in God's family. We might say that election has to do with the past and predestination has to do with the future. Election has to do with what we were chosen from;

predestination has to do with what we were chosen for. It is God's intent to bring us to spiritual maturity so that we can become partners with Him in His eternal purposes.

We were chosen for spiritual maturity "according to the good pleasure of his will." The Father's pleasure is best illustrated by the story of the prodigal son. When the wayward boy returned, repentant and remorseful, he found his father waiting for him. The son had his speech all ready. He was going to say, "Father, I have sinned against heaven, and before thee, And am no more worthy to be called thy son: make me as one of thy hired servants" (Luke 15:18-19). But before he ever reached the part about being made a hired servant, his father interrupted and called for the ring, the robe, the shoes, and the fatted calf. The father had everything ready for the prodigal's return.

Like the father in the parable, God is waiting for us. It is the pleasure of His good will to have everything ready so that in the ages to come the Christian might wear the ring, the robe, and the royal sandals and take his place at God's table as His son.

(4) The Significance of Our Blessings (1:6) "To the praise of the glory of his grace, wherein he hath made us accepted in the beloved."

(a) The Father's Benevolence

To be accepted is one of man's greatest psychological needs, and our psychological needs are echoes of far greater spiritual needs. Our need to be accepted by other people is nothing compared with our need to be accepted by God.

People go to extraordinary lengths to gain the acceptance of those they admire. Many teenagers will do almost anything to be accepted by their peers. They wear outlandish clothing, dye their hair, pose as scholars, or act like slobs—they do whatever is the "in" thing with the group they want to join. Adults do the same, but they are usually more subtle.

Remember, if you will, the story of Oliver Twist. The poor orphan boy was made of tough fiber and refused to do anything to gain acceptance. He would not allow the bully Noah Claypole, for instance, to malign the memory of his mother. Nor would he steal to win the approval of the artful Dodger and old Fagin. The wily Jew, however, knew human nature. He had a plan to wear down Oliver's resistance. He would leave Oliver alone—leave him to his own devices, leave him to wander aimlessly hour after hour in the old house he used as a den. Fagin counted on the natural need for acceptance to wear down Oliver's resistance, so that Oliver would finally seek the approval of the petty thieves and burglars among whom he had fallen, deeming it better than no acceptance at all.

We need acceptance from other people, and we desperately need God's acceptance. But our sinful nature is wholly unacceptable to God. His burning holiness rejects what we are by nature and what we consequently do.

(b) The Father's Beloved

Yet God does accept us! The reason lies in the phrase *the Beloved.* He accepts us, not because of our prayers and promises, not because of our resolves and efforts to be good, not because of our zeal, but because of Jesus. We are accepted in the Beloved.

What a lovely name for Jesus! It was spoken first by the Father when John baptized Jesus in the Jordan. "There came a voice from heaven, saying, Thou art my beloved Son, in whom I am well pleased" (Mark 1:11).

Jesus is Heaven's Beloved, the altogether lovely One, the chiefest among ten thousand (Song of Solomon 5:10,16). God's smile of approval rested on Him throughout His earthly journey. He always did what pleased the Father (John 8:29).

It was God's eternal counsel that the Lord Jesus should first give His life *for* us at Calvary and then give His life *to* us. When we accept Him as personal Savior, the transaction is complete. "For Christ also hath once suffered for sins, the just for the unjust, that he might bring us to God" (1 Peter 3:18). "For he hath made him to be sin for us, who knew no sin; that we might be made the righteousness of God in him" (2 Corinthians 5:21). God now sees us in the Beloved. He looks at us and sees Christ. No angel among the heavenly hosts has more acceptance than we.

An acquaintance of mine who was born in a foreign land became a United States citizen. Once he was accepted, his standing as an American citizen was perfect. I heard him say to an American audience, "I am just as much a *citizen* as your president." Likewise, God placed us in His sight in such a way that we can be perfectly accepted, perfectly at home, perfectly at ease.

Our acceptance by the Father in the Beloved is "to the praise of the glory of his grace." God's glory is greatly enhanced by the grace He has shown to us. It was His idea, not ours. It was His plan to seek us, save us, sanctify us, and seat us in glory. The endless ages of eternity will prove to be all too short a time to sing His praise for such matchless love and grace.

b. The Work of the Son (1:7-12)

(1) Redemption (1:7)

(a) The Person Involved (1:7a) "In whom we have redemption."

We can be accepted by God because of the work of the Lord Jesus Christ. A price had to be paid to redeem us. As the hymn says:

> There was no other good enough
> To pay the price of sin;
> He only could unlock the gate
> Of heav'n and let us in.
> (Cecil F. Alexander)

The price Jesus paid was astronomical—beyond human comprehension. In his short masterpiece, "The Reason Why," Robert Laidlaw faced the question, "How could the Lord Jesus Christ's one life be considered the substitute for the lives of so many, so that God offers salvation to whosoever repents and believes in Christ?" Laidlaw answered:

> That seems a fair question—a problem in arithmetic that can be demonstrated on paper. Christ was God manifest in the flesh—Divinity in humanity—so that the life He gave was an infinite life, which can meet the needs of any number of finite lives. Get a sheet of paper and write down all the big figures you can think of—millions or more—add them up. Now you have a big number; then multiply it by 10—100—by a million if you like—cover sheets of paper, and after all you still have a finite number—a number that has bounds set about it—it has a beginning and an end, however far it may extend. No, by adding finite things together no man has ever been able to make that which is infinite. The *infinite life* of Christ given for sinners is more than sufficient to save all who accept Him as the One who died in their room and stead.[1]

That's the person involved! No wonder our redemption is so great.

(b) The Price Involved (1:7b) "We have redemption through his blood."

In the Old Testament there were two means of redemption—by power and by purchase. The book of Exodus illustrates redemption by power; the book of Ruth illustrates redemption by purchase. It is significant that the first time the kinsman-redeemer Boaz is introduced in the story of Ruth, we are told that he was "a mighty man of wealth" (Ruth 2:1). Only a rich man could redeem. Redemption is a costly business.

Paul wrote, "For ye know the grace of our Lord Jesus Christ, that, though he was rich, yet for your sakes he became poor, that ye through his poverty might be rich" (2 Corinthians 8:9). To secure our redemption, Jesus had to leave the glory of Heaven, enter human life by means of the incarnation, live a perfect life, and then die. He had to suffer the agony of crucifixion, the heartbreak of rejection, betrayal, and abandonment, the sting of ridicule and shame, the horror of being made sin, the torment of God's wrath, and the indignity of death. His blood had to be shed. That was the price. Peter said that we "were not redeemed with corruptible things, as silver and gold . . . But with the precious blood of Christ" (1 Peter 1:18-19). Only God can know how "precious is the flow / That makes me white as snow" (Robert Lowry).

(c) The Pardon Involved (1:7c) "The forgiveness of sins, according to the riches of his grace."

Grace—there it is again! Redemption is by grace. Grace is unmerited favor. It is getting something we don't deserve. Paul strikes this note over and over.

Years ago a converted derelict called Sam Duncannon lived in Scotland. Old Sam haunted the Glasgow mission where he had found the Savior and where his life and soul had been redeemed. He was not an evangelist or a great soul-winner, but he loved his new-found Lord and wanted to brighten the drab lives of the down-and-outers who drifted in and out of the mission. He collected colored pictures, found appropriate verses of Scripture or gospel hymns, and framed the pictures and verses together; then he gave these illustrated verses to people who came to the mission. He hoped the pictures would add a little color to their lives and the verses would bring a little comfort to their souls.

One day Sam found a picture of Niagara Falls that greatly impressed him. He loved the sense of power and inexhaustibility conveyed by the rush of the water over the falls, but for a long time he could not find a verse to go with the picture—a verse that said what he wanted to say.

Then D. L. Moody and his song-leader, Ira Sankey, came to the mission. Mr. Sankey sang a solo and as soon as Sam heard that song, he knew that he had found the words he needed for his picture of Niagara Falls. He could see the finished picture in his mind's eye—the endlessly rushing water and the words of this hymn:

> Have you on the Lord believed?
> Still there's more to follow;
> Of his grace have you received?
> Still there's more to follow.
>
> O the grace the Father shows!
> Still there's more to follow;
> Freely he his grace bestows,
> Still there's more to follow.
>
> More and more, more and more,
> Always more to follow;
> O his matchless, boundless love!
> Still there's more to follow.
>   (Philip Paul Bliss)

In Ephesians 1:7 Paul wrote, "The forgiveness of sins, according to the riches of his grace." In a parallel passage in Colossians 1:14 he added the word *even*—"Even the forgiveness of sins." How wonderful is that word *even*. We read of the Lord Jesus that He "became obedient unto death, even the death of the cross" (Philippians 2:8). Esau cried, "Bless me, even me also, O my father" (Genesis 27:34). When we read, "We have redemption through his blood, even the forgiveness of sins," we could think of the unclean nature of our sins, of the uncompromising nastiness of our sins, of the uncountable number of our sins. No wonder Paul would say, "Even the forgiveness of sins, according to the riches of his grace."

We can thank God that He is rich in grace. What a horror it would be if God had revealed Himself to be a God of infinite power, a God of infallible wisdom, a God of inflexible holiness, and also a God devoid of compassion and sympathy for lost and ruined mankind. How we should praise Him for the riches of His grace!

(2) Revelation (1:8-9)

(a) The Divine Perception (1:8) "Wherein he hath abounded toward us in all wisdom and prudence."

The words "wisdom and prudence" are full of significance. The Greek word translated "wisdom" here is *sophia*, a great word that embraced such ideas as "cleverness and skill in handicraft and art, skill in matters of common life, sound judgment, intelligence, practical wisdom, learning, speculative wisdom, natural philosophy and mathematics."[2] Archbishop Trench said that in the New Testament and Christian writing, *sophia* is reserved for the highest and noblest in wisdom and it is never used in Scripture except to describe God and good men (or in a sarcastic sense). When *sophia* refers to God, it refers to the omniscience that belongs to God alone. The Greek word translated "prudence" is *phronesis. Phronesis* is the product of *sophia*—right thinking leads to right actions. Prudence is the effective use of wisdom.[3]

The Greek word translated "abounded" means "more than enough." The word translated "wherein" refers to the grace in which God has superabounded toward us. This means that God's "more-than-enough" grace operates within the framework of His omniscient grasp of time and space and within the scope of His infallible will always to do what is right. In other words, God's unerring logic and unbounded love are behind His plan of salvation. What a revelation of God! But what He saw in us, so to plan for us and so to love us, is more than tongue can tell.

(b) The Divine Purpose (1:9) "Having made known unto us the mystery of his will, according to his good pleasure which he hath purposed in himself."

Do you recall Moses' explanation of God's love for the children of Israel? In his memoirs he wrote, "The Lord did not set his love upon you, nor choose you, because ye were more in number than any people; for ye were the fewest of all people: But because the Lord loved you" (Deuteronomy 7:7-8). In other words Moses was saying, "He loved you because He loved you!" That is the divine logic. We should not dissect God's love—just enjoy it.

But why did His heart overflow with love toward such graceless, unlovely, sinful people? Why did He use His wisdom to "devise means, that his banished be not expelled from him" (2 Samuel 14:14)? Why did He make a plan that did not violate His holiness or break His laws, yet involved enormous sacrifice and suffering for Himself? Why did He use His will to carry through a plan of salvation for the likes of us?

The answer can only be found in understanding the kind of God He is. He does what He does because He is who He is. He is a God of love, and He wants us to be loving like Him. Moreover, He will never rest until we are.

Even children understand that Jesus loves them. But the most mature will never completely unravel what Paul called "the mystery of his will." It will remain far beyond our understanding. All we know is that it was God's "good pleasure" to set His love upon us and make us the objects of such marvelous grace that even the angels must have gasped as they saw the plan unfold.

(3) Royalty (1:10-11)

(a) For the Christ (1:10) "That in the dispensation of the fulness of times he might gather together in one all things in Christ, both which are in heaven, and which are on earth; even in him."

No small part of the Father's eternal purpose, of "his good pleasure which he hath purposed in himself," is to glorify the person of the Lord Jesus. It was Jesus who came to earth, incarnated Himself in human flesh, lived a life wholly pleasing to God, and then bled and died in agony to make God's mercy and redemption available to us. God has no plan, no program, no purpose, that does not ultimately rest in the person of the Lord Jesus Christ.

That truth is evident in Ephesians 1:10. The word translated "gather together in one" can be rendered "sum it up" or "head it up." The same word occurs in Romans 13:9 where Paul listed five of the ten commandments then added, "If there be any other commandment, it is *briefly comprehended* in this saying, namely, Thou shalt love thy neighbour as thyself" (italics added). Our duties are *summed up* in the law of love.

God intends to sum everything up in Christ—everything in Heaven and on earth. Satan's rebellion brought in contamination. God's answer to the contamination is Christ. Satan no longer has his home in Heaven, although as the accuser of the brethren (Revelation 12:10) it would seem that he has admittance there. But Satan does have a hold on the heavens as "the prince of the power of the air" (Ephesians 2:2). In that sphere we as God's children, indwelt by His Holy Spirit, join the battle against Satan and his hosts. The Lord intends to clean up that sphere when He comes, just as He intends to clean up things here on earth.

Isaiah 24:21 casts a flood of light on this clean-up: "And it shall come to pass in that day, that the Lord shall punish the host of the high ones that are on high, and the kings of the earth upon the earth." The "high ones that are on high" are Satan's spirit rulers of this world's darkness, his principalities and powers, the wicked spirits in high places who lord it over the heavenlies and hold this world in bondage. All these will be cast down when Christ returns.

In Revelation 12:7-9 we learn that Michael the archangel will be sent to make war on Satan and his angels and to cast them down from the heavenlies. Satan will lose control over this sphere and will be confined to earth—to Heaven's rejoicing, his rage, and mankind's ruin (12:10-12). The kings of the earth who live on the earth will be dealt with at Armageddon (16:12-16; 19:11-21).[4]

During the millennial reign of Christ on earth, the believers of this present age—those who comprise the church, the body of Christ, and who are God's heavenly people—will reign with Christ on high. Our place will be in the heavenlies; our home will be the heavenly Jerusalem. From the heavenlies, we shall exercise enormous power and authority over the earth. In other words, we will be seated where Satan now sits as usurper. We will exercise for God a power for good on the earth just as Satan and his hosts today exert relentless power for evil.

In the same way and at the same time, Gentile world rule will end and the Jews (God's people) will replace the Gentiles in all the seats of power. The Lord Jesus will sit on the throne of David in Jerusalem; the twelve apostles will sit on twelve thrones and judge the twelve tribes of Israel; the Jews will govern the nations for God.

Such will be "the dispensation of the fulness of times," as Paul called it in Ephesians 1:10. Things will be summed up in Christ indeed.

(b) For the Christian (1:11) "In whom also we have obtained an inheritance, being predestinated according to the purpose of him who worketh all things after the counsel of his own will."

John Graham of Claverhouse was known as "Bonnie Dundee" and won his spurs as a handsome soldier of fortune in France and the Netherlands. He then led a Scottish uprising to support the deposed Roman Catholic monarch, James II of Britain.

On his return to Scotland he was made captain of the dragoons and was sent to suppress the Presbyterian Covenanters fighting for the right to worship God according to their own consciences. The Covenanters, however, came from a fighting breed. When the Claverhouse cavalry tried to break up one of their meetings, the Covenanters turned on their enemies and soundly defeated them. The enraged Claverhouse returned three weeks later and thrashed the Covenanters at Bothwell Bridge.

Scotland then experienced a wretched time. Claverhouse sent his dragoons to comb the heather and search the moss-hags for outlawed preachers. Some they shot on sight. Others they hauled to prison and treated with utmost barbarity. Not a week passed without the name of "Bloody Claverhouse," as he was called, being roundly cursed by Covenanters.

The Covenanters met for worship where they could—in dens, on the hills, in hideouts. One day a Scottish lass was making her way to one such meeting, following by-paths through the heather, when she was overtaken by a troop of Dundee's dragoons. The leader demanded to know where she was going so early on a Sunday morning. She knew her danger and the danger she posed to her fellow saints if she told the truth. But she could not lie. She looked the captain in the eye. "Sir," she said, "My Elder Brother has died and they're reading his will, ye ken. I want to be there to see what he has left for me."

It's great to have an inheritance, to be remembered in someone's will. Paul said that in Christ we have obtained an inheritance. Peter said that our inheritance is incorruptible and undefiled, that it will not fade away, and that it is reserved in Heaven for us (1 Peter 1:4). Paul told the Corinthians: "Eye hath not seen, nor ear heard, neither have entered into the heart of man, the things which God hath prepared for them that love him" (1 Corinthians 2:9).

From all eternity, God has had our well-being in mind. His eternal purpose was to bring into existence human beings upon whom He could bestow all the inexhaustible riches of His grace. No small part of that "counsel of his own will" is still in the future as far as we are concerned. What God has in store for us is beyond anything we can imagine. We find ourselves yearning for it at times with deep soul-longings that are beyond all utterance. We catch occasional, fleeting glimpses of that "sweet bye and bye" in a passage or two of Scripture, such as those in the closing chapters of the Apocalypse, although the reality will be far better, as Paul put it in Philippians 1:23. In the meantime we can rest assured that God has taken care of our inheritance. That part of our salvation is included in God's predestinating will.

(4) Rejoicing (1:12) "That we should be to the praise of his glory, who first trusted in Christ."

The Lord Himself gives us our first glimpse of rejoicing in Heaven. He tells us in His peerless parable of the Good Shepherd that when He finds His lost sheep, He brings it home rejoicing. So:

> All thro' the mountains, thunder riv'n,
> And up from the rocky steep,

> There arose a glad cry to the gate of heav'n,
> "Rejoice! I have found my sheep!"
> And the angels echoed around the throne,
> "Rejoice, for the Lord brings back His own!"
>   (Elizabeth C. Clephane)

As though the story of the lost sheep were not sufficient emphasis, the Lord then added the parables of the lost coin and the prodigal son. "They began to be merry" is the Lord's own description of the feast that was spread when the prodigal returned home (Luke 15:24). Music and dancing, the robe, the ring, and the fatted calf all contributed to the joyful celebration.

Not only do we have an inheritance in Christ; He has an inheritance in us and all Heaven joins in songs of happiness and praise over that. Just think, our salvation sets the joy bells of Heaven ringing and they echo in the everlasting hills. Our conversion causes joyful commotion in Heaven because the salvation of a sinner brings satisfaction to the Savior and glory to God. Eternal ages will be far too short to sing His praise and those anthems will never cease.

c.   The Witness of the Spirit (1:13-14)

(1) His Word: A Witness to the Christ (1:13a) "In whom ye also trusted, after that ye heard the word of truth, the gospel of your salvation."

Paul was recalling his first cordial reception in the synagogue by the rabbis and the congregation and the division that followed when some trusted Christ after they heard the word of truth. Then revival broke out among the Gentiles, attracting the attention of the whole city, and Paul diligently went from house to house until he could say he was pure of all men's blood (Acts 20:26). The people in Ephesus to whom he was writing were the fruit of this ministry. The Holy Spirit had taken the gospel of Christ—the word of truth— and had so powerfully used it to witness to the Lord Jesus that multitudes had been saved.

Nobody can be saved apart from the word of truth. Human cleverness, persuasiveness, or eloquence cannot save souls, nor can oratory in the pulpit or artistry in the choir. God has not promised to bless programs or performances. He always blesses His Word. The witness of the Spirit is to the Son of God by means of the Word of God. Along the way God uses other vehicles, but His chosen channels for bringing light to an individual's soul and conviction to his conscience are His church and His saints who share His Word.

(2) His Work: A Witness to the Christian (1:13b-14)

(a) The Proof of Our Faith (1:13b) "In whom also after that ye
     believed, ye were sealed with that holy Spirit of promise."

Sealed! What a comforting word. It suggests a finished transaction, absolute assurance, eternal security.

An illustration of God's sealing is found in Revelation 7 where we
read that during the postrapture judgment age 144,000 chosen
Hebrew witnesses will be sealed by God to bear worldwide witness
to the gospel of the kingdom. The beast—the devil's messiah—will
be enraged, but he will not be able to harm them because they are
sealed. They will spread the gospel from shore to shore with
astonishing speed, and countless millions of Gentiles will be saved.
These witnesses, a special and privileged company of God's people,
will then be translated to Heaven (Revelation 14). The seal of God
will have kept them safe. The beast's seal, marked in the flesh of his
followers, seems to be a Satanic imitation of God's seal on the hearts
of His people.

In this age we are sealed by the Holy Spirit—sealed not to escape
life's perils and persecutions, but sealed against any possibility of
losing our salvation after we respond to the word of truth, which is
the gospel of salvation.

Seals are not used much these days except when a company uses
its corporate seal to make documents official. Years ago, however,
seals were commonly used. When I was starting out in the business
world, I worked for a large multinational British bank. In those days
when contracting parties entered into a legal agreement, the
documents were "signed, sealed, and delivered." On numerous
occasions the bank manager called for the sealing wax. Both
contracting parties would sign the documents and the bank manager would sign as a witness. Then he would affix the heated sealing
wax to the documents. After being signed and sealed, the documents were "delivered" to the contracting parties. The agreement,
ratified by the seal, was then in force and was binding on all parties.

In a sense, salvation is a legal document. The Holy Spirit spells
out the terms of the agreement in the "word of truth, the gospel of
your salvation." In that gospel, everything is linked to Christ and His
shed blood. The Holy Spirit makes it clear that our salvation is free
and will last forever. All the doing has been done. All we have to do
is by faith accept the Lord Jesus Christ as our personal Savior and Lord.

God has already signed the contract in the name of Jesus. The
glorious name of Jesus is prominent everywhere: "Thou shalt call his
name Jesus: for he shall save his people from their sins" (Matthew 1:21);

"Neither is there salvation in any other: for there is none other name under heaven given among men, whereby we must be saved" (Acts 4:12); "Whosoever shall call upon the name of the Lord shall be saved" (Romans 10:13).

When we hear the gospel, the Holy Spirit reveals God's terms of salvation to us, convicts us of our sin, and urges us to accept Christ— the One in whom God's offer of salvation centers. When we personally accept God's terms of salvation by receiving Christ as Savior, we in effect put our names on the contract. Immediately God applies the seal. He seals us with the "holy Spirit of promise." He gives us the Holy Spirit.

The gift of the Holy Spirit is God's seal on the document of salvation. He has signed it; we have signed it. The agreement is sealed; the contract of unconditional salvation goes into effect and is binding on all parties. Since God does all the doing, no failure on our part (all failure having been anticipated long, long ago) can invalidate the contract.

In my banking days, the manager would usually deliver the original contract to a bank officer who would place it in the vault for safekeeping. Everything that could be done was done to ensure that the contract was preserved and its terms were put into effect. We can rest assured that God has taken every precaution against His promise ever being broken. As far as we are concerned, God has sealed us with that Holy Spirit of promise. Our salvation is as certain as God's character and throne can make it.

(b) The Pledge of our Future (1:14) "Which is the earnest of our inheritance until the redemption of the purchased possession, unto the praise of his glory."

The Holy Spirit is not only the seal; He is also the earnest. He is not only the proof of our position in Christ; He is also the pledge of our possessions in Christ. He not only confirms our faith; He also confirms our future. He not only guarantees our eternal security; He also guarantees our eternal satisfaction.

We do not use the old-fashioned word *earnest* anymore in ordinary conversation, but real estate agents still use it in some business transactions. When my wife and I first came to the United States, we wanted to buy a house. The real estate agent showed us a number of homes, and we finally found a suitable one in our price range. We made our offer, and then the agent said, "I will need some earnest money." We had never heard that expression before and asked him what it meant.

"Well," he said, "I am going to take your offer to the owner of the house so that he can decide if he wants to accept it. I will need your check for one thousand dollars to show him that you are in earnest about this offer. Your check will prove to him that you really mean business and that you are not going to back out halfway through the deal." The check I wrote that day was not for the full amount of the offer. In fact it was only a token amount. I would have to pay much more money when it was time to complete the deal.

Similarly the Holy Spirit is the earnest of our inheritance as Christians. God gives the Holy Spirit to each believer as evidence that He is in earnest about our salvation. He means business. He is not going to back out. And there is much more to come. The great transaction is underway but is not yet completed. We are still waiting for the rest of it—"the redemption of the purchased possession."

Opinions differ over what Paul meant by the "purchased possession." Doubtlessly it includes the redemption of the body. One day we will have bodies "like unto his glorious body" (Philippians 3:21)—bodies free from disease, disability, defilement, and death. The believer's new body will be controlled by a human spirit that is fully yielded to the Holy Spirit. It will be a body in which the supernatural will be as normal as the natural.

The "purchased possession" may refer to this world, which is now under the curse but will one day be brought into the glorious liberty of the children of God (Romans 8:21). The glowing Old Testament promises of a global paradise will all be fulfilled at the second coming of Christ. God has no intention of leaving this world in its present ruined condition. The book of Ruth teaches us that our kinsman-redeemer has purchased not only the believer's person, but also his property.

The "purchased possession" may be the church. No one has ever seen the church as it exists in God's mind and heart. For the most part we see Satan's counterfeit. The church is torn and divided into sects and schisms, racked by heresy, and rendered powerless through apostasy. As the book of Acts and the Pauline Epistles show, it did not take long for dissensions and distortions to appear in the early church. The true church, however, is God's masterpiece. One day it will be displayed as such "unto the praise of his glory."

The "purchased possession" may include all of these and much more besides. In any case, the Holy Spirit is the earnest of it all. That alone should tell us how magnificent God's full and ultimate reality for us is going to be, and it will all be to the praise of God's glory. God always has an eye on His glory. That is the key to all hermeneutics, to all of God's eternal purposes. The unifying factor is God's glory.[5]

Thus Paul ended the first segment of this remarkable Epistle. He showed us where we stand. He dealt with basic principles: the will of the Father, the work of the Son, and the witness of the Spirit. And he left us nearly breathless with the wonder of it all, wanting to pray and praise God for His goodness and grace. Paul himself went on to pray, as we see in the next segment.

2.   Why We Stand: Believing Prayer (1:15-23)

a.   A Church-centered Prayer (1:15-16)

(1) The Cause of It (1:15)

(a) Paul Had Heard How They Trusted the Savior (1:15a) "After I heard of your faith in the Lord Jesus."

We must remember that this Epistle was most likely a circular letter. It was not just intended for the church at Ephesus where Paul knew most of the believers well. (Many of them had been won to Christ during his three-year stay in their city.) The letter was also intended for other churches springing up in the surrounding area. Although most of the believers in these churches would be strangers to Paul, he could properly speak of having heard of their faith in the Lord Jesus Christ.

Other people's converts were as precious to Paul as his own and after hearing of their faith, Paul began to pray for them. They too had come into the enjoyment of all the magnificent blessings he had just described. He poured out his heart in prayer for them, and what a model prayer this is! Because Paul was in prison, he could not visit these new converts, but he could write to them and pray for them. The devil had as much reason to fear Paul's prayers as he had to fear Paul's preaching and Paul's pen.

(b) Paul Had Heard How They Treated the Saints (1:15b) "And love unto all the saints."

Most of the Lord's people find it easy to love some of the saints, but it is not so easy to love all of the saints. How do we love the saints who disagree with us—saints who hold doctrinal positions radically different from our own? What about the saints whose dispositions and temperaments are the opposite of ours? And how do we love the saints whose culture clashes with ours?

It was easy for Paul to love Timothy—his son in the faith, his most ardent admirer and helper. It was also easy to love Luke, his physician. It was not too difficult to love Peter, even though he must have irritated Paul sometimes. On one occasion Paul had found it necessary to confront Peter face to face; yet there was much that was lovable about bighearted, impulsive Peter. But one wonders how easy it was for Paul to love James, who was stern, ascetic, legalistic, and narrow-minded.

Paul loved God's people, and his love was infectious. The believers at Ephesus had caught it, and so had their converts. Paul was delighted to hear that their love was overflowing to all those who loved the Lord. Love for God's people, after all, is one of the acid tests of genuine conversion. "We know that we have passed from death unto life, because we love the brethren" (1 John 3:14).

(2) The Constancy of It (1:16) I "cease not to give thanks for you, making mention of you in my prayers."

His prayers are among many evidences of Paul's love for all saints. We might wonder how he could find time to pray so consistently for such a large and growing circle of friends. His admonition to "pray without ceasing" (1 Thessalonians 5:17) strikes us as a great goal, but seems to many to be quite impractical. How did Paul find time to pray?

Paul was an active missionary—ever on the move, busy planting churches, evangelizing, soulwinning, counseling, training converts, writing letters, and planning new mission enterprises. Often he would put in a full day making tents to raise the funds he needed for his support. There he would sit with the stiff material, already cut out according to pattern, spread out before him. All he had to do was ply the needle—stitch, stitch, stitch—not an occupation calling for a great deal of mental activity. So he prayed! In and out of the cloth went the tentmaker's needle. In and out of the throne room of the universe went the great ambassador to the Gentiles.

Then, too, Paul could pray during his journeys. Driven out of Phillipi, he walked to Thessalonica, a 100-mile hike, and he prayed as he walked. Driven out of Thessalonica, he walked 40 or 50 miles to Berea. Driven out of Berea, he walked to Athens, a 250-mile hike. What precious time for prayer! Probably Paul never noticed the distances. His feet were tramping up hill and down dale, but his head was only mechanically noting the sights and sounds along the way because he was in Heaven, busy at the throne.

What an example for us! No time to pray? We could employ countless moments each day if we really cared.

b.   A Christ-centered Prayer (1:17-23)

(1) Paul Wanted Them to Know More of the Person of Christ
     (1:17) "That the God of our Lord Jesus Christ, the Father of
     glory, may give unto you the spirit of wisdom and revelation in
     the knowledge of him."

Paul rarely prayed for the things that loom so large in our
prayers—better health, more money, job conditions, family problems, world crises. Paul prayed that people might know God better,
that they might become better acquainted with Jesus.

Knowledge of God must come from God. Paul described Him in
Ephesians 1:17 as "the God of our Lord Jesus Christ, the Father of
glory." In 1 Corinthians 2:8 Jesus is described as "the Lord of glory."
So God the Father is the Father of glory, and God the Son is the Lord
of glory. God the Holy Spirit is the revealer of glory (1 Corinthians
2:9-11). The spirit of wisdom and revelation that gives us the
knowledge of Him must come from the Holy Spirit.

A person can only be known through a process of revelation. A
clever Sherlock Holmes might be able to say, "Elementary, my dear
Watson," and proceed to produce a string of startling facts about
another person, but a process of reasoning cannot go much further
than that. Through reasoning we can learn *about* another person.
But if we are ever to know that person, that person must *reveal*
himself—show what he is like through words and actions, express
his thoughts and feelings, hopes and ambitions, likes and dislikes,
frustrations and fears, wants and wishes. Reason takes us just so far
on the road to knowing another person; self-revelation is essential
if we are to go farther.

Likewise God can be known in small measure through the
evidence we have of Him in creation—"even his eternal power and
Godhead," as Paul put it in Romans 1:20. We can know about God,
but we can only know Him in all the glory of His personality as He
reveals Himself to us.

He has revealed Himself in two ways—in the inspired Word and
the incarnate Word. He has *said* what He is like in the one, and He
has *shown* what He is like in the other. Our responsibility is to get to
know Him by getting to know the Scriptures and the Savior. There
is no greater or grander occupation here on earth.

Paul prayed that his fellow believers might have a spirit of wisdom
and revelation and that they might be occupied in gaining knowledge of God. "Get to know Him" is Paul's basic answer to all of life's
problems and perplexities. Knowing God would solve most of the

present-day problems that cause people to run to the psychologist or the family counselor. Knowing God would affect how people cope with all areas of life.

(2) Paul Wanted Them to Know More of the Portion of Christ (1:18)

(a) Our Hope Is in Him (1:18a) "The eyes of your understanding being enlightened; that ye may know what is the hope of his calling."

We enter into the "hope of his calling" by faith. That calling has its commencement in the council chambers of the living God in eternity past (Ephesians 1:4); it has its continuance in our coming to know Christ as Savior and the Holy Spirit as Comforter (1:13); and it has its completion in Heaven (1:14).

The "hope of his calling" embraces the wide sweep of God's eternal purposes in Christ. Our hope is in Him. We have not merely hitched our wagon to a star. We have been caught up in something so big, so basic to the universe, and so far beyond anything we could ask or think, that our minds simply cannot take it all in. No wonder Paul prayed that the eyes of our understanding might be enlightened.

We have become the objects of the triune God's attention and affection. Father, Son, and Holy Spirit are each interested in us and our eternal well-being. They have turned aside from their occupation with the details of the hundred billion galaxies to concentrate on us. Angels and archangels, cherubim and seraphim, "thrones and dominions" desire to look into these things (1 Peter 1:12). The sinless sons of light find human life more interesting than galactic life.

When God's Beloved stooped down from Heaven's heights to be born in that Bethlehem barn for us, it was an event so momentous that Heaven's hosts crowded down the skyways and starways to peer in wonder into that musty manger, adore the newborn babe, and shout the tidings across Judea's echoing hills. And God has not finished with us yet! Our hope in Him stretches out beyond our threescore and ten years to the endless ages of eternity. What awaits us on the other side is more than tongue can tell.

Paul wanted us to be occupied with thoughts about our hope in Christ. They help us put the mundane things of time and sense into perspective. Here is that fulcrum outside the earth for which Archimedes longed. Here is that lever, long enough to exert the pressure needed so that one lone Man could lift the whole wide world.

(b) His Heritage Is in Us (1:18b) "The riches of the glory of his inheritance in the saints."

God gets something out of our salvation too! What we get out of it defies description; what He gets out of it transcends comprehension. What we get is Him. What He gets is us. A poor bargain for Him, it would seem. But evidently He considered us eminently worth saving. The only explanation is His amazing, divine love—a love that is its own reason and logic.

We note the *fact* of His inheritance. Paul spoke of His inheritance in the saints; He has no inheritance in the sinner. His redemptive work gives us our value, which must be measured in terms of Christ's precious blood.

We note the *fame* of His inheritance. Paul spoke of the glory of His inheritance. It is the theme of seraph song, the wonder of all wonders in a land specializing in glory.

We note the *fullness* of His inheritance. Paul spoke of the riches of the glory. In some wondrous way we have become a source of untold wealth in the balance sheets of Heaven. We are assets of incredible worth to the living God—the brightest jewels in His diadem.

Such is the portion of Christ. We cannot understand it and can scarcely take it in. We can only marvel that the Holy Spirit tells us these things are so.

(3) Paul Wanted Them to Know More of the Power of Christ (1:19-21)

(a) The Direction of It (1:19a) "The exceeding greatness of his power to us-ward who believe."

We see something of the surpassing greatness of God's power when we turn our giant telescopes toward the sky. Our sun for instance is rated a star of only the fifth magnitude. It shines with a mild, yellow light and is 100,000 times less luminous than its brightest neighbor. Nevertheless the sun evokes our awe. It is 864,000 miles in diameter, consists of some 335 quadrillion cubic miles of violently hot gases, and weighs more than 2 octillion tons. It orbits the center of our galaxy, the Milky Way, once every 200 million years.

With the naked eye we can see only about 7,000 stars. The Milky Way, however, contains about 100 billion orbiting stars and is 100,000 light-years in diameter—an inconceivable 600 million billion miles of stars!

Astronomer Edwin Hubble calculated that there are as many galaxies outside the Milky Way as there are stars in it. Since the galaxies are moving farther and farther away from earth, the entire visible universe is expanding in every direction. The distance between the Milky Way and Hydra—a group of distant galaxies that are "as thick as raisins" and some 2.7 billion light-years away—is increasing at a speed of 38,000 miles per second. The Hydra galaxies are receding, in other words, at one-fifth the speed of light. Such is the exceeding greatness of God's power in the macrouniverse.

We see something of that power, too, in the microuniverse. Atoms are less than one-millionth of the thickness of a human hair. In the nucleus of the atom, numerous protons and neutrons are packed together in an inconceivably small space. Each proton and neutron consists of three even smaller particles called quarks. If a hydrogen atom were four miles in diameter, the nucleus would only be the size of a tennis ball! The remainder of the atom is mostly empty space in which electrons travel around the nucleus, making billions of trips each millionth of a second. Their incredible speed makes the atom behave as though it were solid. Facts such as these make our minds reel, but such is the exceeding greatness of God's power.

We see the exceeding greatness of His power *skyward* and *earthward*. In the redemptive process we see the exceeding greatness of His power *"us-ward."* It took as much power to effect our redemption as it did to effect creation. To create, God only had to speak. To redeem, He had to suffer. A seemingly endless universe is the demonstration of the one; an empty tomb is the evidence of the other. Paul reminded us here of the direction of God's immeasurable power. It is "to us-ward who believe." There's no excuse for any child of God to live a defeated, discouraged life. All the power of the godhead is directed toward us.

The book of Esther contains an illustration of directed power. Under the urging of Mordecai, Queen Esther agreed to approach the imperious King Ahasuerus on behalf of the Jews who were under dire threat of extermination. To approach this despotic monarch unbidden was to court death—even for Esther. Nevertheless, Esther walked that knife-edge of uncertainty. Arrayed in her royal robes, she approached and then stopped within sight of the king. "And it was so, when the king saw Esther the queen standing in the court, that she obtained favour in his sight: and the king held out to Esther the golden sceptre that was in his hand. So Esther drew near, and touched the top of the sceptre" (Esther 5:2).

All the power of the throne was suddenly turned toward Esther.

From then on, step by step, the power of that throne was exerted on her behalf and on behalf of her people. That is what has happened to us who believe. We have all the power of God who sits on the throne of Heaven directed toward us.

(b) The Dimensions of It (1:19b) "The working of his mighty power."

The Greek word translated "power" here, *kratos*, means "strength or power put forth with effect." We catch echoes of this word in several English words: "aristocracy" (government by the best), "democracy" (government by the people), and "theocracy" (government by God). The Greek word translated "might" is *ischus*, which means "strength as an endowment." *Ischus* is physical strength such as that mentioned in Mark 12:30: "Thou shalt love the Lord thy God with all thy heart, and with all thy soul, and with all thy mind, and with all thy strength." The word translated "working" is *energeia*, which means "strength put forth, energy." God made an enormous expenditure of His strength, power, and energy in the work of the cross and the subsequent emptying of the tomb in order to redeem us from sin.

(c) The Demonstration of It (1:20a) "Which he wrought in Christ, when he raised him from the dead."

Men had done their worst! They had beaten Christ until His face was scarcely recognizable and scourged Him until His back was as furrowed as a farmer's field. They had crowned Him with thorns so that blood ran in rivers down His head. They had wrenched His beard. Then they nailed Him to a wooden cross and hung Him up to die. Every bone in His body was out of joint; sheer physical exhaustion and raging thirst levied their toll. Agonizing minutes crept on until, after six hours of torment, He imperially dismissed His Spirit, bowed His head, and died. To make sure He was dead, a soldier took a spear and stabbed Him.

Christ was taken down from the cross. Loving hands bathed His mortal remains and swathed them in spices and bandages, layer upon layer. His body was put into a rock-hewn tomb and the entrance, closed with a massive stone, was secured with the Roman governor's seal. Then a guard was detailed to patrol the site and keep intruders away. That was that! Christ was dead and buried— or so men thought.

Soon it would be safe to remove the guard. The natural process of corruption and decay was at work. A little longer and the much-feared three days to His foretold resurrection would have come and gone. Then Jesus could be written off as a notable impostor. His story would be interred in the rubbish heap of history. Christ's claim to be God manifest in flesh would never survive the dissolution of His body in the tomb.

The hours passed slowly. His enemies bet that Christ would not rise again and that the Jesus movement would collapse. But God on His throne in Heaven was laughing and Christ was proclaiming His triumph to the souls of the departed in Hades. His body lay in stately grandeur on its granite slab, quietly sleeping, defying the ordinary processes of death.

Then when the third day dawned, Christ burst the bands of death, rose bodily through the hampering graveclothes, and marched out in the power of an endless life through the sealed door of the tomb. With a wild yell of mortal terror the soldiers fled for Jerusalem. Christ's resurrection appearances began, and the empty tomb became the evidence that He did rise again. Raising Jesus from the dead was the demonstration of God's energy.

(d) The Distinction of It (1:20b-21)

i.   All Seats of Power Are Beneath Him (1:20b-21b)

a.   Where He Is Seated (1:20b) God "set him at his own right hand in the heavenly places."

The same mighty power that raised Christ from the tomb would now raise Him to the heavenly throne. He stood there for a moment on Olivet to say a final fond farewell to those He had come to redeem, to look one last time into the faces of Peter, James, John, Thomas, Matthew, Philip, Andrew, Nathanael, and the rest of the disciples. He gazed one last time into the face of His beloved mother who now had joined the ranks of His own. Then raising His hands He summoned the angel escort and slowly rose toward the sky. The clouds wrapped around Him, the earth receded, the starry hosts rolled past in grand array, Heaven's gates appeared, and in He went.

Amid the hallelujahs of Heaven He made His way along the streets of gold, across the crystal stream, and up to the very throne of God. Then in a battle-scarred body of transfigured human clay, He sat down at the right hand of the Majesty on high.

That is where He is seated still, all other seats of power beneath Him. Around that throne are twenty-four other thrones, but those who sit on them cast their crowns before Him. At the four corners of His throne stand the four living creatures who only exist to sing His praise. Myriads of angels who fill Heaven's halls with ceaseless songs, hang on His words and rush to do His will.

b.   What He Has Subdued (1:21a-b)

1.   All Spiritual Seats of Power (1:21a) "Far above all principality, and power, and might, and dominion."

Principalities and powers are Satan's allies. Angelic beings of enormous power, they help him hold fast to his domains in the spirit world. They are his agents too in holding the world of men in subjection to him (Ephesians 6:12).

Sin did not begin on earth; it began in Heaven. Sin did not originate with the fall of man, but with the fall of Lucifer. Revelation 12 suggests that Satan's rebellion infected a third of the heavenly hosts. But not all the angels fell when Satan fell. The word *dominion* in Ephesians 1:21 may refer to the angelic rulers in the spirit world who side with God in the age-long battle against sin. *Might* and *dominion* here and *thrones* and *dominions* in Colossians 1:16 probably refer to the same ruling powers, and the thrones are probably the same as those mentioned in Revelation 4:4.

The Lord Jesus is enthroned far above all spiritual seats of power. Satan is no match for Him. Satan's hosts cannot hope to win. All they can do now is put on a brave show. As for Heaven's ruling hierarchy, they gladly acknowledge the vastness of the gulf that separates them from Christ by casting their crowns at His feet.

2.   All Secular Seats of Power (1:21b) "And every name that is named."

Whatever forms of government there are and whatever the names or titles of those in power may be, all are subject to Christ. Earthly kingdoms and empires wax and wane, coming and going like ocean tides. Christ reigns on high and overrules them all. All who govern must learn the lesson God taught Nebuchadnezzar: "The heavens do rule" (Daniel 4:26).

Babylonian despot or Persian satrap, Greek conqueror or Roman caesar, pope or prince, holy Roman emperor or Muslim sultan, British monarch or German dictator, American president or Russian commissar—all must learn that "the powers that be are ordained of God" (Romans 13:1). God has set *His* king on His holy hill of Zion. No power in Heaven, earth, or Hell can alter that. All secular seats of power are subservient to His.

Why has the invincible sovereign power that now rests wholly in Christ's hands seemingly been held back? That is part of the mystery of an age of grace.

ii.   All Spheres of Power Are Before Him (1:21c) "Not only in this world, but also in that which is to come."

In this age where sin abounds, grace much more abounds (Romans 5:20). Because we are living in an age of grace, injustice often seems to triumph and the abuse of power often goes unchecked. God deliberately holds back His arm of omnipotence—to the puzzlement of many thoughtful people. A young soldier on active duty with me asked, "Why doesn't God stop this terrible war?" My answer was glib: "Why should He? He didn't start it." But the truth is, He could have averted the war or stopped it, but He didn't because this is not the age of intervention.

An even greater mystery revolved around the cross. I think it was Archbishop Trench who said:

> He might have built a palace at a word,
> Who sometime had not where to lay His head;
> Time was when He who nourished crowds with bread
> Could not one meal unto Himself afford.
> Twelve legions girded with angelic sword
> Were at His back, the scorned and buffeted;
> He healed another's hurts, His own side bled,
> Side, feet and hands with cruel piercing gored.
> Oh wonderful the wonders left undone!
> And scarce less wonderful than those He wrought;
> Oh, self restraint, passing all human thought,
> To have all-power and be as having none;
> Oh, self-denying love, which felt alone
> For needs of others, never for its own.

If God stayed His hand at Calvary when twelve legions of angels arrayed for battle strained over the battlements of Heaven with drawn swords, it is no wonder that He stays His hand today. This is not "the day of vengeance of our God." The Lord Jesus made that abundantly clear when in the Nazareth synagogue He broke off His Scripture reading in the middle of a sentence (Luke 4:18-19; Isaiah 61:1-2). This is God's day of grace and man's day of opportunity.

The day will come, however, when His power will be displayed. Man's day will end and the day of the Lord will begin. Then it will be evident that the Lord Jesus is seated "above all principality, and power, and might, and dominion, and every name that is named."

(4) Paul Wanted Them to Know More of the Position of Christ (1:22-23)

(a) Paul Wanted Us to Consider the Lord's Feet (1:22a) "And hath put all things under his feet."

There is something gloriously appropriate in these words from Ephesians 1:22, since men once pierced His feet. Christ will put His feet on the necks of His enemies and the earth will be His footstool.

When John the beloved disciple saw the Lord he loved in all the splendor of His unveiled glory and majesty—His face shining like the sun, His feet glowing like burnished brass, His eyes flaming like fire—he fell at His feet as if dead! If such was the reaction of His closest human friend on earth, what will happen to His foes when they see Him? What about Caiaphas, the self-seeking, cynical high priest who so dreadfully disgraced what should have been the highest and holiest office in the land and used his position to manipulate Christ's unjust trial and bring about His death? What about Herod, who with his soldiers scoffed at Jesus? What about Pilate, who signed the death warrant of a man he knew was innocent? What about the man who punched Him in the face and said, "Prophesy unto us, thou Christ, Who is he that smote thee?" (Matthew 26:68) What about all the people who have cursed His name, spurned His grace, refused His salvation, or done despite to the Spirit of grace? They, like Satan, are under His feet. Christ will yet trample on that old serpent and crush his head.

(b) Paul Wanted Us to Consider the Lord's Fullness (1:22b-23)

i.   The Church Finds All Its Fullness in Him, the Head (1:22b) "And gave him to be the head over all things to the church."

When many people think of the church, they think of the vast, organized system of religion that emerged in the second or third centuries of the Christian era. That system became the state religion of the Roman empire and today is represented by the Roman Catholic and Eastern Orthodox churches and the various Protestant denominations. This vast conglomeration is not the church; it is *Christendom.*

The *church,* on the other hand, consists of blood-bought saints of God who have put their personal faith in the Lord Jesus, who have been baptized by the Holy Spirit into the body of Christ, and who are now indwelt by Him. That is the church. Its members are found in all parts of Christendom. It knows no denominational boundaries. It is not limited by race or creed, color or class, time or space. (More of its members now live in Heaven than on earth.) Its unity is not an organizational unity, but an organic unity. The church is universal, mystical, invincible.

Christ, who is head over all things in the universe, is head over all things in the church. He is in Heaven, seated on high, enthroned at God's right hand. The head of the church is what gives the church its dignity and destiny. Members of the true church find their fullness in their relationship to the head.

ii.   The Christ Finds All His Fullness in Us, the Body (1:23) "Which is his body, the fulness of him that filleth all in all."

This statement should make us gasp. Indeed, we would consider such a statement to be blasphemy or the word of a madman if it were found anywhere but in the Bible. But this is the Word of the Holy Spirit, written in the Word of the living God.

We cannot comprehend this statement or exhaust it. It is God's solemn word that the Lord Jesus—who fills all in all, who is higher than the high, who conceived and created the universe through His omniscient and omnipotent power, who is the object of angelic worship and the ceaseless theme of seraph song—is incomplete without us. We can understand that we are incomplete without Him, but that He should be incomplete without us is incomprehensible.

This incompleteness is not a trivial thing, as when a man who dresses for a formal occasion forgets his top hat. Christ is as incomplete without us as a head would be without its body.

1. R. A. Laidlaw, "The Reason Why" (New York: Loizeaux, revised 1959), 31-32.
2. Liddell and Scott, quoted by Kenneth Wuest, *Ephesians and Colossians in the Greek New Testament* (Grand Rapids: Eerdmans, 1953), 42.
3. See Wuest, 42-43.
4. See John Phillips, *Exploring Revelation* (Neptune, NJ: Loizeaux, 1987).
5. See Phillips, *Bible Explorer's Guide* (Neptune, NJ: Loizeaux, 1987).

B. The Revolution of the Christian Life (2:1-22)

1. The Great Dispositional Change (2:1-10)

a. The Past (2:1-3)

(1) We Were Dead (2:1) "And you hath he quickened, who were dead in trespasses and sins."

This statement only deepens the mystery of God's dealings in grace. Those who are "the fulness of him that filleth all in all" were once "dead in trespasses and sins."

We were not just dead; we were dead in trespasses. The Greek word translated "trespasses" is *paratōma*, which means "a falling aside when one should have stood upright." This word conveys the idea of falling aside from truth and uprightness and is used to describe Adam's disobedience (Romans 5:15-18). The law was introduced so that this form of sin, *paratōma*, might be thought of as criminal in the mind of the sinner—just as it is in the mind of God.

We were also dead in sins. The word translated "sins" is derived from *hamartono*, which means "to miss the mark, to wander from the right path, to go wrong, to do wrong." Sin entered the world when Adam fell (Romans 5:12).

The natural consequence of falling aside, of missing the mark, was death. Thus, in our natural state, God sees us as dead in trespasses and sins.

When a man sets out to make something, he usually starts with the best possible materials—the purest clay, the finest marble, the choicest wood. But God goes to the refuse heap and selects materials that are worthless. He begins with people who are dead!

It is amazing what modern medicine can do for a patient. Doctors can remodel disfigured faces, transplant kidneys, implant lenses, bypass arteries—as long as the patient is alive. Once the person is dead, doctors can do nothing more than pull a sheet over the body and transfer the corpse to the morgue. But God begins with people who are dead in the fullest sense of the word—dead in trespasses and sins.

(2) We Were Deluded (2:2a) "Wherein in time past ye walked
according to the course of this world, according to the prince of
the power of the air."

Before we accepted Christ as Savior, our utter deadness to
spiritual things was evident in our behavior. We walked according
to "the course of this world." In other words, the spirit of the age
held us in its iron grip.

The word translated "course" is *aion.* This means an age or a period
of time during which certain things happen or a certain spirit or
attitude prevails. We live in a world that always displays a spirit of
hostility toward God. Whether the prevailing mentality is one of
adventure, persecution, discovery, or tolerance, the general spirit
will be worldly, fleshly, and devilish. Why? Because this world is the
sworn enemy of God. The Bible warns of this enmity repeatedly: "If
any man love the world, the love of the Father is not in him" (1 John
2:15). John summarized the spirit of the world as "the lust of the
flesh, and the lust of the eyes, and the pride of life" (2:16). The spirit
of the age is determined by the spirit of the world.

Once we walked according to the spirit of the age and our noblest
thoughts, our most generous impulses, our loftiest ambitions, and
our most religious aspirations were utterly devoid of spiritual
content. We were dead. The spirit of the air also had a hold on us.

The Bible clearly says that there are spirits in the unseen world of
the air. These spirits are fallen, malignant, and bitterly hostile to
man, and they are ruled by the dread prince of the power of the air.
This dark lord, who roams the heavenlies, is Satan. He is the one
who brings evil influences to bear upon the world of men. Our state
of spiritual death was demonstrated by the fact that we walked
according to the spirit of the power of the air. Satan had such
complete control over us that his influence was as all-encompassing
as the air. The air is all about us. It exerts constant but unnoticed
pressure on us. It can at times be felt, but in its essence it is invisible
and intangible. Such is Satan and his influence on the human race.

The reference to "the prince of the power of the air" in Ephesians
2:2 is deliberate and definitive. The Holy Spirit, who is Himself
likened to the wind (John 3:8), uses the title to depict Satan and his
sphere.

In our unregenerate state, we were completely deceived by Satan.
We walked according to the course *(aion)* of this world and according to the spirit of the power of the air. We were so devoid of spiritual
life that we were unaware of our deadness to spiritual things. The
fact that people are spiritually dead explains much that goes on in

the name of religion, philosophy, science, culture, and education even to this day.

Paul borrowed the terminology of the Gnostic heretics to expose who was really behind their anti-Christian ideas. The Gnostics taught that the universe was ruled by *aeōns,* emanations of deity. The prince *(archōn)* of the power *(exousia)* of the air ruled the air. The whole body of *aeōns* made up the fullness *(pleroma)* of the spirit world. These, according to the Gnostics, were the ultimate realities and they stood in contrast with the material world. The strength of Gnostic teaching lay in the fact that, although false and deadly in its hostility to Christianity, it was not altogether void of some vestiges of truth. All subtle doctrinal error contains a mixture of truth and error.

(3) We Were Disobedient (2:2b) "The spirit that now worketh in the children of disobedience."

The force of these words is far stronger than our translation suggests. Paul was not simply saying that we were disobedient children, for the Greek word rendered "children" is derived from *huios. Huios,* meaning "a son," has special reference to one's origin, nature, and relationship to his father. Therefore Paul was saying that we were sons of the disobedient one—Satan. We had the nature and character of that evil spirit who prompts people to disobey God. Through one man's disobedience sin entered the world, so we are heirs to a disobedient spirit.

One of the first behaviors a child displays, as soon as it is able to express its developing personality, is disobedience. No one ever has to teach a child to be disobedient. Rather, a child has to be taught to obey, and the lesson has to be reinforced often. Disobedience comes naturally. Satan has an enormous advantage—our fallen natures are allied to his.

God has to overcome this disobedient spirit in man. That is one reason He took redeemed Israel to Sinai, gave them the law, and instituted an age-long course of discipline. That is why He found such delight in His Son, who did "always those things that please" the Father (John 8:29), and why in this age He commands all men everywhere to repent (Acts 17:30).

So complete are the results of the fall that we have no natural interest in obeying the gospel; our first inclination is to disobey God. Even after we accept Christ, we find it difficult to tread the path of obedience, to believe that God's will for us is "good, and acceptable, and perfect" (Romans 12:2). All too often Satan still manages to persuade us that our own way is best, and that God's will is irksome, unpleasant, and even downright dangerous. "If you let God have His way," Satan whispers, "He'll send you to serve in a leper colony," or "He'll spoil all your fun." Satan slanders God with such suggestions. Our all-wise and all-loving God would never call us to do something for which He had not adequately prepared us and given the appropriate measure of His grace.

(4) We Were Defiled (2:3a) "Among whom also we all had our conversation [manner of life] in times past in the lusts of our flesh, fulfilling the desires of the flesh and of the mind."

Before we accepted Christ, we were controlled by natural desire. Natural desire is what Paul meant by "lusts of our flesh." The word "flesh" here refers to human nature. The Greek word translated "lusts" is *epithumia,* meaning "strong desire," not necessarily evil. For instance, Jesus said, "With desire I have desired to eat this passover with you before I suffer" (Luke 22:15). Paul wrote to Timothy, "If a man desire the office of a bishop, he desireth a good work" (1 Timothy 3:1). Even in unregenerate people, natural desire may produce some commendable results and fine endeavors, though devoid of spiritual worth. But there is a dark side to human desire. Paul had this side in mind when in Ephesians 2:3 he spoke of "fulfilling the desires of the flesh and of the mind." ·

We were also controlled by natural depravity. Fallen human nature gravitates to low things—to gross lusts of the body and contaminating lusts of the mind. Man may seek to disguise this depravity by culture and refinement, but underneath, these lusts burn like a seething volcano that from time to time erupts to his sorrow and shame.

(5) We Were Doomed (2:3b) "And were by nature the children of wrath, even as others."

The word translated "children" here means children by natural descent. We were born of sinful parents into a sin-cursed world. We were born possessed of a bent and inherently sinful nature, and exposed to God's wrath. Fortunately for the survival of the human race, God is rich in mercy, a theme Paul later developed with great delight. The fact remains, however, that wrath was all that we deserved. Wrath filled our horizon.

Sin has clouded our ability to think clearly about the nature of God. We have only the sketchiest notion of what God's blazing holiness is like. The shining seraphim who stand before His throne know. So bright is the effulgence of His glory, the burning brightness of His being, that they hide their faces in their wings and cry,

"Holy, holy, holy!" We have no real understanding of how outraged God is by our sin, what an insult sin is to His person, or how sin fires the flames of His wrath.

[Such then was our past condition. We were without God, without Christ, without hope. We were sinners by birth, by choice, and by practice. Our lot was cast in a world controlled by the evil one, and our eternal destiny was to live forever under God's wrath and curse. But the Holy Spirit does not leave the matter there.]

b.   The Present (2:4-6)

(1) God's Love Shown to Us (2:4-5a)

(a) Its Richness (2:4) "But God, who is rich in mercy, for his great love wherewith he loved us."

Thank God for that "But"! The *buts* of the Bible are always arresting; they are hinges on which great issues turn. Think for instance of the *buts* in the lives of Solomon (1 Kings 11:1), Uzziah (2 Chronicles 26:15-16), and the prodigal son (Luke 15:20,22).

(Paul had painted a very black picture of human depravity and divine wrath. Now this glorious "But" draws our attention to God's mercy and love)

God is rich in mercy. It would have been cold comfort merely to be informed that God is rich. He *is* rich. We will never fully know how rich He is until we arrive at our heavenly home. Then we will see how He paves the streets of His city with gold, builds walls of jasper, makes foundations blaze with precious stones, and forms gates of pearl. Ten million times ten million million worlds are His. He makes the ministers of His throne a flame of fire and sits high and lifted up on a rainbow-circled throne bathed in the ringing anthems of celestial throngs. He is rich in wisdom, rich in majesty and might, rich in glory. And he is rich in mercy! He has lavished the vast treasures of His mercy on us. Blessed be His name.

> Oh for a thousand tongues to sing
> My great Redeemer's praise,
> The glories of my God and King,
> The triumphs of His grace.
> (Charles Wesley)

And our merciful God loves us. Paul wrote not of His love, but of "his great love." Only great love could embrace the sin-sodden wretches Paul described in verses 1-3. God does not just pity us. He loves us.

The grown daughter of a man I know is an alcoholic. I was visiting his home one day when she was delivered to his door in the grip of her terrible vice. She had drunk almost an entire bottle of whiskey. Her temper was flaming and abusive. Her face was flushed, her manner belligerent, her actions violent. I thought of the young girl I had met years before—before drink laid its devilish hand on her life. I looked at the picture of the young unspoiled girl that still hung on the wall of this man's home. I pitied the poor soul with all my heart for the terrible shipwreck she had made of her life, for the ruin of her womanhood, and for her slavery to such a cruel and relentless tyrant.

Her father took her gently by the arm, ignoring her abuse. He steered her unsteady footsteps to his car. He carefully settled her in, his face drawn and his eyes filled with pain. She thrashed around, but he patiently strapped her into the seat, drove her home, and put her to bed. I pitied her; he loved her. Multiply her wretchedness by all the misery sin has wrought in this world and multiply her father's love by infinity. Such is God's great love. He did not just pity me. He loved me. As Samuel Medley put it:

> He saw me ruined by the fall,
> Yet loved me notwithstanding all,
> He freed me from my lost estate,
> His loving kindness, oh how great!

(b) Its Reality (2:5a) "Even when we were dead in sins."

God in His great love did not shrink from us even when we were dead in sins.

Sir Henry Rider Haggard provided an illustration of such love in his novel, *Montezuma's Daughter*. His hero, Thomas Wingfield, found himself trapped among the Aztec Indians during the last stages of their empire. He married, half willingly and half by the sheer pressure of circumstances, the lovely daughter of Montezuma, the princess of the Otomie. He cared for her, admired her, and was more than half in love with her. But half his heart was far away in the England of his birth and with the sweetheart of his boyhood days.

Then the Spanish conquistadors forced the Indians into a desperate war. By virtue of his hatred of the Spaniards and his rank among the Indians, Thomas Wingfield was in the forefront of many fierce battles. The Spaniards, however, brought more than war, famine, and rapine—they brought the plague. Princess Otomie contracted it in its most terrible form, but fortunately escaped not only death but also the terrible disfigurement the plague so often left in its wake.

As her husband nursed her through her illness and ravings, he learned of the depth of her love for him and of her secret fear that he might leave her. When Otomie recovered, she asked her husband to give her a mirror and she breathed a great sigh of relief when she saw that she was still beautiful. In telling this part of his story Wingfield said:

> Supposing Otomie was now as many were . . . a mass of dreadful scars, hairless, and with blind and whitened eyeballs, should I then have shrunk from her? I do not know, and I thank heaven that no such trial was put upon my constancy. But I am sure of this; had I become a *leper* even, Otomie would not have shrunk from *me* (italics added).

God's love was put to an even greater test. He loved us when we were dead in trespasses and sins. The apostle's astonishment was expressed in that word *even*. "Even," he said, "when we were dead in sins."

(2) God's Love Shared with Us (2:5b-6)

(a) It Plucked Us from the Tomb (2:5b-6a) "Hath quickened us together with Christ, (by grace ye are saved;) And hath raised us up together."

The only thing to do with a dead person is to bury him. We have no other solution to the problem of death. The corpse can be washed and groomed, and the cosmetics and the skills of the embalmer can be employed. But the body is still a corpse, and the only place for it is the tomb.

(God, however, is not daunted by death. Our trespasses and sins had brought us to the place of death, but then God acted in grace and power. He quickened us. He made us alive, plucked us from the tomb. The resurrection of Christ was the key.) Since all our trespasses and sins were dealt with on the cross, when Christ arose it became possible for us to arise. God raised us from the tomb in which our trespasses and sins had placed *us*, just as He raised Christ from the tomb in which our trespasses and sins had placed *Him*. The debt was cancelled. Sin's penalty was paid. Death's hold was broken. We were quickened together with Him. Grace triumphed over guilt and the grave; God reached down into the corruption of death and raised us up.

(b) It Placed Us on the Throne (2:6b) "And made us sit together in heavenly places in Christ Jesus."

Imagine the awesome wonder of it: God has seated us on His glorious throne! In Christ we are already seated where He is. God has enveloped us in Christ so that when He looks at us, He always sees Him. No matter how or when God looks at us, He sees Christ— sees Him in all the beauty of His holiness, all the glory of His grace, and all the splendor of His person. We are like the boards of the tabernacle in the Old Testament that were hewn from gnarled, twisted acacia wood and then encased in gold. When people looked at those boards, all they saw was the gold. The same is true of us. When God looks at us, He sees Christ.

God has "made us sit together in heavenly places." If we could start at some point on earth and draw an imaginary line upward from earth to Heaven, up to where Christ sits at the right hand of God, at first we might draw our line up beyond the highest mountains. But the line would have to go higher than that. We might reach up beyond the clouds, beyond the stratosphere, beyond the radiation belts that girdle the globe. But our line would have to go still higher. We might trace the line on up until it is among the stars, climbing farther and farther into the starry heavens, leaving the Milky Way and our nearest neighbor galaxies far behind. But still we would have to go higher. At last we might leave behind the remotest star in space and cross the Great Divide between a space-matter-time dimension into an eternal, spiritual dimension. Our line might pass from star land into glory land, climbing past the shining sentinels at the gates of Heaven ever upward to the towering peak of the ultimate Zion. If we finally reached the dizzy peaks and pinnacles of glory, we would see the dazzling throne where God sits, where Christ sits, where He has "made us sit." We sit there together. This is a thought beyond all thought: He has raised us from the tomb and placed us on the throne. The verbs *quickened, raised,* and *seated* in Ephesians 2:5-6 are all in the aorist tense—it is already done.

c.   The Prospect (2:7-10)

(1) Unstinted Grace (2:7-9)

(a) Eternally Revealed Through Us (2:7) "That in the ages to come he might shew the exceeding riches of his grace in his kindness toward us through Christ Jesus."

Man's sin gave God the opportunity to display a side of His character that otherwise might never have been fully revealed. In His work of creation He displayed His wisdom and His power. (The more we learn about astronomy, physics, chemistry, biology, and medicine, the more we learn about God's infinite wisdom and power.) On the stage of redemption God demonstrated not just His grace, not just the riches of His grace, but the exceeding riches of His grace. As Robert C. Chapman put it:

> God is love I surely know
> By my Savior's depths of woe.

That grace will be eternally exhibited through the church—the ultimate vehicle of its expression—to an awed and admiring universe. (All the varied ranks and orders of creation will see God's throne and will see Christ there, bearing in His body the scars of Calvary, the only marks of sin evident in glory. They will also see us there, trophies of God's grace.)

(b) Eternally Revealed To Us (2:8-9) "For by grace are ye saved through faith; and that not of yourselves: it is the gift of God: Not of works, lest any man should boast."

Here is one of the great summaries of the gospel in the New Testament. Some argue over what the gift is, but it seems clear that it is neither grace nor faith. The gift is salvation, made available to us by God's grace and received by us through faith. Since salvation is a gift, it cannot be earned, merited, or otherwise purchased. The Holy Spirit emphasizes, "Not of works; lest any man should boast."

Suppose God were to take people to Heaven on the basis of their good works. It would then be possible for those people to boast, "I am here because I did this." "I am here because I did not do that." "I am here because of my sacrificial giving." "I am here because of my ascetic living." Boasting is an expression of pride and pride was the original sin, the sin that transformed Lucifer into Satan. Because of his pride, Satan was cast out of Heaven and the vast cycle of sin began. Boasting in Heaven about one's works would necessitate another expulsion and give rise to a fresh outbreak of sin, so God has put salvation on a basis that levels the axe at pride and completely eliminates boasting. Salvation is the gift of God. It is not of works.

Every false religion has at its heart the principle that salvation must be earned, merited, purchased at a price. The sinner must do something to deserve God's favor. The gospel strikes at the root of all false religions, for it declares that salvation is God's gift, available to sinners solely because of His grace and unmerited favor. Salvation can be obtained only by believing, but through all eternity the nail prints in Jesus' hands will remind us of the enormous cost of God's free gift.

(2) Unstunted Growth (2:10) "For we are his workmanship, created in Christ Jesus unto good works, which God hath before ordained that we should walk in them."

Good works are part of God's plan. They are not the *price* of salvation, but the *proof*. The believer is not saved as a result of good works; good works are the result of salvation. They are the result of God's working in the believer's heart. They are the evidence that he is alive from the dead. They are the proof of the glorious togetherness that exists between the believer and the Savior.

The Lord, when here on earth, lived a life of good works. He "went about doing good," Peter summarized (Acts 10:38). Now through His indwelling Spirit He continues to do His good works in us. This was all part of the eternal plan. The word translated "workmanship," *poiēma*, indicates that we are His poem, His masterpiece. Each of our lives is the canvas on which the Master is producing a work of art that will fill the everlasting ages with His praise.

A great dispositional change marks genuine conversion, so that a person who is still dead in trespasses and sins is in contrast to the believer who has been quickened together with Christ. If we profess to be Christians but our lives exhibit no evidence of behavioral change, we are self-deceived.

2. The Great Dispensational Change (2:11-22)

a. The Blood That Invites (2:11-13)

(1) Our Natural State (2:11-12)

(a) No Covenant Relationship with the God of Israel (2:11) "Wherefore remember, that ye being in time past Gentiles in the flesh, who are called Uncircumcision by that which is called the Circumcision in the flesh made by hands."

The Holy Spirit here emphasizes the great dispensational change brought about by Calvary and Pentecost. This change abolished the fundamental difference between Gentile and Jew.

Ever since the days of Abraham the rite of circumcision had served as a covenantal sign of the unique relationship that existed between God and the Israelites. The Jews gloried in this relationship and in their insular pride contemptuously referred to the Gentiles as "the uncircumcised." In the early church many Jewish believers felt that the church was merely an extension of Israel and insisted that Gentile converts to Christianity should be circumcised too as part of the process of coming into the good of the covenant. Gentile believers bitterly resented this requirement. The amount of space devoted to the subject in Acts and the Epistles demonstrates what a hot issue circumcision was.

Under the new dispensation, both circumcision and uncircumcision are without spiritual significance. Paul emphasized the obsolete nature of circumcision as a religious rite by referring to it as "the Circumcision in the flesh made by hands." True, circumcision was the sign of the Abrahamic covenant made with the nation of Israel—but the church is not Israel. The seal of those who are in the true church is not circumcision in the flesh, but the Holy Spirit in the heart (Ephesians 1:13). Gentiles are brought into a covenantal relationship with the God of Israel, not by becoming proselytes to Judaism, but by putting their faith in Christ. The same is true now of Jews. There is no difference. Calvary and Pentecost effected a remarkable change. Gentiles, who had no covenantal relationship with the God of Israel such as the one the Jews enjoyed and in which they made their boast, now have just such a relationship in the new covenant.

(b) No Commonwealth Relationship with the God of Israel (2:12)
"That at that time ye were without Christ, being aliens from the commonwealth of Israel, and strangers from the covenants of promise, having no hope, and without God in the world."

This verse describes the natural state of the Gentiles. Prior to the great dispensational change that has now taken place, the only way a Gentile could partake of the spiritual blessings and covenantal benefits of Israel was to become a Jewish proselyte. Gentiles were natural-born aliens and had no part in the great covenantal promises God had made to Abraham, Isaac, Jacob, Moses, and David. Cut off from these covenants, the Gentiles had no hope and were without God. Their natural state apart from the gospel was deplorable; they were outside both the covenants and the commonwealth. (The Greek word translated "commonwealth" is *politeia*, "the body politic.")

The Gentile believers knew they had no hope. Pantheons in

Greece and Rome, Egypt and the East, were filled with gods made in the image and likeness of fallen men—gods who lusted and warred, gods who openly displayed vile and violent passions. The more sophisticated Gentiles may have paid lip service to such gods, but they knew these gods were obscenities.

No wonder so many Gentiles looked longingly at the Jewish religion. But at the same time they were attracted, they were repulsed by the hypocrisy, exclusivism, and pride of the Jews. The Gentiles were attracted by the Scriptures, but repulsed by the Mishna. They were drawn to the synagogue, but repelled by the thought of circumcision. They were attracted by the noble teachings—the moral, spiritual, and ethical content of the Bible—but dismayed by Jewish provincialism and intolerance.

Then the gospel came. No wonder hundreds of thousands of Gentiles instantly recognized its authority, its simplicity, its superiority over Judaism, its glorious availability, and its power. Now they no longer needed to belong to the commonwealth of Israel; they could establish a direct relationship with God themselves.

(2) Our New State (2:13) "But now in Christ Jesus ye who sometimes [once] were far off are made nigh by the blood of Christ."

As Catesby Paget put it:

> So near, so very near to God
> Nearer I cannot be;
> For in the Person of His Son
> I am as near as He.

God made this nearness possible through the shed blood of the Lord Jesus. What grace! Men put Him to death on a cross of shame. It was the crime of the ages. No greater crime could have been conceived. The crucifixion of Christ was the ultimate expression of man's hatred of God, an act of high-handed rebellion and outrage. Yet God turned the crucifixion into the means of His grace, the ultimate expression of His love for us. No greater manifestation of kindness can be imagined.

Once we were prodigals of the universe dwelling in the far country. We had spent our substance in riotous living and were in the grip of famine and want. Nobody cared. Our place was with the swine, and our daily bread was the husks that they ate. In our sin we were a disgrace to the One who had created us. We did not even have the good sense of the prodigal mentioned in the Lord's parable (Luke 15), for we did not know our way home. We groped in darkness and blindly longed for a God we did not know. But when we were yet a great way off, the Father saw us and had compassion on us. He ran and fell on our necks and kissed us. Now we who "were far off" are "made nigh by the blood of Christ."

b.   The Body That Unites (2:14-18)

(1)   Peace Procured for Us (2:14-16)

(a)   The Old Barrier Abolished (2:14-15) "For he is our peace, who hath made both one, and hath broken down the middle wall of partition between us; Having abolished in his flesh the enmity, even the law of commandments contained in ordinances; for to make in himself of twain one new man, so making peace."

The enmity between Jew and Gentile was deep, acrimonious, ancient, and enduring. Jews regarded Gentiles as unclean scavenger dogs. Gentiles despised Jews as grasping, canting, religious hypocrites. Jewish ritual laws, especially the laws concerning clean and unclean food, made it virtually impossible for a conscientious Jew to have table fellowship with a Gentile, so social intercourse was practically forbidden. The commercial instincts of the Jews—developed in Babylon, practiced in Biblical times, and brought to a fine art in later ages—made the Jews moneylenders to the world. Gentiles were often obliged to borrow Jewish money, but that did not endear the Jews to them. The Gentiles used the Jews, but detested them.

So there was what Paul called a "middle wall of partition" between Jew and Gentile. Paul chose this phrase with care. In the temple at Jerusalem a stone palisade about 4-1/2 feet high warned Gentiles, on pain of death, to go no farther. They could enter the court of the Gentiles, but there they had to stop. The Jews fanatically defended the farther temple courts from Gentile intrusion. Indeed, Paul almost suffered death at the hands of a Jerusalem mob when the rumor circulated that he had taken some Gentiles beyond the wall (Acts 21:28-31). The physical "middle wall of partition" was not destroyed until the temple itself was destroyed.

Paul used that physical barrier as a type—a picture—of the great division in the ancient world between Jew and Gentile. Christ, Paul wrote, has broken down that barrier; in Him Jew and Gentile meet on common ground. We are all one in Christ. The cross has swept away the obstacles created by Jewish rituals and laws. Just as Jews and Gentiles united to crucify Christ, so Jews and Gentiles are now united in Christ and His church. The old barrier has been abolished.

(b) The New Bond Established (2:16) "And that he might reconcile
     both unto God in one body by the cross, having slain the enmity
     thereby."

   The church is the body of Christ. In this body all believers are
common members. There are no divisions based on racial origins,
religious backgrounds, class distinctions, national boundaries, or
color prejudices in the true church. All believers are equal members
of this marvelous, mystical body. A new bond has been established.
   This truth is seen only faintly now perhaps, because of human
failings. But it is an eternal truth in the counsels of God and one that
will be universally displayed when the church is finally seen as that
"one new man" mentioned by Paul in Ephesians 2:15.
   Glimpses of this unity can be seen even in the present imperfect
state of the church. At one time I met regularly with a number of
Christians—Britishers and Germans, Russians and Armenians, Jews
and Arabs. Week after week we gathered around the Lord's table.
We were all one in Christ. United in His church, we enjoyed
harmony and peace even when out in the world our national groups
warred and squabbled.

(2) Peace Proclaimed to Us (2:17-18)

(a) All Difference Gone (2:17) "And came and preached peace to
     you which were afar off, and to them that were nigh."

   The Gentiles were afar off; the Jews were nigh. Yet both were
equally lost. They were at war not only with each other but also with
God. Then peace through the blood of Christ was proclaimed to
both, and all differences were gone. In Romans 3:22-23 Paul wrote,
"There is no difference: For all have sinned, and come short of the
glory of God." The smug and surly elder brother was just as lost as
the profligate prodigal. One was afar off, the other was nigh, but
both were equally estranged from the father and needed to be
reconciled. The differences between them were in the outward
expressions of their pride, self-will, and rebellion; they both had the
same inner need of forgiveness and grace.
   The gospel reduces all people to the same level. All people are
brought into the great equation of salvation through the same
common denominator: repentance toward God and faith in the
Lord Jesus Christ. The flood in Noah's day destroyed the people
who stood on the highest mountains and those who cowered in the
deepest valleys. All in the ark equally experienced God's mercy and

salvation. The gospel teaches that all people who do not trust in Christ are equally lost—the distant Gentile and the nearby Jew.

(b) All Distance Gone (2:18) "For through him we both have access by one Spirit unto the Father."

Father, Son, and Holy Spirit unite to bring us back to God and give us access to the Father. The Jews of the Old Testament had acceptance by virtue of sacrifices, but they did not have access. They could not go into the holy of holies. Only the high priest had that kind of access, and then only once a year, under the most stringent of conditions, after the most elaborate of precautions, and for the briefest of moments.

When the Lord Jesus "through the eternal Spirit offered himself without spot to God" (Hebrews 9:14), God reached down and rent the temple veil. He thus rendered Judaism obsolete and at the same time opened up the way for all believers—Jews and Gentiles alike—to enter His presence. All distance is gone.

One day a little boy named Willie stood wistfully at the gates of Buckingham Palace. He longed to go in and see the king. Between him and the king, however, were iron gates, rigid protocol, armed soldiers, and watchful police. What he wanted was quite out of the question.

A policeman who was ordering the lad to leave suddenly stiffened and sprang to attention as a well-dressed, confident man approached. A brusque nod from the man and the policeman unlocked the gates and stood aside. "Come with me, sonny," said the man, taking the little boy's hand. "We're going in to see the king."

Into the palace they went. Inside were forty housemaids, fifty footmen (including one man who did nothing but wind clocks all day), and six hundred rooms. Willie and the man walked on and on—to the north wing, up stairs, along endless passages, to the king's corridor on the main floor, and into the master suite. (They were a quarter of a mile away from the kitchens!)

The man seemed to know the way and chatted about the rooms they passed: the magnificent ballroom that contained two majestic thrones on a raised dais; the stamp rooms that housed the world's most valuable collection; the Belgian suite with its forty-four rooms for the use of state visitors; the royal wardrobe; the music room; the dining room with a table as large as a skating rink; the dazzling green drawing room.

Finally they arrived in the king's presence, and the man spoke.

"Hello, Father. Here's a little boy who wants to meet you. Meet my friend Willie. Willie, this is the king." The little boy had taken the hand of Edward, prince of Wales, the king's son. Through him, Willie gained access to the king.

We too have taken the hand—the nail-printed hand—of the King's Son, the Prince of Peace. Through Him and Him alone, Jews and Gentiles alike have access by one Spirit to the Father.

c.   The Building That Delights (2:19-22)

(1) The New Household (2:19) "Now therefore ye are no more strangers and foreigners, but fellowcitizens with the saints, and of the household of God."

In Ephesians 2:19-20 Paul used the illustrations of a fellowship, a family, and a foundation to explain the new relationship Gentiles now have with God through Christ.

The first illustration is that of a *fellowship*. Once the Gentiles were strangers and foreigners (sojourners). In Old Testament times if they resided among God's people, they were known as "strangers within the gates." Their status was that of tolerated aliens, unless they became proselytes. They did not enjoy citizenship and had no part in the divine covenants. No matter how good or godly such a sojourner might be, he was never known as a saint—although such men as Uriah the Hittite and Araunah the Jebusite are royally mentioned in the holy Scriptures.

For many years I have lived in the United States and enjoyed life among warmhearted, generous Americans. But as a Canadian citizen, my rights in the United States have been limited. I have been free to work, travel, own property, raise a family, and pay my share of taxes! But I have not been free to vote or have any say in government. For a long time I was required to register my whereabouts every year with the Department of Immigration, and at all times I have had to carry a card identifying me as a registered alien. In other words, I am constantly reminded that I am a stranger and a sojourner.

This is reminiscent of the situation of the Gentiles living amidst the Old Testament people of God. No matter who they were or what they did, no matter how good their intentions were or how exemplary their lives, the Gentiles were simply resident aliens. There was friendship with the Jews perhaps, but not true fellowship. How could there be when the Gentiles were uncircumcised strangers from the covenants and commonwealth of Israel?

But now, through Christ, Gentiles are fully integrated into the body politic of the true commonwealth. There is a new fellowship. Gentiles are fellow citizens with the saints. The Greek word translated "fellowcitizens" is *sumpolitēs*. *Sumpolitēs* comes from the word *politēs*, from which we derive our word "politics." *Sumpolitēs* means "a member of a city or state" and conveys the idea of belonging to a country. In Ephesians 2:19 the word implies full union, the possession of the same citizenship.

In Christ Gentiles enjoy a new citizenship. They are full citizens in the heavenly Jerusalem, and the seat of their government is in Heaven. Jews and Gentiles alike now share in the same fellowship. They are equal members of a new society, of another and better country, of a new and far more glorious commonwealth.

The second illustration is a *family*. Jews and Gentiles alike are now members of a new household, the household of God. No longer are Gentiles excluded from the family because of their birth. It was a rare privilege in Old Testament times to be born into a Hebrew family, to be a child of Abraham and an heir of the covenants of God. Now, by virtue of the new birth, both Jews and Gentiles become full-fledged members of God's family. They are Abraham's true spiritual descendants, heirs of the new covenant, children of the living God, members of His household, and brothers and sisters in the royal family of Heaven.

(2) The New Habitation (2:20-22)

(a) The Foundation of the Building (2:20) "And are built upon the foundation of the apostles and prophets, Jesus Christ himself being the chief corner stone."

The third illustration used to explain the new relationship Gentiles have with God is a *foundation*. Paul described the church as a glorious building that rests on a magnificent foundation: Christ and His apostles. The Holy Spirit says, "Other foundation can no man lay than that is laid, which is Jesus Christ" (1 Corinthians 3:11). Everything rests on Him. Without Him there would be no building. If we build on anything else but Christ, we build in vain, for we build on sand (Matthew 7:24-27).

Before their conversion the Gentiles were building on men's idle philosophies or on vain pagan religions. The Jews were building on burdensome rabbinical traditions. None of those foundations could last. They were sandy foundations, firm enough to stand for a while but inadequate when storm tides came. After accepting Christ, both Jews and Gentiles rested on the enduring foundation described in Ephesians 2:20.

The Holy Spirit identifies the apostles and prophets as being part of the foundation of which Christ is the chief cornerstone. They are included because the New Testament revelation was committed to them (John 14:25-26; 15:26-27; 16:12-13). It was the apostles who received the Holy Spirit's inspiration to declare New Testament truth. It was the apostles who received the Holy Spirit's illumination to disseminate New Testament truth. Thus in a sense the apostles and prophets of the New Testament were God's foundational gifts to the church. Their ministry ceased when the New Testament was written and published; their particular kind of work was no longer needed.

Christ is called the chief cornerstone because of its key position in the foundation. The cornerstone was hewn out first, and its corners, planes, and angles were all true. It was dropped into place last to bind all the other stones together and to ensure that all the foundation's lines were accurate. The cornerstone is called "the stone of testing." Likewise the doctrines of the church must line up squarely with what Christ revealed.

A Mormon once asked me which church I attended. I told him and he replied, "Does your church have apostles, prophets, evangelists, pastors, and teachers?"

I answered, "We have evangelists, pastors, and teachers, but we do not have apostles and prophets."

"How can your church be the true church," he said, "if it does not have all the gifts mentioned in Ephesians 4:11?"

"You are overlooking Ephesians 2:20 and Ephesians 3:5," I responded. "These Scriptures are as important as Ephesians 4:11, for they make it clear that the work of the apostles and prophets was to build the foundation of the church. When I build a house my first concern is to get a proper foundation laid, so I call in men who know how to do that. Once the foundation is in, I don't need them anymore. Instead I need carpenters, bricklayers, plumbers, electricians, roofers, and painters. It would be foolish to keep foundation men on the payroll once their job was done. The apostles and prophets completed their foundation-building job in the first century when they wrote the New Testament and then shared it with the world. The church no longer needs them."

"What would you say," he asked, "if I told you that God has raised up a new prophet for these latter days?"

"I should want to know what he prophesied," I replied, "because if it's in the Bible, I don't need it, and if it's not in the Bible, I don't want it."

"I am here," the man said, "to testify to you, sir, that God has raised up another prophet. His name is Joseph Smith, and the new revelation is the Book of Mormon."

"Well sir," I could only say, "based on Ephesians 2:20 and 3:5, Joseph Smith is a false prophet and the Book of Mormon is a book of lies."

The ultimate touchstone, the true cornerstone, is Christ Himself. Mormon doctrine concerning Him is from the evil one.

(b) The Framework of the Building (2:21) "In whom all the building fitly framed together groweth unto an holy temple in the Lord."

In this Epistle Paul compared the church to a body, a building, and a bride. Two of these metaphors stand in remarkable contrast. A healthy body is complete at birth; a building grows by addition.

When a normal baby is born, all his parts are already in place. His body will grow, but not by addition. David wrote, "In thy book all my members were written, which in continuance were fashioned, when as yet there was none of them" (Psalm 139:16). Likewise the church was complete in the purposes of God from the council chambers of eternity. Its growth as a body is directed toward maturity.

A building, on the other hand, starts from a plan and grows when parts are added a bit at a time until it is complete. This is the growth Paul had in mind in Ephesians 2:21. His dear friend Luke had described this kind of church growth in the progress reports in the book of Acts (Acts 2:41,47; 5:14; 6:1,7; 11:21; 14:1; 17:12,34; 18:8; 19:10).

It is fashionable in some church circles to decry numbers. "This is the day of small things," some say. Others say, "The Lord said, 'Fear not, little flock'" (Luke 12:32). This attitude is as wrong as the one that takes pride in large crowds and great numbers. Numbers in themselves can be misleading and they are no certain yardstick for measuring success in a ministry, but the church should experience steady growth. There should be an increase in numbers as well as growth in grace.

(c) The Function of the Building (2:22) "In whom ye also are builded together for an habitation of God through the Spirit."

In Old Testament times God chose to dwell among His people in material buildings: first in the tabernacle and later in the temple. The types of the temple are millennial; the types of the tabernacle are mystical. The one relates to Israel, the other to the church.

The tabernacle was built of fifty boards. Each board had been part of an acacia tree, the gnarled tree of the wilderness. After the tree was cut down—its old life terminated—the boards were fashioned. Each board was completely encased in gold so that the board itself was hidden forever. Each board stood on a socket of silver, shoulder to shoulder with its fellow board. The boards were held together by four visible bars and one invisible bar that ran through the heart of each board.

Today God dwells not in a material house, but in a spiritual one. Believers are "an habitation of God through the Spirit." Like the acacia trees, each believer was once firmly rooted in this desert world until the axe of conviction laid him low. Cut off from the old way of life, he is put "in Christ" and made to stand on redemptive ground, shoulder to shoulder with other believers. Four visible ties hold believers together: the apostles' doctrine, fellowship, breaking of bread, and prayer (Acts 2:42). One invisible bond unites us: the Holy Spirit, whose great work runs through the heart of each believer. Together we form the church, whose function is to be the habitation where God is pleased to dwell today.

The word translated "habitation" in Ephesians 2:22 occurs in only one other place in the New Testament. Describing the fall of commercial Babylon, the imperial city of the beast to be built on the banks of the Euphrates, John recorded the angel's words: "Babylon the great is fallen, is fallen, and is become the habitation of devils, and the hold of every foul spirit, and a cage of every unclean and hateful bird" (Revelation 18:2). Evil spirits will take up their abode in the haunted ruins of that cursed Vanity Fair of the beast's empire. In contrast, God resides on earth in His glorious church through His Spirit. Thank God that as long as He dwells on earth, the devil can never set up a permanent habitation here.

C. The Revelations of the Christian Life (3:1-21)

In Ephesians 3 Paul embarked on another of his famous digressions. He reminded his readers of the enlightenment, the ennoblement, and the enablement that they possess in Christ.

1. Our Enlightenment (3:1-9)

a. Paul as a Prisoner for the Truth (3:1) "For this cause I Paul, the prisoner of Jesus Christ for you Gentiles."

The stewardship of the revelations Paul received had been costly to him. These revelations are not to be taken lightly. Paul staked his life and liberty on them; he would die for these truths. He was a prisoner because he had dared to proclaim them. He was in chains because of the opposition of the Jews, but he considered himself a prisoner of Jesus Christ, not a prisoner of the Jews or Nero.

The Jews were infuriated when Paul taught that believing Gentiles were full members of God's family and the fellowship of saints. The Jews' national pride was stung. Even in the church many Jewish believers thought that Gentiles should become Jews in order to be Christians, or at least they should be regarded as second-class citizens in the kingdom. Paul's emancipating gospel annoyed many Jews, even within the church. They disliked his wholehearted acceptance of Gentiles into the church, free from all Jewish laws, traditions, and customs. They resented his vocal and tireless championship of the Gentile believers' cause. They felt threatened by his zealous, far-reaching efforts to bring more and more Gentiles into the church. The vast majority of unbelieving Jews regarded Paul with horror and considered him a dangerous heretic. Paul, however, did not criticize the Jews for opposing him. He knew where they were coming from; he had been there himself.

b. Paul as a Pioneer of the Truth (3:2-4)

(1) The Truth Entrusted to Him (3:2) "If ye have heard of the dispensation of the grace of God which is given me to you-ward."

The Greek word translated "dispensation" here comes from a word meaning "stewardship." God had entrusted Paul with great truths.

Paul was their custodian, their steward. He was under obligation to communicate them to others. He discharged this trust nobly through his preaching and writing.

Today we are living in an age—a dispensation—of grace, during which God deals with people on the basis of His grace. God's grace is reigning supremely. This age stands in contrast to the age of law that preceded it and the age of judgment that will follow it.

When we speak of an age of grace, we do not mean that God did not demonstrate His grace in other ages. Obviously He offered grace to men who were under the law; the entire ceremonial law illustrated God's grace. It is equally obvious that God will offer grace to men in the judgment age because millions will be saved during that period (Revelation 7). It is also evident that during our age of grace, God's law—that is, His moral law—still has a vital role (Romans 13:9) and at times God acts in judgment (Acts 5:1-11).

(2) The Truth Enlightening to Him (3:3-4)

(a) How It Was Communicated To Him (3:3a) "By revelation he made known unto me the mystery."

In Galatians 1:16-17 Paul told us that he did not receive his gospel from men; immediately after his conversion he "conferred not with flesh and blood," but sought out the vast silences of Sinai. There, alone with the Hebrew Scriptures and the Spirit of God, he thought through the Old Testament in the light of Calvary. He had to discard much of what he had been taught while studying to be a rabbi. He had been obsessed with the vain traditions of men, but the risen Lord now filled Paul's vision and colored all his concepts. The Holy Spirit came upon him and revealed new truths. He went into Arabia with Genesis, Isaiah, and the Psalms in his luggage, and he came back with Romans, Ephesians, and Thessalonians in his heart.

Paul did not have the enormous advantage of being Jesus' constant daily companion. He did not sit at His feet like Peter and John. The great truths of the New Testament that Paul so gloriously preached were given to him through God's direct revelation.

(b) How It Was Communicated By Him (3:3b-4) "As I wrote afore in few words, Whereby, when ye read, ye may understand my knowledge in the mystery of Christ."

Perhaps Paul was referring to a previous letter in which he had briefly mentioned the mystery (for instance, Romans 11:25; 16:25-26;

1 Corinthians 2:7; 15:51-52). Perhaps he was referring to earlier remarks in this same letter to the Ephesians (1:9-10). In any case, he communicated the great mystery, the great secret, in writing. It was far too important to be passed on simply by word of mouth. Because Paul communicated in writing, all of us can study the mystery and benefit from his reflections on the revelations given to him.

The revolutionary truths Paul wrote about were not his own spontaneous ideas. They were the product of divine inspiration and personal insight. The word translated "knowledge" in Ephesians 3:4 is *sunesis*, which refers to natural insight and reflective thought. Paul was one of the greatest intellectuals of all time, but mental ability alone did not conceive the mystery. God revealed it to him. On the other hand, divine illumination alone did not account for Paul's grasp of this new truth; he made the effort to think it through and write it down.

c.   Paul as a Partner in the Truth (3:5-6)

(1) How the Truth Was Concealed (3:5a) "Which in other ages was not made known unto the sons of men."

It was no secret, of course, that God intended to bless the Gentiles, just as He had blessed the Jews. His intentions were revealed in many Old Testament prophecies, including His first great promise to Abraham (Genesis 12:3). Paul quoted some of these prophecies in Romans 15:9-12, drawing on all three sections of the Hebrew Scriptures to emphasize his point. The promises to the Gentiles were often ignored by the Jews in their insular pride of religion and race.

It was no accident, surely, that the promised land was a bridge connecting Europe, Asia, and Africa, and that the great arterial highways of international commerce, communication, and conflict passed through it. God had always intended that His chosen people would become a spiritual blessing to all mankind—a truth that had too easily been forgotten.

Even in the deportations and dispersal, God intended for His chosen people to have a redemptive impact on other nations. The book of Acts makes it abundantly clear that Jewish communities around the world formed a natural springboard for global evangelism.

(2) How the Truth Was Revealed (3:5b-6)

(a) Its Custodians (3:5b) "It is now revealed unto his holy apostles and prophets by the Spirit."

In embryonic form, the great truths of the Epistles were first revealed to the disciples by the Lord. For instance, Jesus announced the truth about the universal church and the local church to the disciples (Matthew 16:16-19; 18:1-35). Jesus was also the first to teach the distinctive Pauline concept of being "in Christ" (John 15:1-8). The Lord promised that the Holy Spirit would superintend the writing of the Gospels (John 14:26), the Epistles (John 16:13), and the book of Revelation (John 16:13). But the Holy Spirit waited until after Pentecost to enlighten the apostles with the full measure of New Testament truth.

The apostles and the prophets—the custodians of this truth—had the foundational gifts necessary to produce and propagate the New Testament writings. Chief among these custodians was Paul. His giant intellect wholly yielded to the Holy Spirit became the human vehicle to discern and explain God's great mysterious truths.

(b) Its Contents (3:6) "That the Gentiles should be fellowheirs, and of the same body, and partakers of his promise in Christ by the gospel."

The new equality of the Gentiles was a bitter pill for most Jews to swallow. For centuries they had prided themselves on being God's chosen people. They had nurtured a growing contempt for Gentiles and wallowed in religious and racial snobbery. They had considered themselves to be God's favorites. Now all this superiority was shattered. It turned out that all along God had loved the Gentiles just as much as He had loved the Jews (witness the events in the book of Jonah, for instance). Now God was proving this truth in an astonishing way by bringing Jews and Gentiles together in a new body that ignored the special privileges the Jews had enjoyed for some thousand years. Gentiles were not going to be added to the existing corporate body of the Jewish people, the nation of Israel. There would be an entirely new body to which Jews and Gentiles would be added on equal terms.

Jews and Gentiles would share equally in the same *legacy*. They would be "fellowheirs." There would be no double portion for the Jews. Jews and Gentiles alike would receive the same blessing.

They would share equally in the same *life* too. There would be one body, its head being Christ and its members believers. Jews and Gentiles were all one in Him—all washed by His blood, all partakers of the same Spirit of life, and all equally dependent on Him and on one another.

Jews and Gentiles would also share equally in the same *light*. In

Christ, there were no longer any special promises to Jews, no revelations made to them alone. The full blaze of New Testament truth was the property of the church, not Israel.

It made no difference that Saul of Tarsus had been a Hebrew of the Hebrews, a trained rabbinical scholar, a tribal member of the nation of Israel, and a practicing and zealous Pharisee. In the church he was an equal partner with the Philippian jailor and the runaway slave Onesimus.

d. Paul as a Propagator of the Truth (3:7-9)

(1) The Working of It (3:7) "Whereof I was made a minister, according to the gift of the grace of God given unto me by the effectual working of his power."

Paul realized that the revelations of truth he received were gifts of God's marvelous grace. That he had been chosen to be the steward of such far-reaching revelations never ceased to astonish Paul. His insights were certainly not generated by the strength of his own intellect. They were just one more evidence of God's mighty power working within him.

God's grace and power are at work today in members of the body of Christ. When a brother gifted as an evangelist speaks, the Holy Spirit works, people are convicted, souls are saved, and trails of blessing follow him everywhere.

A brother who is an able expositor can open up the wonders of the Word. Because he has received a gift of grace, God's people are blessed and enriched by his ministry through pulpit or pen. God's grace and power are at work in his life.

Another brother is a successful administrator. He knows how to organize and motivate people. Under his ministry the church grows. His abilities are a gift. God's grace and power are working within him.

A sister is a true "mother in Israel." Her home is a haven for her family and a lighthouse for her neighborhood. Her children rise up and call her blessed. All the little ones in the area know her and love her. She mothers them, listens to them, talks to them, laughs and cries with them, and leads them to Christ. Other women in the community consider her a true friend. Tradesmen sense God's presence when they deal with her. Her husband is blessed. Her church feels the impact of her prayers. God's grace and power are at work in her life too.

God's grace and power—His gift to us all—should be at work in all our lives.

(2) The Wonder of It (3:8a) "Unto me, who am less than the least
of all saints, is this grace given."

With these words, Paul guarded against the natural tendency to
take pride in the extraordinary gifts God had given him, particularly
the apostolic gift that enabled him to be the custodian of divine
revelation and New Testament truth. He was, he said, less than the
least of all saints, and was awed that God had chosen him to receive
this gift.

We detect here a growing development of heartfelt, genuine
humility in Paul. In 1 Corinthians 15:9 he wrote that he was "the
least of the apostles, . . . not meet to be called an apostle" because
he had persecuted the church. In 1 Timothy 1:15 he called himself
the chief of sinners. He never forgot the wonder of being chosen to
be a custodian of divine truth.

At times Paul was driven to defend his apostleship because attacks
on him were really attacks on what he taught. He reluctantly but
resolutely declared, "I suppose I was not a whit behind the very
chiefest apostles . . . though I be rude [the Greek word rendered
rude can be freely translated *layman*] in speech . . . . in nothing am
I behind the very chiefest apostles, though I be nothing" (2
Corinthians 11:5-6; 12:11). But he even defended his apostleship
with as much self-depreciation as the occasion permitted.

(3) The Wealth of It (3:8b-9)

(a) Its Hidden Resources (3:8b) "That I should preach among the
Gentiles the unsearchable riches of Christ."

The Greek word translated "unsearchable" here means
"untrackable" and suggests a labyrinth or maze. The wealth we have
in Christ is hidden treasure. We cannot track it down, but the story
of it has been told. Paul had a glimpse of it and vouched for the fact
that the Lord Jesus was rich (2 Corinthians 8:9).

A story about another kind of hidden treasure was told by
Alexandre Dumas in *The Count of Monte Cristo*. It was a standing joke
among prisoners in the dungeons of the Chateau D'If that the
learned abbe Faria was insane because he claimed to have knowledge of a fabulous hidden treasure. The abbe befriended Edmond
Dantes, a fellow prisoner. Faria educated him and adopted him as
his son. Dantes carefully avoided the subject of the treasure, not
wanting to awaken traces of his friend's former madness. But there
was no imbalance of mind in the abbe. As he was dying, the abbe put
the secret of the treasure into Dantes' hand.

In time Dantes escaped from the terrible prison and found the treasure in an underground grotto. It lay in an oaken coffer, bound with steel and closed with a lock and padlock. Hardly believing his good fortune, Dantes pried open the treasure chest, scarcely daring to breath lest the secret be a cruel hoax. But it was true! There before him lay the wealth of an empire: heaps of golden coins; stacked bars of gold; and an accumulation of diamonds, pearls, and rubies worth the ransom of a dozen kings. The treasure transformed the poor, victimized Dantes into the avenging Count of Monte Cristo.

We, the children of Adam's ruined race, also have been victimized. We have been born into a sin-cursed world; we are heirs to a fallen nature; we have been born in sin and shaped in iniquity. Our every prospect is blighted by the law of sin and death. But we have in our hands the secret of a hidden treasure, a treasure hidden in Christ. All spiritual wealth is vested in Him, and all that limitless wealth is ours. It transformed us when we became Christians from spiritual paupers into wealthy sons of God—joint-heirs with Jesus Christ. Now we can avenge ourselves on the prince of this world, on the lord of darkness, on evil spirits that rule the high places. We can use our new-found resources to live godly lives in Christ Jesus and introduce others to all that God has for those who believe in Him.

One thing is sure: We can never find that wealth apart from Christ. It is untrackable. Science, psychology, politics, social reform, education, or culture cannot lead us to that treasure. The spiritual treasure we need is found in Christ and in Him alone.

(b) Its Heavenly Resources (3:9) "To make all men see what is the fellowship of the mystery, which from the beginning of the world hath been hid in God, who created all things by Jesus Christ."

No wonder we cannot find this treasure on our own. It is in Heaven! It is hidden in Christ in God. God entrusted the news of this treasure to Paul to share with all men. He shared the news in his preaching and teaching, but he could only reach a small percentage of people. So under the Spirit's leading, he wrote down the good news that spiritual things hidden from the world's beginning are now universally available to mankind.

Perhaps his imprisonment in Rome made Paul realize the uncertainties of life, the absolute certainty of his eventual death, and the urgency of putting the good news into writing. Doubtless Paul realized that he was now writing under the Holy Spirit's direct inspiration, but he could scarcely have envisioned the results of penning a letter to a congregation of Gentile Christians. His letter would be treasured and duplicated countless times. Everyone would want a copy. The letter would find its way into the divine library. For centuries the letter would be read, memorized, quoted, discussed, and expounded. It would be translated and published and it would bear fruit in lands around the globe. And no wonder! The letter revealed a glorious secret about God's Son and the Gentile world.

Paul revealed a secret that God had kept to Himself. He had kept it hidden when He visited fallen man in Eden, when He talked with His friend Abraham, and when He gave the law to Moses. He told David, a man after His own heart, many things, but He did not tell him this secret. He spoke to Isaiah and Jeremiah, to Ezekiel and Daniel, but still He kept His secret. He did not tell the twelve minor prophets, and then He kept this burning secret for four more silent centuries.

Finally God sent His Son, who was involved in the secret. Jesus dropped hints of it here and there, but He did not give it away. The day of Pentecost came and the church was born. Peter preached, souls were saved, and the secret was out, but still men did not grasp it. So God saved Saul, shared the secret with him, and said, "You tell the world."

What a secret it was! God was going to create a church. He would baptize Jews and Gentiles into it, making no difference between them. That church would be the mystical body of Christ. He would raise it higher than angels. He would seat it with Himself in the heavenlies. It would share fully and forever all that Christ has. That church would be His crowning masterpiece. Creation itself, the showpiece of God's eternal power and godhead, would pale before the everlasting splendors of the church.

What a shout of joy there must have been when the secret was first unveiled in Heaven. Imagine Christ Himself, in a battle-scarred human body, sitting down at God's right hand, turning to His Father and saying, "Now, Father, let's send the Holy Spirit to bring home My Bride."

2.   Our Ennoblement (3:10-13)

a.   Our Triumph (3:10-12)

(1) The Manifold Wisdom of God (3:10) "To the intent that now unto the principalities and powers in heavenly places might be known by the church the manifold wisdom of God."

The Greek word that Paul used here to describe God's wisdom occurs nowhere else in the Bible. It means "infinitely diversified" or more poetically, "many-colored." From whichever way you view God's wisdom, new flashes of truth blaze forth. His wisdom is inexhaustible, as has been displayed in creation. The more we study medicine or astronomy or physics or microbiology, the more complex each facet of nature seems.

For instance, the ancient Greeks invented the word we translate "atom" to describe the ultimate, uncuttable, building blocks of the universe. In the late nineteenth century the discovery of radioactivity indicated that atoms themselves have internal structure. Work on cathode rays showed that within the atom are charged particles called electrons. Atoms, scientists realized, are much more complex than originally thought. Then they discovered that electrically positive protons and electrically neutral neutrons clump in the atom's nucleus. Whirling around this nucleus are negatively charged electrons. Scientists envisioned the atom as a miniature solar system, infinitely small and emptier than space. More discoveries followed, and the quantum theory was stated. Three families of subatomic particles have been named: gauge particles, quarks, and leptons. Indeed, the deeper physicists delve, the more elusive final answers seem to be. Such is God's wisdom demonstrated in creation—infinitely diversified and inexhaustible.

What is true of creation is true of redemption. The Bible, in which the plan of redemption is recorded, reveals the many-colored wisdom of God. We are constantly finding new depths in verses that have been familiar friends since we first met the Lord. God's infinite wisdom is now being displayed to principalities and powers in heavenly places.

It would seem that these principalities and powers are the hostile angels in the unseen world. They are the fallen ones who help Satan rule his planet and stand in stark contrast to the holy angels, known as thrones and dominions, who side with God and serve the redeemed. The principalities and powers are God's sworn enemies. They are the Christian's constant foes, with whom he has to do unremitting battle (Ephesians 6:12). These dark lords of the night are blinded by Satan and are destined to spend eternity in fires God has prepared especially for them. It is fitting that the futility of their schemes should be made plain through the church. In contrast to God's wisdom, Satan's "deep things" are exposed in the church as utter folly, the senseless plottings of a tormented and perverted mind. No wonder principalities and powers bitterly hate the church and those in its ranks.

(2) The Majestic Purpose of God (3:11) "According to the eternal
     purpose which he purposed in Christ Jesus our Lord."

God's plans, which center in the church, are part of His eternal
purpose. He made His plans before time began, before the rustle of
an angel's wing disturbed the silence of eternity. God was not
surprised by Adam's sin or Lucifer's fall. God in His omniscient
wisdom foresaw these tragic events that introduced such dimensions as sorrow, suffering, and shame into the universe. His answer
was the cross of Christ, reared on a skull-shaped hill on a rebel
planet in a remote corner of a galaxy. Through the cross He
displayed His wisdom, love, and power as a means of redeeming
fallen man and rebuking fallen angels.

How wonderful it is that God had us in mind before He created
the stars. He wrote our names on His heart before He created the
world, before the dust of the ages was concentrated in that one
primeval atom, before the roar of creation's "big bang."

(3) The Marvelous Love of God (3:12) "In whom we have boldness
     and access with confidence by the faith of him."

We have full access to God's presence. We can draw near to Him
and to His rainbow-circled, cherubim-guarded, highly exalted
throne. We can come without pomp and ceremony, without formal
and ritualistic preparations, without mediators of any sort. We can
come directly to Him at any time, day or night, with the confidence
of a son or daughter. No one on earth, in Heaven, or in Hell can bar
our way. Such is God's love for us!

The Greek word translated "confidence" in Ephesians 3:12
means "confident assurance." One would not have this confident
assurance if he entered a neighbor's house uninvited, opened the
refrigerator, pulled up a chair to the table, and helped himself to
supper. But one would have this confident assurance in his father's
house because that is where he belongs and he knows he is welcome
there.

The Greek word translated "boldness" here usually means "free
speech," as in 2 Corinthians 3:12. The right of free speech is the
privilege of every citizen in a democracy. But Paul had a higher
meaning in mind. In the New Testament the word means every
believer's right to come directly to God, having no other priest,
mediator, or advocate than the Lord Jesus Christ. What arrogance
for a religious system to interpose man-made functionaries between
the child of God and his Father's smile. The only mediator needed

is Christ; in other words the Christian has access "by the faith of him" (Ephesians 3:12).

Imagine showing up at the door of your father's house, only to find someone guarding the door. You say, "Excuse me please."

The guard asks, "Where do you think you are going?"

"I'm going in to see my father," you answer.

He says, "You can't do that! I'll take your message. You can only approach him through me."

"Get out of the way, mister," you say. "I'm his son. My father loves me. I sure don't need you or anyone else to come between us."

You should not allow a priest or a pretender to come between you and your Father in Heaven.

b.   Our Tribulations (3:13) "Wherefore I desire that ye faint not at my tribulations for you, which is your glory."

All of a sudden Paul came back down to earth. Did the rattle of his chain or the changing of the guard make him freshly aware of his physical circumstances? Had the soldier assigned to Paul impatiently jerked the manacles that made him almost as much a prisoner as his captive? Perhaps the soldier laughed out loud at the contrast between Paul's spiritual claims and his physical chains (if the soldier spoke Greek, he could understand every word that Paul dictated to his secretary).

Paul had been glorying in his limitless resources in Christ and his eternal prospects, while the harsh reality was that he was a prisoner anticipating a trial for treason before Nero. Not much of a future, one might think. Now Paul suddenly seemed to realize how other people might be viewing his situation. After all, he was in trouble only because he preached these glad tidings, and particularly because he preached them to the Gentiles. So he inserted a sentence to reassure his readers since they too might face tribulation for their faith in Christ. Some already had. Paul urged them not to be cast down on his account. He had long since learned to glory in tribulations (2 Corinthians 12:7-10).

Perhaps the best illustration of joy during difficult circumstances comes from *Uncle Tom's Cabin*. Poor Tom had been sold into the cruel hands of the bestial Simon Legree. Simon hated him, tormented him, thrashed him within an inch of his life, and threatened to tie him to a tree and roast him in a slow fire. But Tom remained unmoved by the threats. His soul was in the sky with the Savior. The storm clouds frowned, but Tom's eyes focused on the rainbow. He saw the great white throne, the white-robed throng, the crowns, the palms, and the harps. His ears were filled with seraph songs and the voice that sounded like the voice of many waters. He remained uncowed by Simon Legree and said, "Mas'r, I know ye can do dreadful things but, after ye've killed the body, there ain't no more ye can do. And oh! there's all eternity to come after that!"

Paul focused on the glories of Heaven as he faced trying circumstances on earth. Chains and beatings didn't really matter. He could endure the trials and tribulations of time because he knew that all eternity would follow.

3.   Our Enablement (3:14-21)

a.   The Secret of Our Enablement (3:14-15)

(1) It Is Related to Our Access to the Father (3:14) "For this cause I bow my knees unto the Father of our Lord Jesus Christ."

According to court etiquette in Paul's day, when someone approached the throne he bowed the knee. True, God is our Father, just as He is the Father of our Lord Jesus Christ. True, we are bidden to come boldly to Him. True, He loves us with an everlasting love. True, we have instant access to Him day or night. True, no request is too great or too small to be brought to Him. True, no earthly child in our culture goes down on his knees before his human father. But our Father is *God*. The Scriptures clearly teach that God should be approached with reverence and awe. Evidently Paul knelt when he prayed. This posture helped to remind him of the awesome majesty and nobility of the One he knew he could address as Father.

(2) It Is Related to Our Acceptance by the Father (3:15) "Of whom the whole family in heaven and earth is named."

The Greek word translated "family" here is *patria,* which in this case would be better translated "fatherhood." The link to the word "Father" *(pater)* in the preceding verse would be clearer. The sentence in verses 14-15 can be rendered, "I bow my knees to the Father from whom all fatherhood takes its name."

All fatherhood is derived from God the Father. He is the Father of fathers, the ultimate Father, the one whose fatherhood is the pattern for all fatherhood. All fatherhood should resemble His, for His fatherhood is perfect. The closer the resemblance, the more human fatherhood expresses fatherhood as God intended it to be.

Some of us have had fathers who distorted or destroyed the whole concept of fatherhood. Some of us have had very good fathers.

Some of us have never known our human fathers. Some of us are fathers ourselves and need to conform our fatherhood not to the writings of behavioral psychologists, but to the Father after whom all fatherhood is named.

In any case, all of us in God's family are eternally ennobled by the acceptance of our glorious Father on high. Whether our human fathers were good, bad, or indifferent, we can come to that perfect Father and revel in His marvelous fatherhood.

We have a faint illustration of what fatherhood is all about in Mark Twain's classic, *Tom Sawyer*. The two chief characters in this book are Tom and his sadly neglected friend, Huckleberry Finn. Tom had no father at all. He was raised by his Aunt Polly, a somewhat kindly, but exasperating guardian. Huck had a father, but he was a brute, a bully, and a drunkard who either totally neglected the boy or tyrannized him. At one point Huck was taken under the protective wing of the wealthy, well-meaning widow Douglas, who forced culture on the boy.

In contrast to Huck were the sons of the Welshman. They and their father acted with speedy efficiency when Tom brought the news that he and Huck had unearthed Injun Joe's savage plans to rob and mutilate the widow Douglas. How much better it would have been for Huck if that sturdy Welshman had adopted him. The boy needed fatherhood.

There are many youngsters like Huckleberry Finn in this world of broken homes and ruined marriages, and we can be sure that Satan himself is behind the present-day attacks on the home. The Biblical view of fatherhood needs to be restored as the model. Whether or not a person has a godly father, Christ has made the fatherhood of God available to anyone who comes to God through Him.

b.   The Sources of Our Enablement (3:16-19)

(1) It Is Channeled through the Invincible Spirit of God (3:16)
     "That he would grant you, according to the riches of his glory, to be strengthened with might by his Spirit in the inner man."

The first source of the believer's strength is the Holy Spirit in the inner man.

The governing principle in man does not reside in instinct, as it does in animals. It does not reside in the intellect either, for brilliant people are not always right. It does not reside in the emotions, for feelings often lead us astray. It does not reside in the will, for a strong-willed person can be a tyrant. It does not reside in the conscience, for a conscience can be weak, warped, or wrong. It goes deeper than that. The ruling principle in man resides in the spirit.

God created the human spirit to be the receptacle of the Holy Spirit. He says, "The spirit of man is the candle of the Lord" (Proverbs 20:27). Before the fall, the Holy Spirit was to fill the human spirit and thus control all man's thoughts, feelings, and decisions. The Holy Spirit was to rule his body so that his whole life would be the expression of God.

When man fell, the Holy Spirit vacated the human spirit and this controlling principle was lost. Man living in sin is not what God had in mind when He said, "Let us make man in our image, after our likeness" (Genesis 1:26). A new ruling principle resides in man's soul—sin. Now he is subject to the law of sin and death.

At conversion the human spirit is regenerated. The Holy Spirit returns and relights the candle. The believer can do what no un-believer can do—live in fellowship and communion with God. He has the enablement of the Spirit in his inner man. Paul's great prayer for all believers was that they might be strengthened by the Holy Spirit because that is part of God's plan. His inexhaustible riches in glory are available to us so that we can exhibit them to a lost world.

(2) It Is Channeled through the Indwelling Son of God (3:17a)
    "That Christ may dwell in your hearts by faith."

Once in history a man lived here on earth who was God mani-fested in flesh, man inhabited by God, and man as God always intended man to be. For some thirty-three years He lived and moved and had His being among us. For about 12,600 days He walked and talked, laughed and cried, worked and played. He rubbed shoul-ders with people, experienced pain and pleasure, dealt with pres-sures, was tempted and tried, and lived with human limitations—all without sinning. He went about doing good. He performed miracles for others, but never for Himself. He could have commanded stones to become bread when He was hungry. After all, He changed water into wine and multiplied a little lad's lunch to feed a multi-tude. He could have come down from the cross, but He never did.

Satan put Him to the test to see if He would spoil God's redemp-tive plan by using His deity to override His humanity. Christ's public ministry began and ended on the same note of temptation. In the wilderness Satan taunted, "If thou be the Son of God, command that these stones be made bread" (Matthew 4:3). In other words,

"Use your deity to put an end to your suffering. Why be hungry as a man, when as God you can work a miracle?" At Golgotha passersby reviled Him: "If thou be the Son of God, come down from the cross" (Matthew 27:40). They were saying, "Use your deity to put an end to your human suffering." But Jesus had not come here to spare His life. He did more miracles than men could count, but only to benefit others.

So in His character, conduct, and conversation; as an infant, a child, a teenager, a young man, a man in the prime of life; at all times, in all places, under all circumstances; at home, at school, at work, at play, in the synagogue, on the highway; as a brother, as a friend, as a neighbor, as the babe of Bethlehem, as the child of Mary, as the carpenter of Nazareth, as the preacher from Galilee—Jesus lived life on human terms. He was never less than God and at the same time never more than man. He was content to live on our terms. Filled, anointed, led by the Holy Spirit, joyful in all things, and wholly yielded to the Father, He demonstrated what God had in mind when He created man. His sinless life was filled with love for God and love for other people.

This Jesus, said Paul, still lives. He not only lives in glory at the right hand of God; He also lives in us. Ephesians 3:17 says, "Christ may dwell in your hearts by faith" and can be rendered, "Christ may take up His abode in your hearts by faith."

Our hearts are His home. Our bodies are His temple. Just as He lived His human life in the power of the Holy Spirit and in constant communion and cooperation with the Father, so we are to live our lives in the power of the Holy Spirit and in constant communion and cooperation with Him. His purpose, to use Isaiah's expressive phrase, is thus to "prolong his days" (53:10). He does this by indwelling our lives (Colossians 1:27).

The genius of the gospel lies in the fact that Christianity is Christ. We can't imitate the life that Jesus lived. That is impossible, as most of us have discovered. We have tried and failed. Christianity is the living Christ taking up His abode in us and continuing to live His peerless life in our human bodies.

Christ makes Himself at home in you and me by faith. Faith is the operating principle. The *truth* of Christ's indwelling presence is beyond question. Colossians 1:27 says, "Christ in you, the hope of glory." The *transmission* of Christ's indwelling presence hinges on our faith—that is, our willingness to believe that His indwelling is a fact and to turn over the control of our lives. The enablement to be like Christ comes from Him. His life, not ours, produces in our character, conduct, and conversation what people will recognize as genuine Christianity. He will fill our lives with love for God and love for man.

(3) It Is Channeled through the Ineffable Salvation of God (3:17b-19a)

(a) God's Love Experienced (3:17b) "Rooted and grounded in love."

Most of us have a sentimental view of love. The Bible does not ignore the emotional side of love, but it usually emphasizes the volitional side. Love is not something we add to our Christian lives as time goes on. Love is the root and the foundation of Christian life. In Ephesians 3:17 Paul used two contrasting spheres to illustrate the importance of a right start: the world of the biologist and the world of the builder. A bulb grows and a building grows, but they grow in different ways. They have one thing in common, however. They both must have a right start.

We must be rooted in love. A plant will not grow unless it is rooted in the proper soil. Paul viewed love as the soil in which all Christian experience must grow. If our service for God lacks love, it is like sounding brass and tinkling cymbal (1 Corinthians 13:1). If our Christian lives are not rooted in love, they will wither and fade. Love, the soil of the soul, provides the nutrients necessary to sustain fragrant, fruitful Christian lives. God's everlasting love is what Jesus exhibited in His life and death, and if we are rooted in that love, His love will be reproduced in us.

We must also be grounded in love. The Greek word translated "grounded" in Ephesians 3:17, *themelioō*, relates to the foundation of a building. The Lord Jesus used the same word in His parable of the wise and foolish builders. Speaking of the man who built his house on the rock, Jesus said, "And the rain descended, and the floods came, and the winds blew, and beat upon that house; and it fell not: for it was *founded* upon a rock" (Matthew 7:25, italics added). No matter how great a Christian organization we build, no matter how efficient and seemingly successful we are, no matter how imposing a church we erect, if our efforts are not grounded in God's love, they will amount to nothing.

Some years after Paul wrote to the Ephesians, the Lord Jesus had to warn this same church:

> I know thy works, and thy labour, and thy patience, and how thou canst not bear them which are evil: and thou hast tried them which say they are apostles, and are not, and hast found

them liars: And hast borne, and hast patience, and for my
name's sake hast laboured, and hast not fainted. Nevertheless
I have somewhat against thee, because thou hast left thy first
love. Remember . . . and repent . . . or else . . . (Revelation 2:2-5).

Love must be the basis of the life of a church; otherwise it cannot
last. The church at Ephesus in John's day was insolvent. Its many
works could be compared to spurious coins—coins that had never
known the mint of love. Perhaps Paul sensed what would happen to
the church at Ephesus and that is why he emphasized the need to
base Christian life and church life on the foundation of love.

(b) God's Love Examined (3:18) "May be able to comprehend with
     all saints what is the breadth, and length, and depth, and
     height."

Paul challenged us to try to measure God's love to see if it can be
expressed in finite terms. If we use length, we create a line. If we add
breadth, we create a surface. If we add depth, we create a solid. But
how can we add height? This fourth dimension defies understanding.
    What in terms of physical reality is the difference between depth
and height? If we have depth, we also have height; the two are just
different directions within the same dimension. Height cannot be
considered a fourth dimension unless it symbolizes a spiritual
dimension. John only used three dimensions to describe the celestial city (Revelation 21:16). But Paul introduced a spiritual dimension to help us comprehend the love of God.
    Let's examine the dimensions of God's love.
    The length of God's love. How long is God's love? When did God
start loving us? Was it when we first loved Him? Was it when we first
responded to the Spirit's call? Was it when we were born? Was it
when He created man and first saw us in Adam? Was it when He
made the worlds and planned a planet to be our island home in
space? Was it when He first decided to create us, knowing that if He
acted in creation He would also have to act in redemption? When
did God's love start? It never started! It has always existed. It is
everlasting, as eternal as God is eternal.
    When will God *stop* loving us? If we are disobedient, fall into sin,
and bring shame and dishonor to the name of His Son, will He stop
loving us then? What if we keep on sinning? What if we exceed the
seventy times seven times (Matthew 18:21-22)? God will never stop
loving us. He has not even stopped loving the people who are

eternally lost. He loves them even though it is His holiness that predominates in their experience. The length of God's love stretches back beyond our farthest thought and forward on and on forever.

The breadth of God's love. How wide is God's love? It is wider than the sea, wider than the world, wider than the universe. When God demonstrated His love by becoming a man and living on earth, that love was not narrow, parochial, or prescribed by creed or custom. He loved the rich young ruler and the woman caught in adultery. He loved Nicodemus and Zaccheus the publican. He loved Judas who betrayed Him. He loved Caiaphas and Annas, the scheming political priests who judged Him during a trumped-up trial in the dead of night and who used cheap tricks to try to get Him to incriminate Himself. He loved Herod, who murdered John and mocked Him. He loved poor, weak, self-seeking Pilate, who was torn between justice and ambition. He loved Nero, Hitler, and Stalin. And wonder of wonders, He loves us too! His love is wide enough to embrace everyone.

The depth of God's love. How deep is God's love? Christ came down from the towering battlements of Heaven to the dark recesses of the tomb. He came from Heaven's glory to Galilee and was content to be raised in a despised provincial town and to be known as the carpenter's son. He tread the long and lonely road from Galilee to Gethsemane where He wept His heart out over the horror of our sin and the torment of the approaching cross. From Gethsemane He went to Gabbatha to be bullied, baited, falsely accused, scourged, and crowned with thorns in Pilate's judgment hall. Then He went from Gabbatha to Golgotha where He was nailed to a cross, hung up to die, and exposed as an object of derision. He plunged into the eerie darkness of that midday midnight when as the sin bearer He was abandoned by God and crushed beneath the weight of the world's sin. From Golgotha He went to the grave and on down into Hades itself. How deep is God's love?

Years ago sailors venturing into uncharted seas would let out a sounding line to locate the bottom. "No bottom with this line," the sailor might report to the bridge. Another length of line might be added. "Deeper than that, sir," the officer of the watch might report. The sailors might even attach all the line they had on board to the sounding weight. "Deeper than that" they might note in the log.

We too can let out our sounding lines into the depths of God's love. In the end we can only say, "It's deeper than that. No bottom with this line." Love took our Savior all the way from glory to the grave.

The height of God's love. How high is Christ's love? He has

ascended to glory and is sitting at the right hand of the Father. In
those heights Christ reigns in splendor and brightness beyond that
of the noonday sun. He is adulated and adored, worshiped and
praised, by the shining and sinless sons of light who throng around
His throne.

Will Jesus forget us, now that He is on the throne of the universe
with galaxies swirling around His feet and ten thousand times ten
thousand angels hanging on His words and rushing to do His will?
No!

Our thoughts go back to Joseph, unfairly imprisoned by the
captain of pharaoh's guard on false charges brought against him by
the man's own wife. He ministered to pharaoh's cupbearer, also in
prison, and assured him that he need have no fears for he would
soon be lifted up and exalted again. "When it is well with thee, think
of me," said Joseph. The king's cupbearer was indeed restored to his
high estate. "Yet," says the Holy Spirit with an economy of words that
bespeak a prodigal pathos, "Yet did not the chief butler remember
Joseph, but forgat him" (Genesis 40:23).

But Jesus will not forget us. We are already seated with Him in
heavenly places. And He has promised, "I will come again . . . that
where I am, there ye may be also" (John 14:3).

(c) God's Love Exhibited (3:19a) "To know the love of Christ,
    which passeth knowledge."

We can know Christ's love! Calvary love surpasses creature love.

A traveler in the African bush came to a place where a fire had
recently burned. Beside his path he saw the charred embers of a
nest, and on that nest the carcass of a mother hen. Idly he touched
the remains with his foot and to his astonishment, out from under
the heap ran some baby chicks. Mother love had caused that hen to
give her life for her brood. But that was only creature love.

What can we say about Calvary love? What can we say about the
love that is stronger than death? What can we say about the love that
many waters cannot quench? What can we say about the love that
will not let us go? What can we say about the love that suffers long
and is kind?

Years ago in Britain D. L. Moody met a young man named Henry
Morehouse. Fascinated by the great evangelist, Morehouse begged
a favor. "Mr. Moody," he said, "if I come to Chicago, will you let me
speak in your church?" Not thinking it likely that this youth would
ever come to Chicago, Moody carelessly agreed.

Sometime later the young man knocked on Moody's door in

Chicago. "Hello, Mr. Moody. Remember me? I'm Henry Morehouse. I've come to speak in your church."

Reluctantly, Moody made the arrangements. "Never mind," he assured his deacons. "It will only be for one service. He can't do much harm in half an hour. In any case, I'll get up afterward and put things right."

That night Morehouse preached on John 3:16 and spoke of God's love with Holy Spirit power. Moody was deeply moved. The church leaders asked Morehouse to preach again and again. He preached every night for an entire week on John 3:16. Moody had never heard preaching so powerful. Indeed, Morehouse became known as the man who moved the man who moved the multitudes.

The last night came. Again the young visitor announced his usual text and said: "I have been trying to tell you how much God loves you. Suppose I could borrow Jacob's ladder and could climb that shining staircase until at last I stood on the sapphire pavements of the city of God. Suppose I were to seek out Gabriel the herald angel and were to say to him, 'Gabriel, you stand in the presence of God. Tell me, how much does God love the world?' I know exactly what he would say. He would say, 'Henry Morehouse, God so loved the world that He gave His only begotten Son that whosoever believeth in Him should not perish but have everlasting life. That's how much God loves the world.'"

We can know that love, but paradoxically it passes knowledge.

(4) It Is Channeled through the Infinite Sufficiency of God (3:19b)
"That ye might be filled with all the fulness of God."

God Himself is the source of our enablement. We are to be progressively filled, right up to the measure of God's fullness. This truth is beyond all understanding. Yet Paul prayed that we might experience the fullness.

D. L. Moody did. He rarely spoke of his experience because it was too sacred, but it is recorded in his biography. He had been walking the streets of New York City, oblivious to the crowds and traffic, wrestling with God about a claim God was making on his life. Suddenly he gave in and felt an overwhelming sense of God's presence sweep over him like waves. He went to a friend's house, declined the offer of a meal, and asked for a room where he could be alone. Time passed. He was alone with God in a way he had never known before; he was filled with the fullness of God. At last Moody cried out to God to stay His hand, for he could take no more. After that experience his ministry was never the same. An anointing on him surpassed all that had gone before.

If ever there was One who was filled with all God's fullness, it was the man Christ Jesus. Of course, even when He lived on earth He never ceased to be God. But He accepted life on our terms, and as a man was always filled with God's fullness. There was never a time— as a babe, as a boy, as a man—when He was not filled with the Spirit. Jesus was not anointed for His ministry until John baptized Him in the Jordan and the Spirit came down on Him, but He was always filled with the Spirit. John 3:34 says, "God giveth not the Spirit by measure unto him."

What would God be like if He were a boy of twelve? To answer that question, we only have to look at a boy named Jesus who was filled with all God's fullness. What would God do if He were like us? If He were fiercely tempted, what would He do? To know the answer, we only have to look at the man Jesus, who was filled with God's fullness.

What would God do if He were confronted with all the sorrows of mankind? With this world's sick, poor, bereaved, and demon-possessed? With this world's prodigals? What would He do if He were confronted with religious error, with His nation's oppressors, or with a close friend who harbored treachery in his heart? What would He do if His family decided He was insane or going to extremes? What would He do with His money, with His extraordinary talents, and with His time? What would He do if He faced betrayal and injustice? What would He do if someone spit in His face? What would He do if He were forced to endure a painful, horrible, and lonely death? To answer these questions, we only need to look at the One who was filled with all the fullness of God. All we need to do is look at Jesus.

When Paul prayed that we might be filled with all of God's fullness, he was praying that in our character, in our conduct, and in our conversation, we might be like Jesus. What then, in human terms, was the secret of Jesus' life? Obedience! "Lo, I come," He said, "(in the volume of the book it is written of me,) to do thy will, O God" (Hebrews 10:7). He "became obedient unto death, even the death of the cross" (Philippians 2:8).

Imagine for a moment that we tiptoe into the garden of Gethsemane. We creep past Peter, James, and John, who already are asleep. We see Jesus staring aghast into the cup of suffering that our sins have filled. We see the sweat and blood on His brow. We hear Him say, "Father, if it be possible, let this cup pass from me:

nevertheless not as I will, but as thou wilt" (Matthew 26:39). In the garden we have learned the secret to being filled with the fullness of God; the secret is obedience.

c.   The Scope of Our Enablement (3:20-21)

(1) A Power Inexhaustible (3:20)

(a) Inexhaustible in Its Ability (3:20a) "Now unto him that is able to do exceeding abundantly above all that we ask or think."

God is able to do all that we *ask*. No man could do that, no matter how rich, powerful, or willing he might be. What are we asking for? Peace in the midst of storm? The salvation of a loved one? Help in an emergency? Guidance in a decision? Victory over sin? Blessing on a ministry? No matter what we might ask, God is able to do it.

God is able to do all that we ask or *think*. We all have thoughts that we never express. We have secret yearnings, hopes, ambitions, and dreams. We have longings that are so intangible we can barely put them into words—unspoken prayers for holiness, happiness, godliness, love, and fulfillment. God reads those thoughts. No matter what we long for, God is able to do it.

God is able to do *all* that we ask or think. He has not restricted us to one request. He is not small, parochial, or limited. He is pleased when our thoughts and prayers are commensurate with His omnipotence.

A man once did Alexander the Great a service, and Alexander told him to ask for any type of reward he wished. The man made such an enormous demand on the treasury that the imperial treasurer refused to pay it. The man appealed to Alexander, who said, "This man knows the greatness of Alexander and has asked accordingly. We are greatly honored. Grant his request."

God is able to do *above* all that we ask or think. He can take what we ask and enlarge it. He can take our thoughts and go beyond them. We can only see the here and now; He can see the then and there.

God did above all that Paul could ask or think for Ephesus, though his prayers were not answered the way he expected. Paul wanted to evangelize Asia Minor and Ephesus during his second missionary journey, but God kept on saying no. In Acts 16:6-9 Luke recorded:

> When they had gone throughout Phrygia and the region of Galatia, and were forbidden of the Holy Ghost to preach the word in Asia, After they were come to Mysia, they assayed to go

into Bithynia: but the Spirit suffered them not. And they passing by Mysia came down to Troas. And a vision appeared to Paul in the night; There stood a man of Macedonia, and prayed him, saying, Come over into Macedonia, and help us.

Although God knew that Paul desired to evangelize Asia Minor, He led Paul to Europe where he planted church after church and changed the history of the world. Only after his stint in Europe did God lead Paul back to Ephesus (Acts 18:19-21). Then during his third missionary journey, God enabled Paul to plant a great, flourishing church there (Acts 19:1-20). God did not veto Paul's thought; He simply improved it.

God is able to do *abundantly* above all that we ask or think. He doesn't just make minor improvements in our plans. He overrules them and gives them a magnificence worthy of Himself.

For example, Paul wanted to go to Rome. He wrote to the saints there about his desire to visit them and how often he had intended to come (Romans 1:10-13). But God always seemed to hinder him. Why? Because He was going to do abundantly above all that Paul could ask or think.

By hindering Paul, God caused him to write to the Romans, thus giving us Paul's doctrinal masterpiece. How impoverished the church would have been through the centuries if Paul had simply gone to Rome and had never written to the church there.

But that was not all God did. In the end He sent Paul to Rome— in chains! How could that be viewed as doing abundantly above all that Paul could ask or think? Surely Paul never asked to go to Rome as Nero's prisoner, accused of high treason and facing the possibility of a terrible death. But out of that imprisonment came the Epistles to the Ephesians, the Philippians, the Colossians, and Philemon—not to mention Paul's bold witness that reached into the palace and into the ranks of the powerful Praetorian Guard. Truly he could write, "I would ye should understand, brethren, that the things which happened unto me have fallen out rather unto the furtherance of the gospel" (Philippians 1:12).

God is able to do *exceeding* abundantly above all that we ask or think. Only eternity will reveal how marvelously God has answered all our prayers. (And we thought that He had ignored them!) He has some wonderful surprises waiting for us on the other side of the sea. God's infinite power is inexhaustible in its ability to enable us.

(b) Inexhaustible in Its Availability (3:20b) "According to the power that worketh in us."

The Greek word translated "power" here is *dunamis*. It means God's untrammeled, unequaled, unlimited power—the power that energized the galaxies. Yet God is so gentle we can barely see His power at work in our lives.

Think of the life-transforming power that took a cursing, cowardly fisherman named Peter and transformed him into the peerless preacher of Pentecost; of the power that took Saul of Tarsus, the arch-persecutor of the infant church, and turned him into the great apostle Paul; of the power that took the Lord's pharisaical and unbelieving brother James and made him a pillar of the church! That is the power "that worketh in us." When we get to Heaven we will meet myriads of people, all of whom will be able to tell of the working of that power in them. It is as gentle as the forming of a dew drop, as imperceptible as the growth of a tree, and as lasting as the throne of God.

(2) A Purpose Inescapable (3:21) "Unto him be glory in the church by Christ Jesus throughout all ages, world without end."

God does everything for His glory. That is a basic axiom of sound hermeneutics. That is an important key to understanding His ways and interpreting His Word. God's grace, God's government, and God's greatness may be other keys to understanding the Scriptures and God's ways with men and nations. But these keys only unlock certain doors. God's glory is the master key that unlocks all doors. God does everything for His glory, and Paul ended his magnificent doxology on this note.

God enables us because His supreme purpose is to bring glory to Himself. Our lives are to glorify God *personally*—"Unto him be glory." To glorify and worship a creature—no matter how splendid, powerful, and great that created being is—robs God of glory. All idolatry, however well-meaning, is high treason against God because it gives His glory to another.

Satan tempted Christ by offering Him a crown without a cross. Satan offered the kingdoms of this world with all their power and glory, but at a price. "All these things will I give thee, if thou wilt fall down and worship me" (Matthew 4:9; also see Luke 4:5-7). Jesus, refusing to give glory to anyone but God, instantly stabbed Satan with the Sword: "It is written, Thou shalt worship the Lord thy God, and him only shalt thou serve" (Matthew 4:10).

Our lives are also to glorify God *publicly*—"Unto him be glory in the church by Christ Jesus." In our public worship, in our gatherings as His people, in our corporate testimony, we are to glorify God. We are to display to the spirit hosts in the heavenlies and to all mankind on earth the person of Christ. He is the head of the body; we are its members.

Our lives are to glorify God *perpetually*—"throughout all ages, world without end." When we stop praising God, we defraud Him and demean ourselves. The hosts of Heaven who surround His throne are always praising Him. The chant of the cherubim is a ceaseless "Holy! Holy! Holy!"

The psalmist brought the Hebrew hymnbook to a resounding close with thirteen calls to praise the Lord. "Praise ye the Lord!" He began the last Psalm with that call and he ended it with that call. That Psalm is what we call "an envelope Psalm"—it ends the exact way it begins. It is what we would call today a "round"; that is, as soon as we come to the end of it we have really arrived back at the beginning, which means we go through it again—and again and again.

We are to praise Him perpetually. That will be our joy through the ages . . . down here, generation after generation . . . up there, as the eternal ages roll. Thus Paul completed another major section of this matchless letter. Left breathless and speechless, all we can say is "Praise the Lord!" Then in typical Pauline fashion, he rattled his chain and brought us back to earth again in Ephesians 4:1.

PART III

The Christian
and His Behavior

Ephesians 4:1 – 6:9

III. THE CHRISTIAN AND HIS BEHAVIOR (4:1–6:9)

A. In His Mystical Relationships (4:1-16)

1. The Greatness of the Mystical Body (4:1-6)

a. Its Uniqueness (4:1-3)

(1) It Is Undaunted (4:1a) "The prisoner of the Lord."

With these words Paul dignified his chains. He was not the prisoner of Nero. He was the prisoner of the Lord. A mere caesar could not arrest an apostle without God's permission. Paul was undaunted. Since he had to wear a chain, he wore it like a chain of office. If every move he made had to be accompanied by the rattle of fetters, he made each clank of iron a note in a melody of praise to God. He converted his prison into a palace. He considered himself shut up with God.

Since Paul could no longer roam the world in evangelistic zeal, he became a prayer warrior. Soldiers barred the way to this world, but no soldier could close the way to Heaven. Since Paul could not preach, he prayed. Since he could not plant churches, he upheld those who could at the throne of grace. Since he could not go to Spain, he prayed for Spain. He prayed for Timothy, Titus, Luke, and Aristarchus. He prayed for the saints at Jerusalem, Antioch, Philippi, Ephesus, and Rome. He prayed for the caesar, the senate, the Roman people, the world, and the soldier who shared his cell. God shut Paul up with his pen and his prayers, so Paul praised Him by writing letters and interceding at the throne.

(2) It Is Undivided (4:1b-3)

(a) Its Character (4:1b-2) "I . . . beseech you that ye walk worthy of the vocation wherewith ye are called, With all lowliness and meekness, with longsuffering, forbearing one another in love."

A Christian's character must be in keeping with his calling. And what a calling it is! Paul had to ransack his vocabulary to find words to describe what is ours in Christ in the heavenlies, and then he said that we are to walk worthy of that calling. We are going to be like

Christ for all eternity so we need to begin being like Him now. The place to begin is at home, at school, at work, at play, in the church, and in our community. We must begin with one another, with those whose lives are linked with ours.

The word *lowliness* refers to humility of mind. Thoughts of God's wisdom, love, and power should put an end to all our pride.

The word *meekness* challenges us to cultivate the spirit of the Lord Jesus (2 Corinthians 10:1). Meekness is not much admired among men because they too readily mistake it for weakness. But meekness is admired in Heaven. Only a strong person can display complete self-control and restraint in the face of extreme provocation. This kind of meekness is a fruit of the Spirit (Galatians 5:23).

Longsuffering is an expression of love. Paul said, "Charity [love] suffereth long, and is kind" (1 Corinthians 13:4). How impatient we can be when we don't get our own way or when someone does or says something to irritate us. Jesus never responded with impatience. He urged us to be forbearing, to put up with one another.

As members of the mystical body of Christ—with His Spirit indwelling us, with the Lord Himself as the head of that body, with Christ living His life in us and through us—how much like Him we should be!

(b) Its Curriculum (4:3) "Endeavouring to keep the unity of the Spirit in the bond of peace."

The Greek word translated "endeavouring" literally means "studying" (2 Timothy 2:15). We have to study to keep the mystical body undivided. We are in the school of God, where the chief subject in the curriculum is Christ. We are to study to be like Him; we are to apply our minds to the problems He sets before us. The problems are not merely academic. Often the problems are practical, like getting along in a Christlike way with other people—sometimes with difficult, defeated people we dislike.

In the school of God there are tests so we can evaluate our progress in becoming Christlike. We can evaluate whether Christ is being expressed in and through our bodies and the mystical body of Christ, for this is what the Christian life is all about.

b.   Its Unity (4:4-6)

(1) Its Functional Unity (4:4a-b)

(a) The Diverse Life It Shows (4:4a) "One body."

We look at the church today and we see it torn and divided. In the words of hymnist S. J. Stone,

> . . . with a scornful wonder
> Men see her sore oppressed,
> By schisms rent asunder,
> By heresies distressed.

Men look at the church and see it divided into Catholic, Protestant, and Orthodox communions. They see state churches, countless nonconformist groups, and the endless splintering of the professing church into denominations, sects, and factions. They see liberals and fundamentalists, charismatics and conservatives. They see churches divided on doctrine, churches espousing opposite views on church government, churches bitterly divided on issues. And the confusion over all these divisions is aggravated by a multitude of heresies and cults all claiming to be Christian.

There is, however, only one church. Where man sees disunity, God sees unity. He sees a church comprised of men, women, boys, and girls who have trusted in Christ for salvation, who have been washed from their sins in His blood, and who have been born from above. They are all one in Christ—some living on earth, even more living in Heaven. Life, not light, unites the body of Christ. All who are saved and are members of that body share one life—the life of Christ. That is the unity of the church. The shared life of Christ may be expressed in diverse ways, but wherever a person belongs to the body, that life is there. It makes no difference whether the believer is young or old, gifted or retarded, wise or foolish, high church or low church, oriental or occidental, enlightened or confused, victorious or defeated. What matters is that the life of Christ is present.

(b) The Divine Life It Shares (4:4b) "One Spirit."

It is the Holy Spirit who imparts that divine life. His first work is to convict and enlighten. Then He regenerates, adds the new believers to the body, indwells, fills, seals, anoints.

Paul said, "If any man have not the Spirit of Christ, he is none of his" (Romans 8:9). The indwelling Holy Spirit distinguishes the genuine believer from someone who merely professes to be in the church. One has the Holy Spirit; the other does not. One has spiritual life; the other does not.

Those who share new life in Christ do so because of the indwelling Holy Spirit. True believers may be misinformed about Him or wholly ignorant of Him. They may grieve Him. They may sadly distort what He says about Himself and His work. They may go to all kinds of excess, but He patiently continues to indwell them. As for false professors, although the Holy Spirit does not indwell them, He does continue to strive with them.

There are many false spirits and because of this 1 John 4:1-2 warns us to "try the spirits." There is only *one* Holy Spirit, one Spirit who imparts the one life shared by all the members of the mystical body of Christ.

(2) Its Fundamental Unity (4:4c-5)

(a) Of Calling (4:4c) "One hope of your calling."

All believers have a common hope: the second coming of Christ. They may be doctrinally divided as to when He will come, but they believe He will come.

Postmillennialists think He will come when the leaven of the gospel has sufficiently permeated society and made the world morally and spiritually ready for His coming.

Amillennialists, who view the church as spiritual Israel, see all the millennial promises of the Old Testament as being spiritually fulfilled in the church. They believe that there will be no literal millennium; Christ's coming will usher in the eternal state.

Premillennialists take the Old Testament millennial prophecies literally. They refuse to allegorize the prophecies and explain them away, believing that Christ will set up a thousand-year reign on this planet, the former scene of His rejection.

Post-tribulationists believe that before Christ can come to reign, the church must go through the fires of the great tribulation and be purified.

Midtribulationists think that the rapture of the church will take place halfway through the last seven-year period of Gentile dominance so that true believers will be snatched away in the nick of time.

Pretribulationists view the coming tribulation period as a time when God will wrathfully judge Israel and the nations, and the church will escape altogether.

Partial-rapture theorists believe that only the watchful, ready portion of the church will be raptured. The rest will be left behind to be purged by persecution (a theory, really, of a ruptured church rather than a raptured church). And so it goes on.

As with all major Bible doctrines, the enemy has succeeded in making this glorious truth of our hope confusing and conflicting.

But the bottom line is, we all have one hope. Our calling is sure: Jesus is coming again. We agree on that because He said so (John 14:1-3). Satan wants us to squabble over the details; God keeps this ultimate, blessed hope before us.

(b) Of Confession (4:5) "One Lord, one faith, one baptism."

"One Lord." That is our way of saying, *"I'm saved."* This is the common confession of the redeemed. We may express the message in different ways, belong to different communities of faith, and hold to different convictions, but we have only one confession: Jesus is Lord.

Paul wrote, "If thou shalt confess with thy mouth the Lord Jesus, and shalt believe in thine heart that God hath raised him from the dead, thou shalt be saved" (Romans 10:9). The evidence of our salvation is the heartfelt confession of Jesus as Lord. This confession turns our lives over to Him and makes Him our center, sum, and circumference for salvation, sovereignty, and security. This is not the glib mouthing of words, for Christ Himself warned that not all who say "Lord, Lord" are His (Matthew 25:1-12). No, this confession is the heart response of those who want to know Him, love Him, trust Him, and obey Him. In this confession the mouth speaks "out of the abundance of the heart" (Matthew 12:34).

"One faith." That is our way of saying, *"I'm sure."* Jude 3 speaks of "the faith which was once delivered unto the saints." That is the faith Paul had in mind here—that great body of assuring truth that Luke called "the apostles' doctrine" (Acts 2:42), the foundation stone on which our certainty of salvation rests (Ephesians 2:20; 3:5).

There is only one faith. The bottom line of all Christian belief is Christ: Christ as He is revealed in the Scriptures; Christ as God the Son, eternal, uncreated, self-existing, omnipotent, omniscient, omnipresent, holy, loving, and true; Christ as the second person of the godhead, coequal with the Father and the Spirit, possessing all the attributes of deity, creator, and sustainer of all things, ineffably sublime; Christ as the Son of man, virgin-born, conceived of the Holy Ghost, immaculate, triumphant over sin's curse, victor over demons and disease and disaster and death; humble and holy, loving and lowly, patient and pure, glorious, gracious, and good.

Christ is the One foretold by the prophets; the One who fulfilled the law; the One who pleased God in His character, career, conduct, and conversation; the One who went about doing good, healed the sick, cast out demons, raised the dead, fed the multitudes, stilled the storm, walked the waves.

Christ is the One who was rejected, betrayed, falsely accused, crucified, and buried; the One who died for us to purge our sins; the One whose body defied the corruption of the grave; the One who rose from the dead and ascended on high; the One who sat down at God's right hand, sent the Holy Spirit, heads the church, and is coming again.

Christ is the essence of our one faith. Hallelujah! What a Savior!

"One baptism." That is our way of saying, *"I'm separated."* Despite arguments to the contrary, Paul had water baptism—not Spirit baptism—in mind here. If he had meant Spirit baptism, he would have linked it with "one Spirit" in Ephesians 4:4, not with "one Lord" in verse 5. Also we must remember that Paul did not address this Epistle to theologians, but to ordinary believers who would naturally think of their own water baptism when they read the unqualified words, "one baptism." In that day, there was only one baptism. The unscriptural idea of infant baptism had not been invented in apostolic times. Baptism of believers by immersion was the New Testament mode of baptism.

This one baptism effectively separated the believers from the world. In many instances it was the crucial test of a person's faith. It was the ultimate confession that could cost him his job, his family, his friends, and sometimes even his life. It still remains the test in some cultures. In Muslim lands, among some Jews, and even in some so-called Christian lands, believers can pay a high price for being baptized.

When performed publicly—in a river or at a seaside resort, for instance—baptism is still a daring confession of faith that announces loudly to a watching world that the believer has died with Christ, has been buried with Him, and is now raised with Him to live in newness of life.

(3) Its Family Unity (4:6) "One God and Father of all, who is above all, and through all, and in you all."

That God is our Father is essentially a New Testament truth. This truth was not entirely unknown to the Old Testament saints (Malachi 2:10), but it was Jesus who really taught us to call God *Father*. Christ's first recorded utterance reveals His glorious awareness of His wondrous relationship to God: "Wist ye not that I must be about my Father's business?" (Luke 2:49) His Father's business was not the work of a carpenter, but the work of the cross.

When Jesus responded to the disciples' request that He teach them to pray, He said, "After this manner therefore pray ye: Our

Father which art in heaven, Hallowed be thy name" (Matthew 6:9). In His parable of the prodigal son and the elder brother, Jesus used the word *father* twelve times. He died with that name on His lips and rose from the dead assuring His loved ones that His Father was their Father.

In His last recorded utterance on the way to His ascension, Jesus used the name again. "Wait," He said, "for the promise of the Father" (Acts 1:4). He then added that the *Father* had put the restoration of the kingdom to Israel into His own power (Acts 1:6-7). Then Jesus was gone! But the name still echoes on earth. It is the greatest of all the names for God. He had been known as a Shepherd, a Shield, a Rock, the Lord of hosts, the holy One of Israel—all the wondrous metaphors by which He revealed Himself to the sons of men. But what name can compare with *Father?*

Our Father is *absolute in His power.* As Paul wrote, there is "one God and Father of all, who is above all." No foe can daunt us. No fear can haunt us. No power in Heaven, earth, or Hell can triumph over Him. He is above all. He rules the galaxies, from earth to the uttermost star. No government on earth can overrule His decrees. He is above all, and He is our God and Father. Blessed be His name!

Our Father is *absorbed in His purpose:* "One God and Father of all, who is . . . through all." The Greek preposition translated "through" here is *dia.* In this context *dia* has the general sense of dividing a surface in two with an intersecting line. *Dia* includes the idea of proceeding from and passing on out. It denotes any cause by means of which an action passes to its accomplishment—the passing through whatever is interposed between the beginning and the end of such action. God is through all. In other words, "Known unto God are all his works from the beginning of the world" (Acts 15:18). God knows what He is doing, where He is going, and how He will accomplish His purposes.

Nowhere is this more evident than at Calvary. There God allowed the opposition of earth and Hell to unite against Him and have its diabolical way. The Greek, Latin, and Hebrew letters on Jesus' cross proclaimed not only His title—"Jesus of Nazareth the King of the Jews"—but also the world's united contempt (John 19:19). Greek reasoning, Roman rule, and Hebrew religion joined to endorse the crucifixion of God's King. Hell triumphed! Satan won! God had sent His only Son. Now He had no more heralds to send. As in the parable, the people said, "This is the heir; come, let us kill him, and the inheritance shall be ours" (Mark 12:7). For a little while, it looked as though God was checkmated by men on earth and by plots of the pit. But not so! God was simply on His way through.

The dark hill of Calvary was not the end of the journey. God was "proceeding from." He was intersecting time, drawing a line through the ages. He was dividing the human race in two: saved and lost, believing and unbelieving, reprobate and regenerate. He allowed men to bury His Son in the tomb. He allowed Jesus' body to lie there while He finished drawing that line. Then, having "proceeded from," He "passed on out." Jesus came out of that tomb, ascended into Heaven, took His place at God's right hand in glory, and began the countdown to Armageddon. Our Father is absorbed in His purpose.

Our Father is also *abiding in His presence:* "One God and Father of all, who is . . . in you all." *En,* the preposition translated "in" here, denotes "being or remaining within, with the primary idea of rest and continuance" *(The Companion Bible).* We are familiar with the concepts of the Holy Spirit indwelling the believer (1 Corinthians 3:16) and the Lord Jesus indwelling the believer (John 15:4). Here we learn that the Father also indwells the believer. The thought is beyond all thought! God the Father, God the Son, and God the Holy Spirit are all at home in our hearts.

2.   The Gifts of the Mystical Body (4:7-13)

a.   Grace to Accompany Gifts (4:7) "But unto every one of us is given grace according to the measure of the gift of Christ."

Paul taught us how the body of Christ functions and grows. The Lord has provided everything that the body needs: grace so that its members can function in harmony one with another; and gifts so that the body can live and grow through the ordinary lives of men.

"Grace" was one of Paul's favorite words. The Greek word translated "grace," *charis,* occurs 156 times in the New Testament. No less than 110 of these occurrences are in Paul's Epistles. *Charis* always conveys the idea of free, undeserved favor. Once we understand that God's free and undeserved favor has given us any gifts we have, we will be more diligent in developing and using those gifts and more humble in enjoying them.

Gifts without grace can be harsh, abrasive, and presumptuous in their effect on others, and tend to create egotism and self-complacency in ourselves. Gifts without grace produce pride, friction, and carnality—a truth all too evident in Paul's letter to the Corinthians. The more gifts we have, the more grace we need. That is why Paul spoke of grace being "according to the measure of the gift."

The Lord Himself has bestowed on us any gifts that we have. As James M. Gray's hymn puts it:

> Naught have I gotten but what I received;
> Grace hath bestowed it since I have believed.

Moreover, all gifts are given so that we can manifest to the world and to one another the marvelous traits and abilities of the Lord Jesus.

b.   Gifts to Accompany Grace (4:8-13)

(1) The Gifts Assured (4:8-10)

(a) The Old Testament Promise (4:8) "Wherefore he saith, When he ascended up on high, he led captivity captive, and gave gifts unto men."

Gifts without grace are undesirable, but so is grace without gifts. The church needs both gifts and grace.

The gifts bestowed by the Lord on His church came at Pentecost in fulfillment of the promise in Psalm 68:18. Interestingly, the Jews used this Psalm in connection with Pentecostal celebrations in the synagogue.

When Paul wrote Ephesians 4:8, he had in mind a picture of a victorious king who has overthrown his foes. He is ascending the mountains, entering triumphantly into his city. He is laden with the spoils of war and bestows lavish gifts on his cheering people. He has freed the hostages held by the enemy and has ravished the enemy's domains. The freed captives are special recipients of his princely gifts.

We can see the parallel. Jesus triumphed in battle over sin and Satan. He carried the war into the enemy's domains and led forth from the lower regions a multitude of captives ("he led captivity captive"). Then Jesus took His place on high and "gave gifts unto men." He bestowed liberal, magnificent gifts on His own.

Paul saw in all this a fulfillment of Psalm 68:18, which he quoted in Ephesians 4:8 with a slight alteration. (We find many amended quotations in the New Testament. The Holy Spirit, the Author of both the Old and New Testaments, certainly had the latitude to use His own material in whatever manner suited Him and to bring out shades of meaning He had in mind from the beginning.) The Jews saw in Psalm 68:18 a reference to Moses' ascent of mount Sinai to receive the law, which he then gave to Israel. They associated the giving of the law with Pentecost. Whatever truth there might have been in this use of the passage, Paul lifted everything to higher ground.

(b) The New Testament Proof (4:9-10) "Now that he ascended what is it but that he also descended first into the lower parts of the earth? He that descended is the same also that ascended up far above all heavens, that he might fill all things."

At His birth, the Lord Jesus descended from Heaven's heights to a Bethlehem barn. At his death, He descended into Hades. There He preached to "the spirits in prison" (1 Peter 3:18-20), presumably the disembodied spirits of all those who had died in previous ages. At that time Hades seems to have been divided into two realms, each separated from the other by an impassable gulf (Luke 16:19-31). In one realm were the spirits of the wicked dead, already in torment though not yet in Hell *(Gehenna)*. In the other realm were the spirits of the blessed dead. (The second realm was called *paradise* by Jesus when He was speaking to the dying thief and *Abraham's bosom* by the Jews in their commentaries.)

Jesus went to these captives in Hades with a proclamation. He proclaimed His everlasting triumph over sin, Satan, death, and the grave. To those in the dark realm, it was a message of eternal despair. During their lifetimes they had rejected Him by rejecting the light God had graciously given them. Now they were without God, without Christ, and without hope. One man in their ranks represented them all—the thief who while dying had cursed Christ and blasphemed His claims. With what horror-filled eyes he must now have looked on the One he had so rashly scorned but a few hours before.

To those in paradise the Lord's message was full of unspeakable joy and glory. How the prophets must have rejoiced at the fulfill-ment of their often misunderstood and barely comprehended prophecies! How Abraham, David, and all the others must have shouted for joy! One man in their ranks represented them all—the thief who died calling on Christ to remember him in His kingdom. Now he was alive forevermore. With what wonder-filled eyes he must have looked on the One in whom he had so boldly believed a few hours earlier.

After proclaiming His triumph to those in Hades, the Lord arose in triumph, bringing the souls of the blessed dead with Him. Many of them were united with their bodies and shared in His resurrection as the first fruits of the second harvest. Paradise was thus emptied, and we are not told more about this beyond the intimation here in Ephesians that when the Lord ascended, He took with Him the captives He had delivered from the nether regions. Now all who die in Christ go to be with Him, "which is far better" (Philippians 1:23).

(2) The Gifts Assigned (4:11-13)

(a) The Nature of Them (4:11) "And he gave some, apostles; and some, prophets; and some, evangelists; and some, pastors and teachers."

The gifts listed here are different from most of those mentioned in 1 Corinthians 12. There, for the most part, the gifts are bestowed on believers. Here, gifted believers are bestowed on the church. In 1 Corinthians the gifts are viewed primarily from the standpoint of the local church. In Ephesians they are viewed from the standpoint of the universal church, the whole body. The five gifts listed in Ephesians 4:11 can be summarized in this way:

1. Those gifted to deal with *situations*
   a. Those equipped to *guide* the infant church in ways it ought to go (apostles)
   b. Those equipped to *guard* the infant church in what it ought to know (prophets)
2. Those gifted to deal with *sinners* (evangelists)
3. Those gifted to deal with *saints*
   a. Those called to *tend* the flock of God (pastors)
   b. Those called to *teach* the flock of God (teachers)

The gifts of apostles and prophets were foundational (Ephesians 2:20) and unique to the early church. We have missionaries (sent ones) and preachers today, but we do not have apostles and prophets. Those gifts were temporary and transitional, intended to help the church become established according to the Holy Spirit's plans.

There were primary apostles and secondary apostles. The primary apostles were called and commissioned by the Lord Jesus as His sent ones. Paul was such an apostle, although he had been "born out of due time" (1 Corinthians 15:8). Primary apostles were men who had seen the Lord, who had been with Him from the beginning, and who were eyewitnesses of His resurrection. They were given the task of imparting New Testament truth to the church by direct inspiration of the Holy Spirit. Secondary apostles—men like Barnabas, Timothy, and Silvanus—were intimately linked with the primary apostles.

The prophets spoke by direct illumination of the Holy Spirit. Their work was essential too. Their task was to disseminate New Testament truth before the completion and distribution of the New Testament. The Spirit of God empowered the prophets to impart truths (already revealed to the apostles) to local congregations. Occasionally the prophets foretold things to come. Usually, like their Old Testament counterparts, they were "forthtellers" rather than foretellers. They "forthtold" truth already revealed by the Holy Spirit but not yet in general circulation.

The gifts of apostles and prophets died out with the end of the first century and the completion of the New Testament canon of Scripture.

Evangelists are always needed. The evangelist, a man especially gifted by the Spirit of God to win souls, is the church's salesman, so to speak. All believers can be soul-winners, but not all believers can be evangelists. When the evangelist comes to town, sinners turn to Christ in significant numbers. A person either has or does not have the gift of the evangelist. If the person has the gift of the evangelist, something happens when he preaches: people come to Christ. If he does not have the gift, the response to his message is likely to be sparse. Nobody can produce fruit like the evangelist. His message and methods may be shallower than those of the pastors and teachers, but he gets the souls because God has given him the gift. A person who does not have this gift should not fret, but thank God some people do have it.

The pastor is simply a shepherd, as the name of the gift implies. He loves the Lord's people and has a heart for the flock. He cares for the weak, the sick, and those who are going astray. He counsels the young, cares for the needy, and comforts the bereaved. He does these tasks supremely well because he has the shepherd's heart and the pastoral gift.

The teacher expounds the Bible's great truths: its sublime doctrines; its underlying principles; and the broad scope of its history, theology, purpose, and impact. He compares spiritual things with spiritual (1 Corinthians 2:13), shows God's ways with men down through the ages, and communicates God's stirring plans for the future. The teacher develops consistent hermeneutics and discerns a unifying principle broad enough to explain all of God's revealed ways.[1] He teaches others how to divide the Word of truth (2 Timothy 2:15) and opens their eyes to the wonders of Scripture.

(b) The Need for Them (4:12-13)

i.   The Purpose Involved (4:12) "For the perfecting of the saints, for the work of the ministry, for the edifying of the body of Christ."

If we delete the comma after the word *saints*, we receive the full force of this statement: "For the perfecting of the saints for the work of the ministry." The word translated "perfecting" *(katartismos)* only occurs here. Its verb form, however, occurs in many places in Scripture and is translated in a variety of ways in the New Testament. For instance, it is used of mending nets in Matthew 4:21. In Matthew 21:16 Jesus used the word in His response to the chief priests and scribes who objected when people hailed Him with their hosannas: "Have ye never read, Out of the mouth of babes and sucklings thou hast perfected praise?" The word is used in Hebrews 10:5 to describe the incarnation of the Word: "A body hast thou *prepared* me" (italics added). This is a reference to the unique creative act involved in the virgin birth; God brought into being a perfect vehicle through which the incarnate Word of God could fully express God's thoughts, likeness, and ways to men. The thought, then, behind the word *katartismos* is that of making something fully ready, of perfectly equipping someone, of fully preparing something. The proper use of the gifts is to bring the body of Christ to its full potential.

The universal gifts that God has given to the church are intended to build up the local church and the universal church. The Holy Spirit does not intend that those with these gifts should monopolize the ministry. Gifted people should help equip others to carry out the work of winning people to Christ, shepherding the flock, and teaching God's Word.

ii. The Period Involved (4:13) "Till we all come in the unity of the faith, and of the knowledge of the Son of God, unto a perfect man, unto the measure of the stature of the fulness of Christ."

The Holy Spirit wants us to achieve the stature of Christ. What a goal! The same Greek word translated "stature" here is used to describe Zacchaeus, who was "little of stature" (Luke 19:3). It can also be translated "age," as in the account of the man born blind whom Jesus healed and whose parents were interrogated by the authorities. His parents answered, "He is of age; ask him" (John 9:21). In effect they said, "He has grown up." The Holy Spirit wants us to grow up until we display, here on earth, something of Christ's stature and maturity.

This ultimate goal will not be realized until the rapture when all the individual members of the body of Christ will be glorified together with the head. In the meantime, we should not expect the church universal to display this glorious unity and maturity. Denominational differences, doctrinal conflicts, dispositional clashes, and other issues constantly divide the church. However, the goal is certainly achievable within the fellowship of any local church.

If an individual believer is to mature fully, he needs the fellowship of other believers. The idea of an arm or a leg developing in isolation from other members of the body is ludicrous. No one can attain full spiritual maturity apart from the give-and-take of a local church fellowship. The New Testament does not mention freelance evangelists, independent missionaries, itinerant Bible teachers, or other Christians who have no local fellowship and are responsible to no one but themselves.

3.   The Growth of the Mystical Body (4:14-16)

a.   Growth Diabolically Inhibited (4:14) "That we henceforth be no more children, tossed to and fro, and carried about with every wind of doctrine, by the sleight of men, and cunning craftiness, whereby they lie in wait to deceive."

This verse is full of interesting words. The word translated "children," for instance, is derived from a word that literally means "one not old enough to speak"—in other words, a small infant. A child who is not yet old enough to speak is helpless. He is picked up and put down at the will and whim of others. He has no vocabulary with which to express his wishes. The gifts to the church are designed to get us past the highly vulnerable stage of infancy in our Christian lives.

A new convert soon manifests evidence of spiritual life, but his opinions and ideas are unformed and largely inarticulate. His theology embraces little beyond the bare fact of his salvation. Most likely his views on the Holy Spirit, prophecy, or the church are what he has picked up uncritically from others. He is vulnerable and needs the ministry of gifted men to protect him.

The spiritual infant has no doctrinal stability. He is "tossed to and fro." (The Greek word translated "tossed to and fro" literally means "surging like the sea.") His opinions are constantly changing. He has not yet mastered principles of hermeneutics and applied them to the Scriptures. He has not yet, through exegesis of the Bible, formed convictions of his own regarding bedrock truths. Thus a spiritual babe will often enthusiastically espouse one viewpoint for a while, then discard it and adopt another. His viewpoints are fluctuating and might even be out of harmony with the Scriptures.

The expression translated "carried about" means "borne hither and thither." In Mark 6:55 the sick were "carried about." In other words, Paul was painting a picture in Ephesians 4:14 of a person who is helpless in the hands of others.

So in verse 14 Paul gave us three vivid illustrations of the vulnerability and doctrinal peril of those who have not yet matured in the faith. He took us into the nursery, out to sea, and into the hospital.

But Paul was not finished. He used some more word pictures to illustrate how some people take advantage of the spiritual immaturity of some believers. People who are not well established in the Word are easily swayed. They are carried about from one teacher to another "with every wind of doctrine." This weakness is bad enough when the teachers are all saved people, but it can be deadly when false teachers come. They were coming to Colossae, which was not too far from Ephesus. In Acts 20:29 Paul warned the Ephesian elders to watch out for "grievous wolves" who would come in, "not sparing the flock."

Paul had a gambling scene in mind as he continued to illustrate how some people take advantage of the spiritually immature. The word translated "sleight" in Ephesians 4:14 literally means "a cube" and refers to dice. The word metaphorically signifies slyness or trickery. Satan and his teachers play tricks with the truth. For example, cultists are adept at supporting their heretical teaching with a verse of Scripture that is taken out of context or slightly twisted. Someone even quoted John 3:7—"Ye must be born again"— to support his belief in reincarnation!

Paul spoke of the "cunning craftiness" of false teachers. The word translated "craftiness" in Ephesians 4:14 could also be translated "subtlety." Paul used the same word in 2 Corinthians 11:3: "The serpent beguiled Eve through his subtilty." Eve was no match for the devil. But she had God's Word and all she needed to say when Satan tempted her was, "Thus saith the Lord!" Her failure to adhere faithfully to God's Word led to her downfall. God did not expect her to argue with the enemy or dialogue with him. God did expect her to adhere faithfully to the plain, literal sense of His Word.

The same word is used to describe the Lord's enemies when they tried to trip Him up by questioning the lawfulness of paying tribute to Caesar. Luke said, "He perceived their craftiness" (Luke 20:23).

Those who take advantage of the spiritually immature "lie in wait to deceive." The clause, "Whereby they lie in wait to deceive" (Ephesians 4:14), is a translation of a group of Greek words including *pros* ("with a view to"), *planē* ("deceive"), and *methodeia* (which refers to Satan's strategies, wiles, schemes, methods, and cunning devices). *Planē* signifies "wandering" and is the root of our word "planet." At Colossae false teachers were lying in wait to lead people astray. *The Companion Bible* points out that the association of *methodeia* with Satan in 6:11 shows that the deceitful schemes in 4:14 are of the devil, and not merely error. What was craftily and methodically being taught in Colossae—and what is being taught in the cults today—is not just error. It is calculated deception that emanates from the father of lies.

The growth of the body of Christ, then, was being diabolically inhibited in Paul's day. Satan was attacking the church with all his craft and power. No wonder the church needed apostles, prophets, evangelists, pastors, and teachers!

Satan threw everything he had at the early church. In the providence of God, he used every trick of his trade during the first century. Satan has no new tricks for us—only variations of tricks already played. He is bankrupt of ideas. In the apostolic age every wile of Satan was met and answered by the apostles and prophets, and the New Testament furnishes us with all we need to combat Satanic error and delusion. We can thank God for that. Satan overplayed his hand in his desperate attempt to stop the infant church. He shot his bolt. He has been fully unmasked and can only trade now on people's ignorance of God's Word.

b.   Growth Divinely Inherent (4:15-16)

(1) The Law of Love (4:15a) "Speaking the truth in love, may grow up into him in all things."

We can go to two extremes. We can speak the truth but not in love, in which case we are being *ungracious.* Truth spoken in that spirit often offends and does little good because it alienates the people we are seeking to win. Or we can speak in love and suppress the truth, in which case we are being *unfaithful.* People who do not want to hurt someone's feelings may say nothing and allow a sinful situation to continue. They suffer in silence. True love, however, will always speak at the right time, with the right words, in the right spirit, and using the right approach.

Paul spoke the truth in love to the Ephesians. He got down to very practical issues later in chapter 4. He talked about lying, anger, stealing, unclean conversation, and marital relationships, but no one took offense because earlier he made so many warm and positive comments. None of the Ephesian Christians thought that Paul was being harsh or unkind. They all knew that he loved them. We can accept the truth from someone with whom we share mutual love. As Solomon said, "Faithful are the wounds of a friend" (Proverbs 27:6).

(2) The Law of Life (4:15b-16)

(a) The Head Controls (4:15b-16a) We "may grow up into him in all things, which is the head, even Christ: From whom the whole body fitly joined together and compacted by that which every joint supplieth, according to the effectual working in the measure of every part, maketh increase of the body."

Paul returned to one of his favorite illustrations: the church is compared to a body, of which Christ is the head. In other passages Paul developed the theme of the interdependence of the members of the body and our mutual suffering and joy. Here the theme is our mutual development. We are to grow up as individuals and as a body.

Nothing is more wonderful than the way a body grows. Light, warmth, nourishment, exercise, and protection contribute to the fascinating process of growth to maturity. Likewise Christ gave various gifts to His church to stimulate growth. The growth of His body may not be continuous (time-lapse photography developed by Moody Institute of Science shows that in plants there is a period of growth followed by a period of rest), but the process continues until maturity is reached.

Not all parts of a body grow at the same speed or to the same size. The measure of our individual spiritual growth is Christ. How much like Him have we become? To what extent is His glorious life being reproduced in us, the members of His body?

Paul was anxious that the church at Ephesus and all who would ultimately read this circular letter might grow spiritually. He did not want contentment with mere fundamentalism to stunt growth at Ephesus. He did not want intellectualism to stunt it at Colossae. He did not want materialism to stunt it at Laodicea. "Look at Christ," Paul was saying. "Look at Him; live like Him; be like Him."

(b) The Heart Consoles (4:16b) "Unto the edifying of itself in love."

For the second time in two verses Paul mentioned love. Why? Love is the most important ingredient in spiritual life and growth.

> Love never faileth.
> Love is pure gold.
> Love is what Jesus
> Came to unfold.

Paul's emphasis on love in this letter was inspired. By the time the apostle John wrote to the church at Ephesus, the Lord had to write "Ichabod" over its door (1 Samuel 4:21). Revelation 2:2-4 says in effect: "I know all about you—how you are standing up for the truth and how you are standing up in the task. I know how busy you are and how doctrinally sound you are, but I have something against you. You don't love Me anymore." Poor insolvent Ephesus! Love for the Lord was lacking and without that, everything else was spurious. The Lord took such a serious view of this lack of love that He threatened to remove the church altogether unless the believers there repented.

---

1. See *Bible Explorer's Guide.*

B. In His Moral Relationships (4:17–5:21)

1. A Complete Deliverance (4:17-24)

a. A New Life (4:17-21)

(1) The Sinner's Condition (4:17-19)

(a) His Intellect Darkened (4:17-18) "This I say therefore, and testify in the Lord, that ye henceforth walk not as other Gentiles walk, in the vanity of their mind, Having the understanding darkened, being alienated from the life of God through the ignorance that is in them, because of the blindness of their heart."

The behavior of a believer is to be radically different from that of the unconverted. Paul reminded his readers of the blindness of lost people. Certainly no enlightened Christian should let such ignorant people influence what he believes or how he behaves.

What a collection of words and phrases Paul used to describe the heathen and humanistic thought of his day! Never were his words more graphically illustrated than in our day. People who are outside of Christ simply cannot think straight on moral and spiritual issues. They may articulate the issues, but they leave out the spiritual dimensions because they are blind to them. Therefore they cannot come to any true conclusions. In Ephesians 4:17-18 we hear echoes of Paul's terrible indictment of fallen mankind in Romans 1.

The lost walk in the "vanity of their mind." The Greek word translated "vanity" in Ephesians 4:17 is *mataiotēs*. It occurs only two other places in the New Testament. Paul used *mataiotēs* in Romans 8:20 to describe the disappointing misery of the world of nature as a result of the curse: "The creature was made subject to vanity." Nature, red in tooth and claw and groaning in a minor key, is far removed from the pristine bliss of Eden. Then Peter used *mataiotēs* to describe the language of apostates. Although they are "wells without water, clouds that are carried with a tempest; to whom the mist of darkness is reserved for ever . . . they speak great swelling words of vanity" (2 Peter 2:17-18).

Man's thinking, alienated from God, is vanity. He thinks up all kinds of false religions and philosophies, and boasts of how right he is. Yet his notions are empty and dangerous.

The understanding of the lost is "darkened." Paul told the Corinthians, "The god of this world hath blinded the minds of them which believe not, lest the light of the glorious gospel of Christ, who is the image of God, should shine unto them" (2 Corinthians 4:4).

The nonsense some men believe shows how darkened their understanding is. Christian Scientists, for instance, believe that death is not real and that pain is an error of the mortal mind. Mormons believe that they can become gods. Hindus believe that, depending on how we behave in this life, we might come back as a cow, a cuckoo, or a cockroach. The scientific community embraces the theory of evolution. The humanist thinks that man is essentially good and quite able to cope with moral problems. In practice, humanism licenses lawlessness and lust.

Lost people proclaim lies as truth, immorality as morality, high-sounding nonsense as science, and philosophical speculations as religion. Their lack of understanding results from "being alienated from the life of God." The opposite of life is death. Men without God are spiritually dead. No wonder they are unable to think straight in matters of faith and morals.

Man was created to be inhabited by God. God intended for the human spirit to be inhabited by the Holy Spirit. The indwelling Holy Spirit was to enlighten the intellect, ennoble the emotions, and energize the will. Thus the life of man would express, in human terms, the life of God. The fall ruined all that. Sin entered and the Holy Spirit left. Without the life of the indwelling Holy Spirit, the natural man is spiritually dead, "alienated from the life of God."

The genius of the gospel is that when we accept Christ as Savior, we are cleansed by His blood and regenerated by His Spirit. The Holy Spirit takes up residence in the human spirit, making it possible for the saved person to have fellowship with God, cooperate with the Holy Spirit, and begin to live the kind of life God intended man to live—a life governed by the Spirit of God. Before a person receives Christ, he is adrift on life's stormy seas without a compass, rudder, or anchor. He is subject to every wind of error that may blow into his life.

The understanding of unsaved people is darkened because they are cut off from the life of God as a result of indwelling ignorance that is caused by deep-seated, inner blindness. What a vicious circle. The darkness is self-perpetuating. The lost move from darkness to darkness in darkness.

No wonder Christians should not walk as "Gentiles walk." We must never copy the beliefs, thought patterns, convictions, and codes of conduct of unsaved people. Even the most brilliant of them are blind leaders of the blind. Einstein never wanted to believe in God. Marx was an atheist. Darwin jettisoned the faith of his youth. Freud hated Christianity. Nietzsche hated God. Nearly all the well-known philosophers leave God out of their reckoning.

(b) His Inclinations Depraved (4:19) "Who being past feeling have given themselves over unto lasciviousness, to work all uncleanness with greediness."

The next step downward from willful blindness and wicked beliefs is wanton behavior, a theme Paul developed in Romans 1. In Ephesians 4:19 Paul wrote that people gave themselves up. In Romans 1:24, emphasizing the other side of the story, Paul wrote that God gave them up.

Occurring only in Ephesians 4:19, the Greek word *apalgeō* is translated "past feeling." Those who are past feeling have lost their sense of pain. The sense of pain is vitally important to a healthy body. A person with no sense of pain might accidentally put his hand into the fire and not know it until his hand is badly burned. Many of the terrible wounds that lepers suffer are the result of insensitivity to pain caused by their disease.

People who embrace wicked philosophies soon lose their sensitivity to evil and put their precepts into practice. They give themselves up to lasciviousness (also see Mark 7:22) in order "to work all uncleanness with greediness."

The word translated "work" in Ephesians 4:19, *ergasia,* describes a regular, gainful occupation. This word is used to describe how the slave owners used the demon-possessed girl they had in their power (Acts 16:16,19). *Ergasia* is also used in the passage about Demetrius and the silversmiths of Ephesus who "brought no small gain" to themselves by making shrines of the pagan goddess Diana; their wealth was threatened by the conversion of many Ephesians to Christ (Acts 19:24-27). (Incidentally, these confrontations with the slave owners and the silversmiths are the only two occasions recorded in the book of Acts when Gentiles instigated persecution against Paul.) The word is also found in Luke 12:58 where the Lord denounces the blind leaders of Israel: "When thou goest with thine adversary to the magistrate, as thou art in the way, give *diligence* that thou mayest be delivered from him" (Luke 12:58, italics added). Here *ergasia* means "work hard, take pains, do your best."

So in Ephesians 4:19 Paul was saying that those who are past feeling work hard at their vileness. They hope to gain from it and many do. People who run prostitution rings, sell drugs, and enslave people in hellish lusts are so greedy for gain that they disregard the effect their work has on others. Likewise, those who write, print, and sell pornography and glorify sodomy and other kinds of perverted sex are greedy beyond description.

(2) The Saint's Conversion (4:20-21)

(a) The Change (4:20) "But ye have not so learned Christ."

In another flash of genius Paul did not link Christian belief and behavior to a creed or code. He linked them to Christ. He did not link them to a precept or principle, but to a person.

Christianity is Christ. All we have to do is place ungodly philosophies and practices alongside Him and we can see at once how false and filthy they are. When we think of Christ, we think of the sermon on the mount, of His priceless parables, of the Lord's prayer. We think of One who went about doing good, who was humble and holy, loving and lowly, patient and pure, selfless and kind.

If we think of Christ, we reread Ephesians 4:18-19 with a growing sense of horror and shame. Could the contrast be greater? And to think that millions of people choose darkness rather than light! They would rather have lust and corruption than the living Christ. Given the choice, the crowd still cries, "Barabbas!"

"But ye have not so learned Christ," Paul reminded us in Ephesians 4:20. Life with Christ is a life of victory over the mental darkness and moral depravity of the lost. The Lord Jesus clarifies our thoughts, cleanses our lives, indwells our hearts, quickens our consciences, and stiffens our resolve.

(b) The Challenge (4:21) "If so be that ye have heard him, and have been taught by him, as the truth is in Jesus."

We always need to be cautious of the "ifs" in the New Testament. Here the word *ei* followed by the indicative mood means that the hypothesis is assumed to be fact. The classic use of this form of the word "if" is in 1 Corinthians 15:17 where Paul wrote, "And if Christ be not raised, your faith is vain; ye are yet in your sins." The "if" casts no doubt on the fact that Christ has been raised.

Paul used a similar form of argument in Ephesians 4:21. There is no doubt that these Ephesian Christians had heard of Christ. Even the most elementary knowledge of Christ would be enough to provide a contrast between the lifestyle He exemplified and expounded and the lifestyle espoused by the pagans among whom the Ephesian Christians lived. The truth is in Christ Jesus. The way of lust and license is false; it ends in disease, defilement, demoralization, and death. Paul made it clear that a new life is fundamental to being a Christian.

During World War II, I lived in a much-bombed industrial town in south Wales. When a bomb damaged a store or commercial enterprise, the dogged proprietor would most likely clear away the worst of the rubble, board up broken windows, clear a space for the merchandise, and put up a sign that read, "Business as usual." Such a sign said a lot about the commendable determination of the stricken shopkeeper to keep going, but such a sign would be most inappropriate for a Christian life. We are not to conduct "business as usual." We are to conduct business "under new management."

b.   A New Look (4:22-24)

(1)   What Must Be Put Off (4:22-23)

(a)   The Old Disposition (4:22a) "Put off concerning the former conversation."

The Greek word *anastrophē* occurs thirteen times in the New Testament and is always translated "conversation" in the King James text. The English word "conversation" has undergone a drastic change of meaning since the days of King James. The true meaning of *anastrophē* in today's English is "manner of life." Paul was saying that the believer is to put off his former manner of life through deliberate choice and determined action. The old disposition to sin must be "put off," or as some scholars render it, "put away." The believer has a new disposition because he is indwelt by the Holy Spirit. The Holy Spirit brings the disposition of the Lord Jesus into his life.

What a marvelous disposition He exhibited! He was never unkind or selfish. He never lost His temper, never had to apologize, never was rude or impatient. He was loving and thoughtful of other people. We search the Gospels in vain for any flaw in His character. Because our sinful disposition is quite incompatible with our Savior's disposition, we must take off the old disposition. We each have a new suit of clothes, so to speak, and so we take off our old sinstained clothes once and for all. We are not to try to wear the new clothes over the old. We are to take off the old clothes and put them away.

Years ago in Vancouver I saw these words on a sign in the window of a dry cleaning establishment: "If your clothes aren't becoming to you, they should be coming to us." That was a clever slogan, but it does not express Paul's message. He was not telling us to send our old garments of sin to the cleaners and then wear them again. They are not becoming to us at all. They must be put away forever. God has something better for us—something new.

Sometimes the cleaner pins a little note on a garment: "Sorry. This stain will not come out." God knows that a person cannot eradicate the deep stains that sin has left on his character. It is hopeless for him to try. God has a much better solution. He tells him to take off and put away the habits of his old nature once and for all.

(b) The Old Desires (4:22b) "Put off . . . the old man, which is corrupt according to the deceitful lusts."

The "old man" is best described by Scofield as "the man of old," the man the Christian used to be. He was born with the incorrigible nature that God has put to death in the death of Christ (Romans 6:6).

Paul described this Adamic nature as being "corrupt according to the deceitful lusts." The old man has deceitful desires that produce corruption in him just as putrefaction produces corruption in a corpse. There is nothing attractive about a decaying carcass; it fills us with horror and disgust. Its corruption is most offensive. Nobody would want to share life with a corpse.

No wonder Paul urged us to put off the old decaying man. The fact that we need any urging at all shows how deceitful the old nature is. We still feel some fatal attraction, even though the desires of the Adamic nature lead to the grave's corruption, vileness, and horror.

(c) The Old Direction (4:23) "Be renewed in the spirit of your mind."

Many of our problems have to do with the way we have been trained to think. The human mind is brilliant. It can unravel many mysteries of the universe, find ways to split atoms, unravel DNA, and weigh stars. But without God it cannot think properly about matters of faith and morals.

Satan always attacks the mind. Ever since our first parents ate of the tree of the knowledge of good and evil, the human mind has been vulnerable because it has a natural bent toward evil thoughts.

It is attracted by sin. It is blind to spiritual truth, unless it has the Holy Spirit's illumination.

The regenerating work of the Holy Spirit brings the mind of Christ into the human personality. The Holy Spirit gives a new direction to the thought life of a Christian. His carnal mind wants him to continue in the old direction, but he must deliberately put it off. There are some books he is not to read, some shows he is not to watch, some conversations he is not to have, some stories he is not to tell. He puts off such evil, and he is renewed in the spirit of his mind.

(2) What Must Be Put On (4:24) "Put on the new man, which after God is created in righteousness and true holiness."

The "old man" is the Adamic nature; the "new man" is the new nature, the nature of Christ. Just as we inherited Adam's fallen nature by natural birth, we inherit Christ's nature by the new birth. Righteousness and true holiness marked the nature of the Lord Jesus, and as we deliberately "put on" the new nature, righteousness and holiness will be seen in our lives. People will recognize us for what we are. Christlike Christians display the life and loveliness of the Lord Jesus; carnal Christians still wear the rags of the "old man."

2.   A Converted Disposition (4:25-26)

a.   A Transformed Tongue (4:25) "Putting away lying, speak every man truth with his neighbour: for we are members one of another."

Complete deliverance from the old nature is expressed in a converted disposition—including a transformed tongue, which James said no man can tame. In Ephesians 4:25 Paul moved from principles of the faith to the practice of the faith. He started spelling things out, giving specific examples of what happens when we put off the old nature and put on the new nature.

It seems incredible that Paul should have had to tell Christians not to lie. Yet we are all surprised sometimes at "the hidden things of darkness" that lurk in our souls (1 Corinthians 4:5). How easy it is in an unguarded moment when someone asks an awkward question to take refuge in a lie. But a lie on the lips of a Christian instantly grieves the Holy Spirit, who describes Himself as "the Spirit of truth" (John 15:26). Nothing short of confession and an application of the blood of Christ can erase that sin. We are to discard all falsehood.

God is truth, unchanged and unchanging. The lie is the idiom of Satan's language. Lies are the evil one's common currency of speech. He, above all else, is "the father of lies" (John 8:44).

Zechariah wrote, "Speak ye every man the truth to his neighbour" (Zechariah 8:16). (Paul was quoting him in Ephesians 4:25.) Zechariah was a postexilic prophet. One of his great burdens was to urge the restored Jewish remnant not to repeat the sins that had made their exile necessary. Throughout chapter 8, Zechariah reiterated the phrase, "Thus saith the Lord of hosts," as the Lord contrasted His former acts of government and His present acts of grace. One of the fundamentals for staying in the land, the Lord said, was to speak the truth. How significant and sad that centuries later the Jewish people ended up hiring false witnesses against the Lord. They paid for this sin when they were exiled again for nearly two thousand years.

Paul picked up Zechariah's warning and addressed it to Christian believers. But there are some fundamental differences between the restored Jewish remnant and Christian believers. For instance, we are not in the land; we are in the Lord. Our position is not in Canaan; our position is in Christ. We are not concerned with a place; we are concerned with the person of Christ. Israel could lose its position—and it did; we cannot lose our position in Christ.

We have something Israel did not have. Israel had the divine statute, but we have the Holy Spirit! If Israel needed to put away lying, how much more should we. All deceit grieves the Holy Spirit and consequently leaves us bereft of joy, peace, and power.

There is something particularly deceitful about lying to a fellow member of the body of Christ, but all lying is destructive. We are to have a transformed tongue, one that speaks the truth in love.

b. A Transformed Temper (4:26) "Be ye angry, and sin not: let not the sun go down upon your wrath."

The Greek *orgizō*, translated here as "Be ye angry," is imperative; it is a positive command. There is nothing wrong with being angry for a righteous cause. Anger can be wholesome. There are times when we should be angry. Anger can be kindled by the fire of Hell or by the fire from the altar of God. Anger kindled by the old man is always sinful, destructive, and devilish. Anger kindled by the Holy Spirit at the sight of some injustice, some great depravity, or some monstrous iniquity, is intended to give those who are engaging in the sinful activity reason to fear. The person who cannot get angry at the seduction of an innocent girl, at the corrupting of a child, at those who practice and propagate perversion and pornography, must either be spineless or wholly without moral conviction.

Jesus was angry when He drove the moneychangers out of the temple. A beautiful children's hymn written long ago embodies a lovely prayer, but begins with a wholly false concept of the Lord Jesus:

> Gentle Jesus, meek and mild,
> Look upon a little child,
> Pity my simplicity,
> Suffer me to come to thee.
> (Charles Wesley)

Is Jesus gentle? Yes. Is Jesus meek? Yes, indeed. Is Jesus *mild?* A thousand times NO! Surely Charles Wesley used that word only because he could think of no other word to rhyme with *child*.

Jesus was anything but mild, bland, soft, and passive. There was nothing mild about Him when He denounced the scribes and Pharisees for their hypocrisy and called them a "generation of vipers" (Matthew 3:7). There was nothing mild about Him when, whip in hand, He strode into the temple (Matthew 21:12-13). Jesus was angry, but he did not sin. He also wept over the Christ-rejecting city of Jerusalem and its people in view of its impending doom (Luke 19:40-44; Matthew 23:34-39).

The Greek word translated "sin" in Ephesians 4:26 is *hamartanō*, which literally means "to miss the mark." Paul was saying, "Be angry, but don't miss the mark. Control your anger." The apostle was quoting from Psalm 4:4, which in the Septuagint version reads, "Tremble and sin not." Concentrated anger is powerful enough to produce trembling.

We should note carefully how Ephesians 4:26 is positioned in the text. Its neighbor is the tongue (4:25) because it is all too easy for us to say wrong things when we are angry. Its other neighbor is the devil (4:27), because Satan is swift to take advantage of powerful emotions.

We should also note that the Holy Spirit added this caution to Ephesians 4:26: "Let not the sun go down upon your wrath." The word translated "wrath," *parorgismos,* communicates the idea of provocation. If you have to be angry—if the cause is righteous, the provocation severe—then let the storm burst but make sure the expression of your anger is not promiscuous or prolonged. Let calm follow the storm and be sure that your fellowship with God is not broken. Do not let the day end without quieting your spirit and

making sure you have not grieved the Holy Spirit. You must not
nurse anger. A converted disposition includes a transformed temper.

3.   A Conquered Devil (4:27) "Neither give place to the devil."

The author of the bad behavior described in Ephesians 4:17-
19,22,25 is unmasked in verse 27. It is the devil. The mother of all
sin is lust, and the father of sin is the devil. James said that when lust
has conceived, it brings forth death (James 1:15). Sin did not begin
on earth; it began in Heaven. Sin did not begin in the human heart
but in the soul of Lucifer, the highest anointed cherub in glory. Sin
was already hoary with antiquity before the fallen Lucifer introduced it into this planet.

Satan does not like people. He hates us with a hatred that beggars
description. His sole interest in Adam's race is to deceive us,
degrade us, distress us, and then destroy us. Since man was made in
the image and likeness of God, the more Satan can deface that
image, distort it, and turn it into a mere caricature, the more his
distorted soul is satisfied. He constantly opposes us, even more so
when we have been born again and the image of God has been
restored in us.

Regenerated believers are no longer the devil's dupes; they are
his deadly enemies. He fears as well as hates us. From the moment
of our salvation right down to the gates of death, he keeps up the
pressure of his opposition. But we must not give in. Paul said,
"Neither give place to the devil." It is not that the devil is afraid of
us personally. Rather, he is desperately afraid of the Holy Spirit who
indwells us. Satan never knows when we will enter into all that is
available to us—when we will become filled with the Spirit and
triumphantly wage battle in his realm. Paul expected that we *will*
live triumphant lives. We are not to give place, ground, or opportunity to the devil.

Note where Ephesians 4:27 finds its home in the text. Its immediate neighbors are temper (4:26) and theft (4:28). The devil lurks
between anger and dishonesty, waiting to exploit them to ruin our
testimonies and dishonor the Lord's name.

4.   A Conspicuous Difference (4:28-29)

a.   In Conduct (4:28) "Let him that stole steal no more: but rather
     let him labour, working with his hands the thing which is good,
     that he may have to give to him that needeth."

What greater proof of a changed heart and life could there be than for a former thief to seek honest employment, become concerned about those unable to work, and give of his own wages to alleviate the problems of the poor? The idea that a Christian can continue stealing is ludicrous.

One reason for the low ethical standards all too common among professing Christians today is that some leaders no longer preach repentance as a prerequisite to regeneration. They foster an "easy believism" that makes no moral demands on the conscience of the new convert. Yet the very word *conversion* implies a change of belief and behavior. It seems incredible that the Holy Spirit should have to spell it out: "Now that you're saved, don't steal. Go to work." But there it is in Ephesians 4:28. It is a sad commentary on our moral decay that the Bible must be so specific about what should be an obvious fact.

The verse also tells the former thief to work with his hands. There is nothing dishonorable about manual labor, although our society tends to esteem white-collar workers more. When Jesus came, He forever glorified manual labor by becoming a village carpenter. Paul was not ashamed to ply his trade of tentmaking when funds were low. He not only covered his own expenses, but also helped supply the material needs of fellow laborers. Among the Jews it was common practice for all men to learn a trade, even if they intended to become rabbis and teachers. Indeed, more often than not, the local rabbi was expected to earn his living.

b.   In Conversation (4:29) "Let no corrupt communication proceed out of your mouth, but that which is good to the use of edifying, that it may minister grace unto the hearers."

Paul went back to the fountainhead: if the heart is right, character will be right, conduct will be right, and conversation will be right. No corrupt communication will flow out.

The Greek word translated "corrupt" here literally means "bad, rotten, putrid." The word is used to describe decaying animal or vegetable matter. Corrupt language, unbecoming in any person, is unthinkable in a Christian. Nothing will destroy a testimony more swiftly.

Think of Peter's words when Jesus was on trial. The people who gathered around the fire in the courtyard of the high priest's house accused Peter of being a disciple. They said, "Surely thou also art one of them; for thy speech bewrayeth thee" (Matthew 26:73). The comment was astute, but when Peter began to curse and to swear, his accusers held their peace. They had been skeptical of his denials, but now they were convinced he was telling the truth. No follower of the Lord Jesus would curse and swear.

The conversation of Christians should be edifying and directed toward the spiritual welfare of others. Our speech should be marked by grace. Yet rare is the dinner table where conversation promotes godliness. Our guests should leave more edified, uplifted, and ennobled than they were when they came. Surely we should cultivate the habit of wholesome and enriching conversation.

One wonders if some of the parents who weep over erring sons and daughters sowed seeds of disinterest in godliness at the family table. Perhaps the conversation at dinner consisted of gossip and criticism of the fellowship, leaders, decisions, and spiritual temperature of the church. A constant diet of dissecting the message, depreciating the messenger, and constantly undermining what is sacred and spiritual, cannot fail to leave its mark. Let us determine before God that henceforth we will allow no corrupting comments in our homes. Rather, let us direct all our conversation toward positive ends.

5.   A Christlike Demeanor (4:30-32)

a.   An Ungrieved Holy Spirit (4:30)

(1) Who He Is (4:30a) "Grieve not the holy Spirit of God."

The Holy Spirit can be *resisted* (Acts 7:51). Resisting the Spirit is a sin of the unsaved, especially those who have had many opportunities to hear and heed the gospel. This sin is not dispensational, like blaspheming the Holy Spirit (Matthew 12:31). Only people who saw Jesus perform mighty miracles and attributed them to Satan, could blaspheme the Holy Spirit. People in all ages can resist the Holy Spirit. In Noah's day, for instance, God warned, "My spirit shall not always strive with man" (Genesis 6:3).

The Holy Spirit can be *quenched* (1 Thessalonians 5:19). Quenching the Spirit is a sin of the church. Paul warned the infant Thessalonian church about this sin right after he taught them about the rapture. His warning was part of his closing, pithy remarks to that church.

Many local churches today are going nowhere, winning no one, making no impact, losing numbers, and moving in ever-smaller circles because they have quenched the Holy Spirit. Their fellow-ship is undisciplined, inconsiderate, quarrelsome, prayerless, un-happy, unthankful, critical of the preacher, and slack on matters of faith and morals, and as a result the Spirit is quenched. (See the context of 1 Thessalonians 5:19.) The members often try to solve these problems by firing the preacher, streamlining the machinery, livening up the music, buying more advertising, getting on the radio and television, or imitating the methods of "successful" churches. But none of these tactics will work. The results, if any, will be disappointing. Instead of genuine conversions, there will be false professions because "that which is born of the flesh is flesh; and that which is born of the Spirit is spirit" (John 3:6). There will be conversions without repentance, programs without power, and religion without the Holy Spirit.

The Holy Spirit can be *grieved* (Ephesians 4:30). This is a sin of the individual believer. The word "grieve" is a love word. You cannot grieve someone who does not love you. You might annoy, upset, infuriate, or disappoint him, but you cannot grieve him. You can only grieve someone who loves you. You can grieve the Holy Spirit.

The word translated "grieve" in Ephesians 4:30 is in the active voice and means "to cause pain or sorrow." We grieve the Holy Spirit (we cause Him pain) by doing and saying things that are contrary to His character. In the Bible the Spirit of God reveals Himself as the *Holy* Spirit. Because He is holy, the kind of ungoverned behavior that Paul described in the context of this verse must cause Him indescribable pain and sorrow. We are commanded not to grieve Him because of who He is—the Holy Spirit.

(2) What He Does (4:30b) "Whereby ye are sealed unto the day of redemption."

Paul had already told the Ephesians that the seal of the Holy Spirit is the earnest of our inheritance (Ephesians 1:13-14). A seal indicated ownership and possession.

One of the Holy Spirit's ministries is to keep us safe and secure from the wiles of the devil, the weaknesses of the flesh, and the wickedness of the world until we are "saved to sin no more"[1]—until "the day of redemption." That glorious day is coming when the sons of God will come into their own (Romans 8:19), when the saints of God will be displayed to the universe as the exhibit of God's marvelous grace (2 Thessalonians 1:10). We must not make the Holy Spirit's work harder. We must not grieve Him by refusing to cooperate with Him in His maturing, molding work in our lives.

b.   An Ungrudging Human Spirit (4:31-32)

(1) Things to Be Discarded (4:31) "Let all bitterness, and wrath, and anger, and clamour, and evil speaking, be put away from you, with all malice."

This is a typical Pauline list. What an ugly accumulation of human characteristics! They sour our lives, scald our brethren, stain our characters, spoil our testimonies, and sadden the Holy Spirit.

Nothing could be more grieving to the Holy Spirit than a bitter, resentful spirit. Bitterness soured the soul of Simon Magus (Acts 8:23) when Philip preached Christ in Samaria, and showed that Simon's profession of faith was utterly false.

The Greek word translated "anger" in Ephesians 4:31 is the same word used for legitimate anger in verse 26. Anger is listed as an evil that grieves the Holy Spirit because it can easily get out of control. "Wrath" is a translation of a different Greek word that means "a violent outbreak of anger." Wrath boils up and subsides again just as swiftly, but leaves behind all kinds of scars. That kind of anger grieves the Holy Spirit of grace.

The word translated "evil speaking" is *blasphēmia,* from which we derive our word "blasphemy." *Blasphēmia* refers to slanderous, injurious talk and to railing (1 Timothy 6:4). The word is used to describe the mockery of the multitudes who reviled Christ when He was on the cross (Mark 15:29).

"Malice" is a translation of *kakia,* the usual Greek word for depravity, which denotes a vicious disposition. This kind of disposition, so contrary to the Spirit of Christ, undermines character, grieves the Holy Spirit, and produces the crop of noxious weeds listed in Ephesians 4:31. These characteristics have no place in the life of a child of the King. They are to be put away.

(2) Things to Be Displayed (4:32) "Be ye kind one to another, tenderhearted, forgiving one another, even as God for Christ's sake hath forgiven you."

Here Paul emphasized the positive. He told us we must display spiritual graces instead of soul-destroying grudges. How can we do less? We must forgive others, for the sake of the Lord Jesus Christ, just as God has forgiven us for what we did to Him, for the sake of the Lord Jesus Christ.

Wuest translated the beginning of this verse as, "And be becoming kind." We might not be able to achieve the kind of total revolution of inner disposition demanded by the Holy Spirit all at once. God is reasonable. He knows our frame. He makes allowance for us to learn and practice, even though we already have the indwelling Holy Spirit to provide the energizing power needed for change. But God does demand that here and now—right away—we start putting away the old nature and putting on the new.

6.   A Categorical Demand (5:1-7)

a.   Love Is to Be Enthroned (5:1-2)

(1) The Exhortation (5:1) "Be ye therefore followers of God, as dear children."

The new birth places us in a new family where we are God's beloved children. The family of God is the idea of the family raised to the superlative. The world knows nothing about this kind of bond. The world has lodges and fraternities, but it cannot weld people together in families. The family is God's idea. Satan hates the family and has designed and put into operation many forces that can destroy the family.

In the family of God we are to be followers of God. The Greek word translated "followers" here can also be translated "imitators." Just as children in a human family often imitate their parents, so in God's family we are to imitate God. He is our model. Since God is love, we must imitate Him and express love to those in the family of faith and to the lost world outside.

A friend of mind copastors a large church. Thousands attend its services and participate in its ministries. Every Sunday the aisles are filled with people coming forward for salvation, rededication, and church membership. Years ago I asked him what the secret of success was. He replied, "Our people love God, our people love each other, and our people love the lost." No wonder people flock to that church.

In writing to the successful church at Ephesus, Paul reminded the Christians there that love is to be enthroned and exhorted them to imitate God.

(2) The Example (5:2) "Walk in love, as Christ also hath loved us, and hath given himself for us an offering and a sacrifice to God for a sweetsmelling savour."

Paul generally used the word *walk* to describe a person's outward life, the life that other people see. The word depicts progress in the Christian life because the Christian life never stands still. It is a life of movement. As Christians, we are either moving forward or sliding backward. We are becoming more like Christ or we are slipping back into our old ways.

We must keep Calvary before us and make Calvary love the goal toward which we walk. The Lord Jesus is the supreme example of love. At Calvary He expressed His love for us and His love for God.

Jesus said, "Greater love hath no man than this, that a man lay down his life for his friends" (John 15:13). Paul added, "God commendeth his love toward us, in that, while we were yet sinners, Christ died for us" (Romans 5:8). The love that took the Son of God from the heights of Heaven and the throne of the universe to that cross of shame and woe, on a skull-shaped hill called Calvary, to die on our behalf is "more than tongue can tell."[2]

Calvary expressed the Lord's love for His Father too. There was a burnt-offering aspect to the cross (Leviticus 1). In Old Testament times the burnt offering was the highest expression of love for God. Its unique feature was that it was all for God. The burnt offering was one of the three sweet-savor offerings, and there were different grades of burnt offerings ranging from a turtledove to a full-grown bullock. The size of the offering indicated the measure of one's appreciation and love.

When the offering was a turtledove or a pigeon, the priest helped, thus indicating that while the expression of appreciation and love was acceptable and pleasing to God, it was so feeble that a more mature believer needed to help make it known. When the offering was a bullock, the offerer was still considered unable to comprehend all that Calvary meant. But a full-grown bullock represented a mature, virile appreciation and love for God.

All of the full-grown bullock was burnt on the altar except the skin. The skin was given to the priest. Here again the symbolism is significant. The priest represents the fulltime minister of the gospel, the person whose whole life is given to the ministry. Sacred themes occupy his thoughts daily and continually, while secular matters play a minimum part in his life. Reserving the skin for the priest was God's Old Testament way of saying that not even the most consecrated believer can fully understand the devotion of Christ to His Father as expressed in offering Himself on the cross; he cannot get beyond the surface. Yet the goal of our lives is still to love as Christ loved.

b.   Lust Is to Be Dethroned (5:3-7)

(1) God's Demands Are Not to Be Underestimated (5:3-5)

(a) The Principle Is Underlined (5:3-4)

i.   The Holy Spirit States His Antipathy to Lust (5:3-4a)

a.   Immorality in Our Walk (5:3) "Fornication, and all uncleanness, or covetousness, let it not be once named among you, as becometh saints."

The expression translated "not be once named" can be rendered "not be even named." In other words, such sins are unthinkable for a child of God.

In Romans 1:24 Paul linked uncleanness with dishonoring the body through carnal sin. In Paul's day, as in ours, sexual promiscuity was taken for granted. Everybody indulged in it; it was an acceptable lifestyle. Many of Paul's heathen converts had been brought up in a permissive atmosphere where it was common for a man to keep a mistress, frequent houses of ill repute, gratify his lusts in casual liaisons, or accept a partner without bothering with the formality of marriage. These practices were considered natural, not immoral. Yet the Holy Spirit says that such behavior must not even be mentioned in Christian circles. They are the antithesis of genuine Christianity. Moreover, covetousness itself—the root sin from which sexual sins are often the fruit—must be banished from our accepted moral code.

Our society may be tolerant of these sins. Governments may pass laws legitimizing behavior that a generation ago would have brought a prison sentence. The Holy Spirit, however, will not tolerate such immorality. The conduct of a Christian is controlled not by a heathen society, but by the Holy Spirit.

b.   Impurity in Our Talk (5:4a) "Neither filthiness, nor foolish talking, nor jesting, which are not convenient [befitting]."

Just as offensive to the Holy Spirit and just as destructive of spiritual life as immorality in our walk is impurity in our talk.

"Filthiness" comes from the word *aischrotēs,* which signifies something shameful or obscene. A Christian should not tell dirty jokes or talk about things that make other people blush. In our day, open talk about intimate matters is acceptable. Nothing is sacred. The language of the gutter is freely used in books and broadcasts. Vulgar talk that would have been considered pornography a generation ago is now hard to avoid. The tendency is for us Christians to lower our standards also. The world is always trying to pour us into its mold, but the Holy Spirit brings us back to the gold standard of

Christlike behavior; He takes us away from the worthless paper currency of the world's immoral ways.

"Foolish talking" is silly talk. The original Greek is rendered "buffoonery" in the lexicons. "Clowning" would be the more modern word. The trouble with flippant talk is that it degenerates into worse talk. After a serious meeting we often allow Satan to snatch away the seed by foolish talking. Often when a person is facing eternal issues, someone will inject a flippant word and the moment of decision disappears. Flippancy in conversation can become a habit with some people and it is almost impossible to have a serious conversation with them. They turn everything into a joke or a pun.

"Jesting" is ribaldry. This word is used in classical writings to describe cultured insolence. Although some people think it is clever to make cutting remarks, the Holy Spirit expresses His personal antipathy to such ego-building, hurtful words. They are not to be used by God's people.

ii.   The Holy Spirit States His Antidote to Lust (5:4b) "But rather giving of thanks."

Since we have to talk about something, let us elevate our conversation to a higher plane. Let us use our tongues to express gratitude to God for all that He has done for us and use our conversational skills to encourage others to think seriously about spiritual things.

(b) The Penalty Is Underlined (5:5) "No whoremonger, nor unclean person, nor covetous man, who is an idolater, hath any inheritance in the kingdom of Christ and of God."

Paul bluntly wrote that a person who is guilty of non-Christian practices cannot expect to have any share in the kingdom of God. These practices prove that he is not in the kingdom of God; they betray the presence of an unregenerated heart. Jesus told Nicodemus, "Except a man be born again, he cannot see the kingdom of God" (John 3:3).

A cheap form of Christianity is in circulation today. It is not really Christianity at all, just a popular counterfeit. People make professions of faith that entail no repentance, no genuine conversion, no regeneration by the Holy Spirit, and no dynamic new life in Christ. Such people can be deceived into thinking that they are Christians, but they see no need—and feel no impulse from an indwelling Holy Spirit—to give up sinful practices or resist them. It is "business as usual," the same old dirty business as before. Such people are as lost as they were before they went through the meaningless motions of professing to believe, being baptized, and joining local churches. Their penalty is devastating. Hell awaits them. Their lives reveal that their professions of faith were only lies.

Let us make sure we understand that lust is to be dethroned. God's demands are not to be underestimated.

(2) God's Demands Are Not to Be Undermined (5:6-7)

(a) We Are to Recognize Deception (5:6) "Let no man deceive you with vain words: for because of these things cometh the wrath of God upon the children of disobedience."

Paul challenged the notion that people can be saved and still habitually commit the gross and grievous sins he was denouncing. He contradicted the notion that the penalty for such sins in the lives of Christians is simply exclusion from the coming millennial kingdom. There may indeed be millennial loss for negligent Christians, but people who indulge in the vices Paul was describing are not Christians.

"Let no man deceive you," says the Holy Spirit. Those whose teaching undermines God's absolutes in the realm of personal morality are speaking vain words. The word translated "vain" in Ephesians 5:6 literally means "hollow, empty." Teaching that lacks substance and divine authority is deceptive.

We know that people who practice immorality are not Christians because the Holy Spirit calls them "children of disobedience." The expression is also used in Ephesians 2:2 to describe lost people.

In Romans 1:18-32 Paul wrote that the wrath of God is to be poured out on the ungodly. God's parental discipline will assuredly visit His own children who fall into moral sin, as David discovered. But His wrath is reserved for the unsaved who sin habitually. God will not pour out His wrath on those whom He has saved from wrath (1 Thessalonians 5:9).

(b) We Are to Repudiate Deception (5:7) "Be not ye therefore partakers with them."

No true child of God can compromise when tempted to take part in immoral behavior. God demands that we make a clean break with the ungodly lifestyle of our unregenerate days. Such a deliberate break with our past sins is proof that we not only profess Christianity, but we also possess Christ.

7. A Convicting Distinction (5:8-14)

a. Where Light Radiates (5:8-10)

(1) It Brings a Change of Character (5:8) "Ye were sometimes darkness, but now are ye light in the Lord: walk as children of light."

As children of God we cannot be partners in immorality because there can be no fellowship between light and darkness. Light drives out the darkness. Light refuses to coexist with darkness. Biblical morality is always a matter of black or white, light or darkness, truth or falsehood, good or bad, right or wrong. There are no shades of gray.

Paul recognized that once we walked in darkness. Some allowance perhaps can be made for the unsaved, but we are now children of light and there is no excuse for us to live immoral lives. Professing Christians who live immoral lives prove by their behavior that their professions of faith were spurious.

When I was conducting meetings in a small town in Iowa some time ago, the brother who took me back and forth to the airport shared his testimony with me. His story was that he attended an evangelistic service and although he did not understand what was happening to him, the Holy Spirit convicted him of sin. A few days later the pastor and the evangelist visited him, and his conviction grew. That night he and his girlfriend returned to the services being held at the church; he was drawn there by the new stirrings of God in his soul. When the invitation was given, he turned to his girlfriend and said, "I'm going forward. What about you? I've got to get this matter settled."

The girl, who had been raised a Catholic, had come into contact with the gospel some months before. She had asked him at the time, "What does it mean when they say you have to be saved?"

His answer had been definite: "Don't let it worry you. That's just their idea. There's nothing to it." But now he knew there was something to it after all. "I'm going forward," he said. "What about you?"

"I'm coming too," she answered.

That night they both accepted Christ. They now had a new problem because they were living together as man and wife although they were not married. No one said anything to them about their situation, but the Holy Spirit did. They knew that they could no longer live in sin. For the time being they decided not to break up their living arrangement, but to use separate bedrooms. For a while they struggled with the complications of their situation.

"I began to devour the Bible," he told me, "looking for some light on what we were doing. I was soon convinced that we could not go on living as we were." They sought pastoral counseling, and within a week they were properly married in the sight of God and man.

When they were still in the darkness of their unregenerate state, they found it easy to come to terms with living in sin. But once they were saved, the indwelling Holy Spirit made such accommodation impossible. As children of light they knew instinctively from the inward voice of the Holy Spirit that living in sin was wholly incompatible with living for God.

(2) It Brings a Change of Conduct (5:9) "The fruit of the Spirit is in all goodness and righteousness and truth."

The phrase translated "fruit of the Spirit" here is sometimes translated "fruit of light." Paul repeatedly emphasized light and the word "light" occurs five times in Ephesians 5:8-14. First John 1:5 tells us that "God is light, and in him is no darkness at all."

If we are "children of light" (Ephesians 5:8), we will display the characteristics of light. If we are children of God, we will display the character of God. That character will be evident to our fellow men through our conduct. God always acts according to His character. He is good, He is righteous, and He is true. Our conduct as Christians will reflect these moral qualities of goodness, righteousness, and truth. We will not habitually be bad, wrong, or false. The conduct of a Christian is the best evidence of his new birth and the best testimony to the unsaved of the regenerating power inherent in his new birth.

The English evangelist Tom Rees told a story about a man who was saved in one of his meetings. The new convert had been a terrible drunkard and a domestic tyrant. His craving for drink had reduced his family to abject poverty. Although he had a roaring, godless camaraderie with his workmates and drinking buddies, he abused his wife and neglected his home.

Then he met Christ. He immediately gave up alcohol. He became a loving husband, a good provider, and a tender father. His home showed evidence of the transformation the new birth had wrought. Food appeared on the table, his wife and children were warmly clothed, and new comforts were added to the home from time to time.

His drinking companions did not like the change. They missed the vile oaths, dirty stories, and ribald songs. They found themselves confronted by a stranger—a man who went to church, sang hymns, read his Bible, gave his testimony, worked hard, and refused to drink with them or waste time on the job. During his lunch hour this transformed man sat alone rather than listen to the filthy conversations of his former friends. He would read his Bible, and the sight of the Bible infuriated his workmates. They began to persecute him. They attacked the Bible and ridiculed him for being foolish enough to believe it.

One of them tackled him with a Scripture passage that is a favorite of those who drink. "Hey Bob," he said, "how about that place in the Bible where Jesus was in somebody's house and turned water into wine? That's a pretty tall story, wouldn't you say? You don't believe *that*, do you?"

The converted drunkard had not been saved very long. He was not a skilled apologist, but his answer was classic. He said, "Fred, I don't know anything about that. I can't say if Christ turned water into wine in that house, but I know that He has changed beer into furniture in my house."

Where light radiates, it brings a change of character and a change of conduct.

(3) It Brings a Change of Criterion (5:10) "Proving what is acceptable unto the Lord."

Is this behavior acceptable to the Lord? That question is the criterion for judging conduct. The criterion is not personal preference, and whether or not the world approves does not matter. The Christian judges conduct according to whether or not the Lord approves it.

It is not difficult to discover what is good, right, and true. All we have to do is stand for a few minutes alongside the Lord Jesus. We only have to read about how He lived, what He did, and what He permitted to be part of His life. From His first breath in the cradle to His last breath on the cross, He spent His life under the smile and approval of His Father in Heaven.

We complicate the problem of judging behavior by considering shades of gray. Nowadays psychology tempts us to make excuses, shift blame, explain away guilt, and wrap up unacceptable behavior in high-sounding phrases. But there are no shades of gray for the Christian whose supernatural life enables him to choose conduct pleasing to the Lord.

The Christian is equipped with this supernatural life by the supernatural experience called the new birth. He is empowered to live this supernatural life by the supernatural indwelling and filling of the Holy Spirit. He is supernaturally added to a fellowship of other supernaturally transformed individuals, who are joined together in a supernatural body known as the church. The church, which was supernaturally injected into history on the day of Pentecost, will be just as supernaturally ejected out of history at the rapture. The believer becomes a member of this mystical, supernatural body of Christ by yet another supernatural work of the Holy Spirit known as the baptism of the Spirit. There is nothing natural about being a Christian! His new life in Christ is supernatural from start to finish. It's just as supernatural as the birth, life, miracles, teaching, character, death, burial, resurrection, ascension, enthronement, and second coming of the Lord Jesus Christ.

The criterion for judging what is to be permitted in our lives is whether or not the conduct is acceptable to the Lord. That standard settles all the issues. It sweeps away all the befuddling, pettifogging compromises and excuses. When Christ is brought into the picture, the choices are clear.

b.   What Light Repudiates (5:11-12)

(1) What Is Done in Darkness Is Not Something with Which We Can Compromise (5:11) "Have no fellowship with the unfruitful works of darkness, but rather reprove them."

Instead of showing a spirit of genial tolerance toward the works of darkness, we are to take a firm stand against them. The Greek word translated "reprove" means "convict." The classic New Testament example of reproof is the account of John the Baptist when he reproved King Herod for stealing Herodias, his brother Philip's wife, and for "all the evils which Herod had done" (Luke 3:19).

This particular Herod was Antipas, who ruled for forty-three years over Galilee and Perea, regions where both John and Jesus ministered. Antipas possessed all the vices of his terrible father, Herod the Great, and none of his father's better qualities. Antipas is described as covetous, greedy, self-indulgent, utterly dissipated, and suspicious. He possessed the cunning of a fox; in the East such craftiness was usually considered good statesmanship.

Philip was the best of the sons of Herod the Great—the best of a bad lot. At one time it seemed as if Philip would be sole heir to his father's domains. The old tyrant changed his will, however, leaving Philip wealthy but bereft of position and power.

This turn of events did not sit well with Philip's unscrupulous and vicious wife. Herodias had married her half uncle Philip when his prospects were bright. So it little suited her pride and ambition that her husband would not sit on a throne.

Then Herod Antipas came to visit his half brother Philip in Jerusalem. At once Herodias saw her chance and began a sordid affair with Antipas. The pair agreed that when he came back from Rome, he would get rid of his wife and marry Herodias. Their adulterous marriage followed, and Antipas did not have to look far for trouble. Herodias became his curse and ruin.

John the Baptist boldly and publicly denounced Herod Antipas for what he had done. This rugged prophet refused to compromise with the unfruitful works of darkness. Safety dictated silence, but John spoke out. He reproved Herod for stealing his brother's wife and accused him of breaking God's law. For this firm stand, John earned the implacable hatred of Herodias, who schemed for ten months to bring about his death. In the end she succeeded in the terrible manner described in the Gospels.

Regardless of the consequences, we cannot compromise with what is done in darkness.

(2) What Is Done in Darkness Is Not Something about Which We Can Converse (5:12) "It is a shame even to speak of those things which are done of them in secret."

This is the day of talk shows on radio and television. Nothing is sacred. All aspects of sex are explored and aired with a blatant frankness that falls discordantly on sensitive ears. No matter how offensive the subject, the stations continue to spill it all out. People tell even the most intimate details and discuss them over the air waves.

Worse yet, shameful perversions are treated as a theme of entertainment, with the same brazen, pandering publicity. If they are not careful, Christians can be caught up in this so-called openness. The Holy Spirit, however, says that we should avoid talking about such evils. If we do talk about them, we are to speak against them. Certainly we are not to make such shameful topics the subject of casual conversation. The base and bestial practices of wicked people are not fit topics for the children of God to discuss glibly.

The word translated "shame" here is translated "filthy" in Titus 1:11. This word can also be translated as "deformed" or "ugly." It is used in Ephesians 5:12 to underline behavior that is indecent and offensive to modesty and purity. People who practice such behavior are shameful, and so are those who talk about them.

c.   Why Light Regenerates (5:13-14)

(1) The Work of the Spirit (5:13) "All things that are reproved are made manifest by the light: for whatsoever doth make manifest is light."

The word translated "reproved" here, *elenchō*, means "to convict, to bring in a verdict of guilty." The Lord Jesus used this same word to describe the convicting work of the Holy Spirit in the human heart: "When he is come, he will reprove the world of sin, and of righteousness, and of judgment" (John 16:8).

The Holy Spirit brings secret works of darkness into the light. Most of us have at one time or another turned over a stone or a log and recoiled at the ugly creatures that make darkness their home and scurry away in terror when exposed to the light. It is a terrible fact that we all harbor sins in the dark recesses of our souls. They live and flourish there, multiplying and reveling in being unseen. But once we let the light shine in, once we let the Holy Spirit do His convicting work in our hearts, the hidden works of darkness will be exposed.

The book of Job tells us how this saint of God faced calamity, criticism, and conviction. We see him first in Satan's hands, overwhelmed by disaster and yet retaining his integrity and faith in God. We see him next in men's hands, being accused and scornfully criticized. His response to them was angry self-defense; in his last speech (Job 29–31) he referred to himself by personal pronoun no less than 195 times. Finally we see Job in God's hands, abhorring himself. The man who had argued vehemently to justify himself when faced with criticism—and who in so doing exposed all the hidden and unsuspected bitterness, sarcasm, pride, anger, and self-righteousness of his soul—was repenting in dust and ashes.

Only the Holy Spirit can expose our sins to the light. When He does, we can see them for what they are—ugly beyond words.

(2) The Work of the Savior (5:14) "Wherefore he saith, Awake thou that sleepest, and arise from the dead, and Christ shall give thee light."

Light and life go together. Life craves light and cannot in its higher forms exist without light.

The phrase "shall give thee light" (another rendering would be "shall shine upon thee") comes from the Greek word *epiphauō*, which occurs only here. It was a word used to describe the rising of the sun. In Ephesians 5:14 *epiphauō* means that Christ will "shine upon" the believer. The whole verse is a paraphrase of Isaiah 60:1-2.

The Christian has new light and new life. The new light chases away the darkness in which he once groveled. The new life replaces the deadness that once possessed him and held him in corruption and uncleanness. Just as Lazarus, coming forth from the death and darkness of the tomb, was glad to be relieved of his vile graveclothes, so the new Christian throws off with horror the conduct and conversation that characterized him before he came to Christ.

Imagine a surgeon wanting to keep on the gloves that he wore while performing an autopsy on a decaying corpse! Obviously the doctor would want to get rid of the contaminated gloves and scrub his hands in antiseptics. Likewise, the idea of a Christian still wanting to walk and talk as he did before he came to know the Savior is incongruous.

8. A Conscious Decision (5:15-17)

a. Concerning Time (5:15-16)

(1) We Are to Be Wise concerning Our Ways (5:15) "Walk circumspectly, not as fools, but as wise."

The Greek word translated "circumspectly," *akribōs,* is one of ten synonyms in the Greek New Testament for the idea of being perfect. This verse could be translated, "Walk carefully or precisely, exactly, assiduously."

In some European countries, property is often protected by a high wall, the top of which is covered with embedded broken glass to discourage intruders who might try to climb over it. One can sometimes see a cat walking along the top of such a wall. The cat walks circumspectly, carefully, precisely, and assiduously. It picks up one paw and carefully places it where there is no glass. When that paw is in place, the cat reaches forward tentatively and gingerly with the next one.

We are to walk circumspectly during our relatively few years on earth. We are to be testimonies to the Lord Jesus Christ.

(2) We Are to Be Wise concerning Our Days (5:16) "Redeeming the time, because the days are evil."

The Greek word translated "evil" is *ponēros,* from which we derive our word "pornographic." We live in a pornographic society. Pornography is becoming increasingly difficult to avoid, especially during our spare time. Some of the books we are given to read plant impure thoughts in our minds. At strategic locations magazines wait to be picked up so their stories and photographs can pollute our minds. And television is the worst pornographer of all.

Once impure thoughts plant themselves like evil seeds in the receptive soil of our souls, they are difficult to eradicate. They grow like poisonous, prolific weeds. Their deadly fruit is temptation and sin.

The way to keep our thoughts pure, of course, is not to allow this world to plant vileness in our minds in the first place. Some contamination cannot be avoided, but much could be avoided if we simply decided to redeem the time. To "redeem the time" means to "buy up the time." We could avoid many traps if we were to buy up our spare time when the temptations of pornography are strongest. We must convert our spare time into another kind of time: time when we study the Bible; time when we turn our thoughts toward the throne of God in prayer; time when we pick up a good book, go for a walk, do some gardening, or visit someone in the hospital; time when we do what we have sinfully neglected because we were "too busy."

b.   Concerning Truth (5:17) "Wherefore be ye not unwise, but understanding what the will of the Lord is."

Failure to do what the Holy Spirit says is the height of folly. The Greek word translated "unwise" here is *aphrōn;* it can also be translated "senseless." Surely it is the height of stupidity to have in one's hand the very Word of the living God—inbreathed by the omniscient, all-wise Creator of the universe—and neglect to read it, study it, memorize it, and obey it! The angels must look at our foolishness in astonishment. We spend years going to college to study medicine, physics, chemistry, business management, engineering, and history. We invest time and money to sit at the feet of those we consider to be learned. We buy their books, attend their lectures, apply our minds to master what they have to say. But we neglect our Bibles. What folly! What an exposure of our warped sense of values!

There is no wiser, no more knowledgeable being in the universe than the Author of the Bible. There is no more patient teacher than the Holy Spirit. There is no greater book than the Bible. There is no greater privilege this side of Heaven than to have a copy of the inspired Word of God. Yet we often let it gather dust.

Refer the average professing Christian to the book of Habakkuk, for example, and he will probably have to turn to the index or flip pages in order to find it. Ask him to name the covenants—what they contain and where they are found—and he cannot do it. Ask him the difference between the sin offering and the trespass offering, and you are speaking to him in a foreign language. Ask which Mary sat at Jesus' feet and he might know, but ask which Herod murdered the apostle James and he will likely be unable to answer.

Ask when Paul wrote Romans or why he wrote 2 Corinthians. Ask whether Isaiah and Jeremiah were acquainted with one another or why David wrote Psalm 24. Ask the significance of the feast of weeks or who reigned when Amos preached. Ask in what ways Daniel filled in the details of the silent centuries between the books of Malachi and Matthew. Ask him to name the twelve apostles or the seven churches of Asia to whom John sent letters. Ask when Jesus was transfigured. Ask him to name the "I Am" sayings of Jesus. Ask him to quote Psalm 23 or give the reference for "Jesus wept." Ask him to name three of David's soldiers or the differences between the beliefs of the Pharisees and the Sadducees. You will be appalled at his abysmal ignorance.

The average church-attending, professing Christian knows little about the one Book in all the world that should mean the most to him and about which he should know the most. That same person may know who starred in *Gone with the Wind,* the score of yesterday's football game, or the Dow Jones industrial average.

No wonder the Holy Spirit says, "Don't be senseless, but understand what the will of the Lord is." The will of the Lord is found in the Word of God. To know the will of God, we must know the Word of God. We must make a conscious decision to study the Bible as much as, if not more than, any other subject.

9. A Captivating Discovery (5:18-21)

a. How to Be Filled with the Spirit (5:18) "And be not drunk with wine, wherein is excess; but be filled with the Spirit."

The Holy Spirit draws a deliberate parallel—one we would not dare to draw had He not drawn it for us first—between a man filled with wine and a man filled with the Holy Spirit. Since He has given us the illustration, we can examine it closely and see what it implies.

Most of us have seen an intoxicated person. First he deliberately chooses to drink intoxicating spirits. Then he drinks more and more until he is drunk. At this point his behavior changes. I have known men who were timid when they were sober, but who became belligerent and pugnacious when they were drunk; men who were hard as nails when sober, but sentimental and tearful when drunk; men who were congenial and friendly when sober, but morose and surly when drunk. I have seen drink turn a moral man into an immoral man and make a filthy-minded man sing hymns learned at his mother's knee or argue about religion. Drink turns a man into another kind of person. It distorts his conduct and degrades his conversation.

Drink temporarily transforms a person's personality, but there is no such thing as permanent intoxication. The man who is drunk on Saturday night is sober on Sunday morning. If he wants to remain intoxicated, he needs another filling. Of course over the long run, drunkenness deteriorates and destroys a person's character.

Being intoxicated illustrates—in reverse—being filled with the Spirit. To be filled with the Holy Spirit is a deliberate choice. In Ephesians 5:18 Paul said, "Be filled." Most of the Holy Spirit's ministries to believers are once-for-all, sovereign acts of God. The indwelling, the baptism, the sealing, the earnest, and the gift of the Spirit are in no way dependent on us. They are wrought in us by the Holy Spirit at the time of our conversion; they are irreversible and irrevocable. The filling of the Holy Spirit, however, is different. It is conditional because it depends on our cooperation with the indwelling Spirit of God.

When a Christian is filled with the Spirit, he is transformed into another kind of person. He exhibits the loveliness of Christ and the fruits of the Spirit. It is evident in his walk and in his talk that something has happened. People take knowledge of him that he has been with Jesus.

The Holy Spirit's filling is not permanent. Paul used the present continuous tense: "Be ye being filled with the Spirit." A person can be filled with the Holy Spirit one moment and grieve the Holy Spirit the next. When he grieves the Spirit, he needs to confess his sin, claim cleansing in the blood of Christ, and seek a fresh filling.

Stephen Olford used an equilateral triangle to illustrate the process of a continuous filling. The base of the triangle can be labeled "The Lordship of Christ." We determine by God's grace that Jesus is to be Lord—

> Lord of every thought and action
> Lord to send and Lord to stay
> Lord in speaking, writing, giving,
> Lord in all things to obey,
> Lord of all there is of me,
> Now and for Eternity.
>   (E. H. Swinstead)

One side of the triangle can be labeled "The Word of God." (The same phenomena associated in Ephesians 5:19 with being filled with the Spirit are associated in Colossians 3:16 with being filled with God's Word.) The remaining side of the triangle can be labeled "The Spirit of God."

With this simple figure in mind, note what happens. As we begin to read the Word of God, the Spirit of God brings some divine truth to our attention: a promise to claim, a sin to confess and avoid, a command to obey. Because we have established the basic premise that Jesus is Lord and made that the foundation of all our behavior, our immediate response is to obey. We yield on whatever issue in the Word of God the Spirit of God has brought to our attention. As we yield, He fills us and we receive the power to turn that teaching into practical reality. As this process continues, the Holy Spirit enlarges our horizons, increases our capacity, deepens our spirituality, and enables us to grow in grace and increase our knowledge of God.

Sin or self can short-circuit this process. A person can be filled with the Spirit one moment and be filled with self or fall into sin the next. Peter's experience just prior to ascending the mount of transfiguration is an example. At the time he was not indwelt and filled by the Holy Spirit, but his experience illustrates how swiftly a change from spirituality to carnality can take place (Matthew 16:13-23). The Lord asked His disciples who people thought He was. The disciples replied that people were ranking Him with John the Baptist, Elijah, Jeremiah, the prophets—the greatest men of the past and present. That answer was not good enough, so the Lord asked the disciples, "Whom say ye that I am?"

Instantly Peter replied, "Thou art the Christ, the Son of the living God."

Jesus responded, "Blessed art thou, Simon Barjona: for flesh and blood hath not revealed it unto thee, but my Father which is in heaven." Jesus then began to talk to the disciples about the cross.

Peter was aghast. "Be it far from thee, Lord," he blurted out.

Jesus turned on him. "Get thee behind me, Satan," He said. "Thou art an offence unto me: for thou savourest not the things that be of God, but those that be of men." Peter was a channel for the Holy Spirit one moment and was speaking in the flesh the next. Such is human nature.

That is why Paul wrote, "Be ye being filled." When we lose the *infilling* of the Spirit, we need a fresh filling. The way back is the way of the cross, the cross Peter so vehemently rejected. We must come back in repentance and with confession to the gracious Spirit of God, beg His pardon for having grieved Him, ask for cleansing, and receive a fresh filling. (We should note that in this age no believer loses the *indwelling* of the Spirit.)

When the truth about the filling of the Holy Spirit is first revealed to us, there is a crisis. We have to choose whether or not to yield to the Spirit. The crisis sometimes coincides with conversion, but more often comes later. Often we spend time in a spiritual wilderness first, and God has to bring us, like Israel of old, to the Jordan for a fresh, more mature comprehension of our spiritual death, burial, and resurrection with Christ.

In the Old Testament, the children of Israel symbolically entered into an experience of death, burial, and resurrection at the Red Sea. In the strength of that experience, they could have gone directly into Canaan. Their unbelief at Kadesh-barnea, however, led to forty years of wilderness life. They had to have a fresh experience of the truth of death, burial, and resurrection at the Jordan before they could enter into victorious living in Canaan.

At the time of his conversion a Christian could enter into the truth of Romans 12:1 and present his body as "a living sacrifice, holy, acceptable unto God, which is [his] reasonable service." However, months—even years—of worldliness, carnality, and defeat often intervene before he has a new experience with God that opens up the way to a Spirit-filled life. That crisis experience, be it early or late in his Christian pilgrimage, is the moment of surrender and yielding that is taught in Romans 6.

Once the lordship of Christ is established, there is a process of a continuous filling as described in the above illustration of the triangle. But what happens when, in the ongoing process of fullness and failure, the Christian discovers unsuspected areas in his life that have never been yielded? Does he have to start all over again? Must he present to the Holy Spirit, one by one, the members of his body and the various areas of his life? Perhaps the following illustration will help answer these questions.

An avid collector of old books is visiting a home. Browsing through his host's bookshelves he notices a battered old book. The cover is frayed, the casing is cracked, the pages are loose—some are even missing—but his collector's eyes gleam. He says to his host, "How long have you had this book, my friend?"

The host glances at it. "That old thing!" he says. "I don't know. It's of no use to me. I was going to throw it away. My wife picked it up off the floor behind the chair there the other day. It must have fallen off the shelf. I think it used to belong to my father. You can have it if you like. Pay for it? Dear me, no. Take it." The guest gratefully accepts the book, lamenting only to himself that some of its pages are missing.

Several days later the collector visits his friend again. "Oh by the way," the host says, "remember that old book I gave you? Well, I moved the chair yesterday, and guess what? I found more pages. If you give me the book back, we can start all over. I will give you the book again, including these missing pages."

Wouldn't that be an odd thing to say? It is not necessary to start all over again each time another missing page is found. The original owner only has to say, "Remember that book I gave you? I found a few more pages. I'm sorry they were missing. Here, they belong to you."

This illustration of the battered book can help us understand the filling of the Spirit of God. When the Holy Spirit shows someone an area of disobedience in his life, something not yet surrendered, there is no need for him to go back and start all over again. All he needs to do is say, "Gracious Holy Spirit, here is an area where I have been holding back what belongs to You. I meant for You to have all of me when I first surrendered to You. Please take this area of my life too."

So the message of Ephesians 5:18 is "Be ye being filled." It is the filling of the Spirit that enables us to do all that the Spirit of God demands of us in the previous verses and all that will be required in the verses that follow.

b. How to Be Thrilled in the Spirit (5:19-20)

(1) Joyful Acclamation in Song (5:19) "Speaking to yourselves [to one another] in psalms and hymns and spiritual songs, singing and making melody in your heart to the Lord."

When Christians are filled with the Spirit, there will be joyful ministry. Our hearts will overflow with music and song in public worship. The second fruit of the Spirit, after all, is joy. The Christian faith is a happy, joyful, singing faith, which is one reason why we have so many hymnbooks.

Several explanations, most of them rooted in the practices of the early church, can be given for the three categories of music that Paul listed here. What do these categories suggest to us today?

"Psalms" suggest what we might call *Scriptural* music—the singing of the Psalms themselves, for instance, or other portions of Scripture. Attempts have been made to fit tunes to the actual words of Scripture, but without the rhythm and rhyme we normally associate with western-style music, the songs are often stilted and awkward. The *Psalms of David in Metre,* which are used in the Church of Scotland, are perhaps better for singing. Many of these are remarkably true to the Biblical text. They lend themselves to our kind of singing because they can be sung to well-known tunes. Probably the best-known example is the lovely rendering of Psalm 23, which we so often sing to the haunting tune of "Crimond" that Jessie S. Irvine composed a little more than a century ago.

> The Lord's my shepherd, I'll not want;
> He makes me down to lie
> In pastures green; He leadeth me
> The quiet waters by.

"Hymns" suggest what we could call *spiritual* music—classical compositions that form the backbone of our better hymnbooks. These great hymns are clearly Biblical in content and have stood the test of time.

Each generation produces music; many hymns have a brief day, but some always survive. For instance, hymns of Martin Luther, Charles Wesley, and Isaac Watts will be sung as long as the church remains on earth; some hymns born out of the Moody-Sankey revivals have won their place in the ranks of the immortals. Our own day has its contributions too.

"Spiritual songs" suggest what we might classify as *soulful* music, including choruses, lighter compositions, and popular Christian ballads. A few survive for a generation or two, but most die as quickly as they are born. They serve a purpose, however, if they lift our hearts and souls to God in joyful adoration. They can put a new spring in our steps or give us words to express our aspirations to know God better. They can help us express our resolve to love God more, grieve Him less, and serve Him better.

Hymnbooks are an excellent means of teaching and reinforcing truth. Wise indeed are the parents who teach their children to learn and love good Christian music and the great, doctrinal hymns of the church. How often the words of a hymn leap to the mind of a preacher as the best way to communicate a truth.

Not only will joyful ministry emanate from our Spirit-filled lives in public worship; there will also be joyful music in private worship. Overflowing with music and song, we will sing and make melody in our hearts to the Lord.

(2) Joyful Acceptance of Wrong (5:20) "Giving thanks always for all things unto God and the Father in the name of our Lord Jesus Christ."

All things? Are we to give thanks when things go wrong? When injustice comes? When death or sickness enters? When a loved one goes astray? Can we still sing when times are hard?

Paul could. We only have to picture him and his dear friend Silas in the Philippian jail to see what it means to be filled with the Spirit. Their backs were torn, their limbs were cramped by the stocks, and their future was uncertain, yet they were singing! That prison cell was so shaken that its doors burst open; the other prisoners were so spellbound they could not budge. The jailer himself was so moved that his first words were, "What must I do to be saved?" (Acts 16:30)

One reason the church today is so weak is that it has forgotten how to sing. Often we make Christianity dull and dreary, a drudgery rather than a delight. No wonder the world reacts as did the man who was offered a tract by a sour-faced Christian. The man looked at the Christian's face and said, "No thanks. I've enough trouble of my own." Let us get back our joy in the Lord.

c.   How to Be Drilled by the Spirit (5:21) "Submitting yourselves one to another in the fear of God."

This verse summarizes the practical implications of being filled with the Spirit, and it introduces the next major section of the letter. The next section deals with human relationships and reviews our various roles and positions in life. The key to each relationship is submission, the kind of submission the Son yielded to the Father when He lived on earth as a man. That kind of submission, so often contrary to human nature, is an evidence of the filling of the Spirit. The Holy Spirit will drill us in submission by the pressure of human relationships. It may take time, but eventually we learn that the path of submission is best; we learn to fall in line with the will of the Holy Spirit.

All of life and society should swing around the pole of obedience to divinely ordained authority. Sin entered the world through one man's disobedience; our salvation was wrought through another's obedience unto death, "even the death of the cross" (Philippians 2:8).

Looking back over the section of the Epistle that concludes with Ephesians 5:21, we see that yielding ourselves to the Holy Spirit is the key to all our *moral* relationships. Looking ahead to the sections following Ephesians 5:21, we see that yielding ourselves to the Holy Spirit is also the key to all *marital* relationships and to all *material* relationships.

---

1. William Cowper, "There Is a Fountain."
2. J. E. Hall, "More Than Tongue Can Tell."

C. In His Marital Relationships (5:22–6:4)

1. As a Partner (5:22-33)

a. Some Priorities of the Marriage Relationship (5:22-29)

(1) The Wife: Loyalty Revealed in Surrender (5:22-24)

(a) The Exhortation (5:22) "Wives, submit yourselves unto your own husbands, as unto the Lord."

This verse, taken out of context, has caused many husbands to repress their wives and many wives to be resentful and rebellious. Standing alone, this verse seems arbitrary and unfair. But it does not stand alone. No verse of Scripture stands alone. This verse is preceded by the command that we submit ourselves one to another in the fear of God. What a pity that preachers so often ignore this context when beginning a series of messages on husband-wife relationships. The context includes not only the Holy Spirit's instruction for mutual submission, but also His teaching about the Holy Spirit's infilling—the blessed oil that makes the machinery of marriage run smoothly.

Two words dominate the Biblical teaching in Ephesians 5:22-29: *submission* and *love*.

The Greek word translated "husband" in Ephesians 5:22 is *anēr*. *Anēr* is one of the words translated "man" in the New Testament. Paul was telling the wife to submit herself to her own man. The thought that comes to mind at once is that the husband is to be just that—a man. *Anēr*, which never refers to the female sex, is used here like an honorable title.

The wife is required by the Holy Spirit to submit to her man—her husband—"as unto the Lord." That perspective lifts this command to a higher, holier, and more heavenly plane. What woman in all the world who has met and fallen in love with Jesus would not willingly do anything for Him? Never in the Gospels do we find a woman treating Him badly, speaking against Him, or doing anything to harm Him. The women of the New Testament loved and honored Jesus. He was so manly, so honorable, so attractive, so thoughtful, and so kind. It is the men in the Gospels who opposed Him, not the women.

(b) The Example (5:23) "The husband is the head of the wife, even as Christ is the head of the church: and he is the saviour of the body."

God has ordained a hierarchal structure throughout the universe. First Corinthians 11:3 reveals that God has established the principle of hierarchal structure in all of life's relationships: "The head of every man is Christ; and the head of the woman is the man; and the head of Christ is God." A hierarchy is discernible also in the unseen spirit world. We read about principalities and powers, the rulers of this world's darkness, and wicked spirits in high places. We read about Satan as the prince of the power of the air who presides over all these fallen demonic forces. There are also hints of a hierarchy in the ranks of the unfallen angels—thrones and dominions, angels and archangels, cherubim and seraphim.

Indeed, order is the unifying factor in all of God's creation. Sin introduced disorder and chaos into the universe. Sin began on earth when Satan challenged our first parents to defy God's authority.

God's order in human relationships goes back to the garden of Eden. God created the man first, investing in Adam the position of headship. God created the woman second, giving Eve a subordinate (but not subservient) position in relation to the man. Adam was made to be ruled from his head; Eve was made to be ruled from her heart. But Satan persuaded Adam and Eve to change roles. Eve took the lead and the place of headship. Satan cleverly aimed the temptation at Eve's *mind* and engaged her in an intellectual discussion on whether or not she should do something that God had expressly forbidden. The result was that she was deceived. When Adam approached, Satan withdrew and allowed Eve to tempt him, thus aiming the temptation at Adam's *emotions*. The Bible says that Adam was not deceived; he disobeyed.

In the new creation, God reestablishes the original order. Man is to be the head, under Christ; the woman is to acknowledge the headship of the man. This sounds strange and chauvinistic to today's "emancipated" woman, but it is God's order for society nevertheless. We can ignore God's order only at great risk to the home, the community, the nation at large, and the individuals involved. Nothing is more unsightly than to see a woman developing dominant masculine traits or a man exhibiting marked feminine traits.

In the Christian home God's order is to be firmly established. The governing principle is not merely God's order in creation. Everything is lifted to a higher plane. Christ, rather than creation, is set before us as the model. Ephesians 5:23 says, "The husband is the head of the wife, even as Christ is the head of the church: and he is the saviour of the body." ("Body" refers to the church, His mystical body.) The analogy is deliberate. The church owes its obedience to its head—to Christ. The wife owes her obedience to her husband, who is to mirror the Lord Jesus to her through his behavior. Just as Christ is the Savior—the deliverer and defender of the church—so the husband is to be the protector of his wife, who is one flesh with him.

(c) The Expectation (5:24) "As the church is subject unto Christ, so let the wives be to their own husbands in every thing."

We are to consider the marital relationship on this lofty plane. The relationship between Christ and His church is unique. Nearly all of the brides mentioned in the Bible illustrate this relationship. We can see it clearly in the stories of Jacob and Rachel, Boaz and Ruth, and David and Abigail. We can see it too in the progressive stories of Adam and Eve, Isaac and Rebekah, and Joseph and Asenath. Taken together, these last three marriages are pictures of the church's past, the church's present, and the church's prospects.

The story of Adam and Eve illustrates the past and shows how the church was formed. Adam was put to sleep in the will of God. Then God opened his side and took from him what was needed to form his bride. This scene is reminiscent of Calvary, where the Lord Jesus entered into the sleep of death in the will of God. Jesus' side was opened and out gushed water and blood, the elements that made possible the creation of the church—His bride.

The story of Isaac and Rebekah illustrates the present. Their love story typifies the work of the Father and the Spirit in finding the bride for the Son. In Genesis 22 Isaac went to mount Moriah as a willing sacrifice, obedient unto death. But in Genesis 24 he was a passive observer, waiting with his father for the coming of the bride. All the action was in the hands of the unnamed servant whom Abraham sent to seek, invite, persuade, and bring the responsive bride to his son. In this present age the Son's work is finished and He sits on His Father's throne. The Holy Spirit is the active One. He is here to seek out a bride—the church—for the Father's beloved Son, who is waiting at His right hand in glory.

The story of Joseph and Asenath illustrates the prospects of the church (Genesis 41:45). Asenath was taken from obscurity and elevated to share the lofty position occupied by Joseph at the right hand of pharaoh. In the same way, our past is blotted out and our destiny is to sit with Christ on His throne and share His glory for all eternity.

The point here is that since the brides of the Bible are obviously intended to typify the unique relationship between Christ and His church, the marriage of every believer should do the same. Every married Christian couple should be an illustration to the world of the relationship that exists between Christ and His church.

In Ephesians Paul discussed the whole concept of marriage in the Lord on this high level. The marriage relationship is unique and as sacred as the relationship between Christ and His church. This perspective should end all carnal quibbling over who is responsible to do what. All marriages are to function like Christ and His church. All marital decisions are to be made on the spiritual plane.

(2) The Husband: Love Revealed in Sacrifice (5:25-29)

(a) The Exhortation (5:25a) "Husbands, love your wives."

The Holy Spirit's word translated "love" here is *agapaō,* the highest kind of love—spontaneous love, love irrespective of rights. The word carries the idea of "making much of a person." When a wife knows that her husband loves her with this highest kind of love—love irrespective of rights, love that makes so much of her— she feels no resentment over her responsibility to render loyal submission to him.

"Husbands, love your wives" is a command. We tend to think of love primarily in terms of emotions. That is natural because we are most conscious of love in the realm of emotions. God, however, relates love to the will rather than to emotions. He commands us to love. He commands us to love Him: "Thou shalt love the Lord thy God with all thy heart, and with all thy soul, and with all thy mind, and with all thy strength" (Mark 12:30). He commands us to love our neighbors as we love ourselves. He commands us to love one another. That is because God is love. Love is the greatest revelation of God. "God commendeth his love toward us, in that, while we were yet sinners, Christ died for us" (Romans 5:8).

Obviously if love can be commanded, it does not belong solely to the realm of emotions. The emotions we associate with falling in love sometimes fluctuate. Sometimes they fade away altogether. Emotions need to be cultivated. The word *agapē* refers to love as a principle. The New Testament reserves another word, *phileō,* for love as a feeling. *Phileō* is distinct from love as a fact and is associated instead with the ideas of kissing and fondness. *Agapē,* not *phileō,* is always used to describe man's love for God. God does not tell us to be fond of Him; He commands us to love *(agapaō)* Him.

Phileō, however, is sometimes used to describe God's love for us. God is fond of us! John used *phileō* in describing the Lord's love for Lazarus (John 11:3,36). The Lord not only loved Lazarus; He was very fond of him. In John 11:5, however, where Lazarus's sisters are included in the Lord's love, *agapaō* is used to place the Lord's relationship with Martha and Mary on a more spiritual plane. *Agapē,* the cause and ground for *phileō,* places love on the highest plane—beyond the reach of momentary emotions—where the spirit rules both soul and body.

(b) The Example (5:25b-27)

i.   Love That Travails (5:25b) "Christ also loved the church, and gave himself for it."

Such was the love of the Lord Jesus that He "gave himself" (literally, "gave up Himself") for His beloved. He died that she might live. "Greater love hath no man than this, that a man lay down his life for his friends" (John 15:13).

Any woman would find it easier to defer to a husband she knew would die for her than to a husband she felt might sacrifice her to his fears, lusts, or ambition. The husband is to make sure that his love for his wife is of such a quality that, come what may, she will reign so supremely in his heart that no sacrifice would seem too great for him to make for her. He must keep before him the example of Jesus and His great love for His church.

One might hesitate, perhaps, before using Samson as an example. Yet, despite his glaring imperfections, Samson was a striking type of Christ in his determination to take a Gentile bride. His parents could not understand why he would want a Gentile bride, a pagan woman. But Samson's heart was already engaged. (Besides, God's plans were involved.)

The day came when Samson went to meet the woman his heart so greatly desired. On his way he met a roaring lion. But Samson was strong and filled with the Spirit. (There are more references to the Holy Spirit in connection with Samson in the book of Judges than all the other judges combined.) Samson was not worried about a mere lion, however fierce. He tore that lion apart with his bare hands and went on to claim his bride. That she proved unworthy of him only adds to the sad parallel. She allowed fear and family pressure to turn her away from him. Samson's subsequent vengeance

on those who dared to interfere with his beloved wife also adds to
the parallel.

One can imagine Samson alone with his bride. For the first time
she sees the marks on his body from his battle with the lion. "Oh
Samson," she might have said, "those are terrible marks! Why are
you so marred?"

And Samson may have replied, "These, my beloved, are the
tokens of my love. I was willing to die for you."

On a greater and grander scale, Christ demonstrated love for His
church. Husbands are to have love like Christ's for their wives.

ii.   Love That Transforms (5:26-27) "That he might sanctify and
       cleanse it with the washing of water by the word, That he might
       present it to himself a glorious church, not having spot, or
       wrinkle, or any such thing; but that it should be holy and
       without blemish."

Paul's eloquence began to soar above time and sense. In Ephesians
5:26-27 husbands, wives, and the ordinary and orderly arrangements of a human home are left behind. All we see here are Christ
and His church. We see love that finds us in our sins, love that
regenerates, love that transforms, love that enables, and love that
ennobles. We see love that is not content with leaving us as it found
us; it is actively at work making us beautiful beyond description.

All too often we only see the spots, blemishes, faults, and failings
of God's people. We major on the negatives. We see that the church
is weak and divided. We do not yet see the church as Christ sees it,
as He has always seen it. He sees it as perfect and complete, glorious,
bright as the morning, fairer than day, lovely as the flowers of
paradise, sweeter than the dawn. He sees the church as it will be
when His transforming work is done. He sees it without spot or
wrinkle. Without spot—beyond the reach of temptation. Without
wrinkle—beyond the reach of time. Christ sees the church as holy
and without blemish. He sees it as the mirror image of Himself.

This is not hyperbole. This is reality. Because Christ gave Himself
for the church, He is now able to "sanctify and cleanse it with the
washing of water by the word." This washing of course has nothing
to do with baptismal regeneration. We are saved by the *blood* of
Christ, not by the *water* of baptism.

The Greek word translated here as "washing," *loutron,* is only
used one other place in the New Testament: Titus 3:5, which refers
to "the washing of regeneration." *Loutron* primarily means "a vessel
for washing," and seems to refer to the Old Testament laver.

The priest, when he approached God, came first to the brazen altar where an animal was sacrificed and its blood shed. This ritual symbolized the *radical* cleansing for sin, which is the basis of our salvation. Sin is so deep a stain that it can only be washed away in the blood of the Lord Jesus.

Having been to the altar, the priest proceeded toward the tabernacle where God sat enthroned in holiness behind the veil. Coming to the laver, which was made of mirrors, he saw that although he was only a few steps away from the holy place, he was already defiled by contact with this world. He did not need a new sacrifice at this point; he needed to be washed in water to remove the revealed defilement. He needed *recurrent* cleansing.

The blood of Christ secures our regeneration; the water of the Word acts like the laver. Like the mirrors of the Old Testament laver, the Word of God *reveals* to us the defilements we have picked up just by walking through this evil world. The Word of God—also a cleansing agent—*removes* the defilement. Psalm 119:9 says, "Wherewithal shall a young man cleanse his way? by taking heed thereto according to thy word."

The Lord has traveled on earth. He knows what this world is like. We are not yet in His world, in the glory land. He is patient with us. He works with us so that one day we will be seen in all of His glory and perfection. His love travails and transforms; it is the divine model for the husband's role in marriage.

(c) The Expectation (5:28-29)

i.   The Self Motive (5:28-29a) "So ought men to love their wives as their own bodies. He that loveth his wife loveth himself. For no man ever yet hated his own flesh; but nourisheth and cherisheth it."

Paul's explanation moved from the bride to the body and from the body to the bride. His train of thought went from a man and his wife to Christ and His church, from the church as a bride to the church as a body. The roots of his illustrations are as deep as the origin of the human race.

It all began in the garden of Eden. A man was put to sleep in the will of God. His body was opened and a bone was removed from his side. God used that bone to build a body—a bride. The body and the bride are two distinct concepts, yet strangely and mysteriously bound together. When God presented the bride to Adam, He said, "They shall be one flesh" (Genesis 2:24).

On the foundation of Genesis 2:24, Paul built his doctrine of marriage. In marriage two people become one. Marriage is much more than physical union. It is psychological and spiritual union, which is why all violations of the sacred marital relationship are totally damaging to personality and why all casual, unblessed liaisons earn God's judgment and bring inevitable retribution.

Paul was concerned in Ephesians 5:28-29, however, with the husband's duty to love his wife. He particularly emphasized the husband's duty to love his wife as much as he loves his own body.

The "self motive" is here. Most well-adjusted people love themselves. Love of self, of course, can be a very bad thing, especially when it expresses itself in selfishness. There is, however, a normal and wholesome love of one's self that, though it must be kept in its proper place, is not sinful. The believer's motivation goes far beyond mere selfishness; it is based on the essence of what God planned marriage to be. In marriage two persons become one person. After God married Adam and Eve, He "called *their* name Adam" (Genesis 5:2, italics added). They were two people with one name. This precedent is followed today when a bride gives up her family name and takes her husband's family name. In a sense, she loses her identity in his.

A man is to love his wife in the tender, caring way he loves his own body. A man instinctively provides for the comfort of his body. Using plain common sense, he protects his body from harm, heeds its signals, and desires its well-being. When a man becomes over-tired, famished, or gnawed by a toothache, he will do whatever he can to solve the problem.

Life is too uncomfortable when we ignore bodily demands, so we usually waste little time responding to them. For better or for worse, we are wedded to our bodies. They can make life blissful or tormenting. We cannot ignore our bodies, but self-indulgence can be as harmful as neglect. In between stoic harshness and epicurean self-indulgence is the happy medium where most of us live. The sane and sensible thing to do is to nourish our bodies and cherish them.

Just as a man must take care of his body, a husband must see to his wife's comfort. He must protect her from harm, desire her well-being, and pay close attention to the signals that she sends. She can, after all, make his life blissful or tormenting. He needs to help her develop her potential, nourish her, and cherish her. These are the sensible things to do if he wants to live in peace and comfort. Paul, however, did not end his injunction to husbands on the level of selfish motivation.

ii. The Supreme Motive (5:29b) "Even as the Lord the church."

The Lord views the church as His bride; it is His body. He loves it, nourishes it, and cherishes it. It is precious to Him. Nothing on earth or in Heaven compares with it. He died to redeem it. He watches over it. His Holy Spirit is here to guide it and gladden it. At the Father's right hand, Christ is importunate on the church's behalf. He anticipates with delight the coming day when the church will be complete, when it will be like Him forever, when it will reign with Him over God's vast empires in space. As far as the Lord is concerned, nothing is too good for His beloved. The church is the love of His life, the center of His thoughts, and the object of His purposes.

A man should view his wife in the same way. He should not use his wife's faults and weaknesses as reasons for neglecting her or for failing to give her the love and attention he vowed to her. Does not the Lord see many imperfections in His church? Of course He does. But with love and patience, kindness and forbearance, He ministers to His church. He knows that the day will come when the church will be perfect, glorious, and all that He meant it to be.

Love covers a multitude of sins (1 Peter 4:8). The kind of love described in 1 Corinthians 13 is divine. Such love is a fruit of the Spirit and is possible only through a filling of the Holy Spirit. Every husband should take a weekly tour of that chapter and apply each of its clauses to himself and his attitude toward his wife.

b. Some Principles of the Marriage Relationship (5:30-33)

(1) The Concept (5:30-32)

(a) A Man and Christ's Body (5:30) "We are members of his body, of his flesh, and of his bones."

Having reviewed the priorities of the marriage relationship, Paul turned to the principles of the marriage relationship.

In Christian marriage, the model never to be forgotten is the Lord Jesus. A believer is a member of His body. No more intimate relationship could be imagined than the organic relationship that exists between one member of a physical body and another member. Each member of a body shares the same life, is controlled by the same spirit, is washed by the same blood, and is ruled by the same brain. The idea of a leg, an arm, or an eye existing independently is ludicrous.

Because we are members of Christ's body, the high and holy standard of Christian marriage is reachable; the standard is not just a lofty ideal. The link between each believer and Christ may be mystical, but it is certainly not mythical. Ephesians 5:30 says, "We are members of his body." Christ's life is our life. His love is our love. His Spirit energizes our spirits. His blood cleanses all.

When Paul wrote that husbands are to love their wives "as the Lord the church," he was not being idealistic. He is being intensely practical. Because we are members of His body, our lack of love is replaced by His boundless love. Our little tributaries of love soon dry up, but the ocean tides of His immeasurable love come in and overflow the banks of the narrow channels of our love.

The husband is not to resolve: "I will love my wife as Christ loved the church. I will do my best to imitate Christ." The result would only be an imitation. The Holy Spirit is telling every Christian husband to draw on the fact that he is a member of Christ's own body—"of his flesh, and of his bones," as the King James version adds. A mystical but real, organic relationship exists between the believer and Christ, making it possible for a man to love his wife as Christ loved the church.

If this relationship between Christ and us did not exist, then Paul's whole idea of marriage was just a noble dream. But this relationship is not merely a glorious concept. It is a down-to-earth, hard-fact reality. It is the principle on which all else rests. Our organic oneness with Christ certainly exists. We have God's Word for that. Any breakdowns are on our side, not His.

The key to making the principles of the marriage relationship work is faith. Our problem is that we only half believe them. The principles, however, remain the same. We *are* members of His body. And, of course, this principle applies to the wife in her role, in the same way it applies to the husband in his role.

(b) A Man and Christ's Bride (5:31-32) "For this cause shall a man leave his father and mother, and shall be joined unto his wife, and they two shall be one flesh. This is a great mystery: but I speak concerning Christ and the church."

On the one side, a Christian husband is mystically linked with the body of Christ. On the other side, he is maritally linked with his wife. Now Christ's life and love flow through him to her, completing the circuit. Of course the Christian wife is also directly linked with Christ and His love flows through her too. Faith throws the switch that allows the power to flow and the results to show.

Paul's teaching on marriage, like the Lord's teaching in Mark 10:2-12, is based on Genesis 2:23-24. Marriage was God's idea. Its purpose was to make paradise complete—to bring Heaven down to earth. In instituting marriage, God had eternity's values in view and the ultimate reality of Christ and His church in mind. Sin, however, has dimmed the bright ideal. Even when we know the truth that is found in Christ, our chronic unbelief often hinders us from seeing the truth work in our lives. The fact remains, though, that God intends the Christian home to be an outpost of Heaven in a sin-cursed world. The home is to be a place where family, friends, visitors, and neighbors can come, see, and sense the wonders of God's mysterious purposes at work.

It is no accident that the first and second times that love is mentioned in the Bible occur when and where they do.[1] The first mention of love is *the love of the father for the son* in Genesis 22. Abraham loved Isaac, yet God demanded that he take his only begotten son to mount Moriah and enact Calvary there. "Take now thy son, thine only son Isaac, whom thou lovest, and get thee into the land of Moriah; and offer him there for a burnt offering upon one of the mountains which I will tell thee of" (22:2). The spiritual significance of this illumines all of a past eternity.

The second mention of love is *the love of the son for his bride* in Genesis 24. "Isaac brought her into his mother Sarah's tent, and took Rebekah, and she became his wife; and he loved her" (24:67). The spiritual significance of the marriage of Isaac and Rebekah illumines all of the endless ages yet unborn.[2]

There are hidden depths in Christian marriage that are linked with God's eternal purposes. Paul gave us glimpses, and a comprehensive study of Old Testament brides will reveal more. Some of those brides teach us truth regarding Christ and His church; others (such as Abraham and Sarah, Abraham and Katurah, and Hosea and Gomer) teach us truth regarding Jehovah and Israel.

(2) The Conclusion (5:33) "Nevertheless let every one of you in particular so love his wife even as himself; and the wife see that she reverence her husband."

Paul brought his discussion of the Christian as a partner to a close by restating the principles of the marriage relationship in practical terms. Considering marriage as analogous to the mystical relationship between Christ and the church is interesting and inspiring. But we must bring the discussion "down to earth." After all, the husband-wife relationship is a practical matter, subject to immense stresses and strains.

If we forget all the ideals and mysticism, we must remember this: Husbands are to love their wives just as much and in the same way as they love themselves. No summary could be shorter, simpler, or plainer. Nearly all domestic friction and unhappiness would cease if husbands observed this basic principle. A wife would be unlikely to resist a husband who loved her as he loved himself. (If the husband goes on to love her as Christ loves the church, so much the better.)

Paul had a parting word for the wife too: Reverence your husband. The wife is to put her husband on a pedestal, make much of him, admire him, speak well of him, and defer to him.

In this age of feminism it is common for women to reject God's counsel on this issue. Someone may say, "Ah, but you don't know my husband." Well, God knows him, and God says that he is to be reverenced as a husband.

Someone else may object, "My husband is weak, foolish, and undeserving of my respect. How can I reverence him?" Paul would answer, "By being filled with the Spirit; by counting on your mystical union with Christ in the oneness of the body; and by realizing that in reverencing your husband you are fulfilling God's will and enabling the Holy Spirit to make you more like Jesus and show the world the loveliness of Christ through you."

Alexander Whyte said in his book on Bible characters that when Paul wrote his parting word to the wife, he had one eye on Rebekah. If we read the full Genesis account of Isaac and Rebekah, we discover practical lessons as well as interesting typology. On the practical level, Isaac and Rebekah's marriage deteriorated. A number of factors contributed to the deterioration.

In the first place, Isaac was placid, quiet, and submissive. Not a fighter, he was far more disposed to give in than to stand up for himself. Rebekah, by contrast, was resolute, clear-thinking, and practical. She was a doer who had married a dreamer. Then too, Isaac let Rebekah down when he played the coward for his own safety (Genesis 26:6-9). That would be hard to forgive and, humanly speaking, impossible to forget. Worst of all, as time went on Isaac cultivated another first love: good food. He loved Esau because he brought him venison. Once he had loved Rebekah; now he loved himself.

All of these factors turned Rebekah into a disgruntled wife. She ceased to reverence her husband. The original romance faded and disappeared. The harsh reality of daily life led her to go her own way, assert her dominant personality, and cultivate favoritism. A domestic tragedy of terrible proportions resulted. Egged on by his mother,

Jacob lied, cheated, and deceived Isaac. Esau threatened to kill Jacob. Jacob had to leave home hurriedly, and Rebekah never saw her favorite son again. Isaac belatedly took the spiritual lead when it was almost too late.

For a wife to reverence her husband may be difficult; not to do so will be disastrous. The command does not mean that the wife has to submit to bullying or endorse her husband's foolish decisions. It does mean that instead of tearing him down, she must build him up. It does mean that she must respect the God-ordained, husband-wife role in marriage, conceding that God knows best and could overrule.

A capable, strong-willed woman who is married to an incompetent, passive man certainly has a problem, but it is not too difficult a problem for God to solve. If she will seek the Holy Spirit's filling, if in the power of His enablement she will reverence her husband, build him up, and help him where he is weak and she is strong, her husband will develop the masculine qualities that command her reverence. If she refuses to reverence her husband, she will dominate him and cause him to become resentful. Or she could cause him to develop feminine characteristics that are most unlovely in a man, while she develops masculine characteristics that are most unlovely in a woman.

2.   As a Parent (6:1-4)

a.   The Child's Simple Task (6:1-3)

(1) The Principle (6:1) "Children obey your parents in the Lord: for this is right."

This verse summarizes the whole duty of a child, manward and godward. His sole duty is to learn to obey authority, and his parents are to be his only voice of authority. Later on, parental authority will compete with the school's authority, the government's authority, and possibly an employer's authority.

We are born rebels. Each of us raises the voice of selfishness and rebellion at an early age. We need to learn to obey. Children who learn to defy parental authority will go on to defy other authority and will often grow up to defy divine authority.

There exists of course the sad possibility that parental authority might be arbitrary. Yet God's rule still applies. A child owes obedience to his parents. The larger issues must be left with God, the ultimate source of all authority. He can sovereignly overrule in the end the misuse of parental authority.[3]

Children raised in Christian homes have an awesome privilege. Many children are born into homes where God is hated and atheism holds sway. Others are raised to bow to idols and false gods. Others grow up in cruel environments. Of all the millions of children born every year, relatively few are born into Christian homes. We have no idea how the selection is made, but it has incredible advantages.

Children raised in homes where God is known, where Christ is loved, where the Bible is read and believed, and where the Holy Spirit is honored have great opportunities. From their earliest days, these privileged infants are taught to say the saving name of Jesus, are taught to say childish prayers, are taken to Sunday school, are told Bible stories, are encouraged to memorize the living Word of God, and—above all—are taught the way of salvation through Jesus Christ. While others born the same day are being raised, in China for example, to chant the Communist International, to scoff at the idea of God, to revere Marx and Lenin, and to believe in dialectical materialism, children in Christian homes are being taught John 3:16. While others are being taught to worship Krishna, bow before idols, believe in reincarnation as the secret of life and nothingness as its ultimate and most blissful goal, children in Christian homes are being taught to sing,

> Jesus loves me! this I know,
> For the Bible tells me so.
>   (Anna B. Warner)

Children raised in Christian homes also have an awesome responsibility. A child who rebels against parental authority in a Christian home earns God's displeasure. For him to obey is right. Anything else is terribly and criminally wrong. The whole duty of a child in a Christian home is to obey Mom and Dad. That is God's supreme command to that child.

One could think of instances where a godless parent might demand that a child do things that are morally wrong and contrary to the laws of God and man. Paul was not requiring that children obey orders contrary to the laws of God. He had the Christian home primarily in mind.

We get just one glimpse of Jesus between His birth and His baptism. We see Him when He was twelve years old, already in complete control of the knowledge that He was the Son of God. Yet we read that He went down to Nazareth with Joseph and Mary "and was subject unto them" (Luke 2:51). What a lesson in obedience! To think of Him—the Lord of life and glory, the Creator of the universe, the One who was the express image of God, the One whom angels worshiped—being in willing subjection to a village carpenter and his wife!

(2) The Precept (6:2) "Honour thy father and mother; which is the first commandment with promise."

The Decalogue—the ten commandments found in Exodus 20—is the essence of the law. It is the heart and core of divine legislation; the other six hundred commandments are expansions and expositions of it. The Decalogue divides man's duty into two categories: his duty to God and his duty to man. The commandment concerning children, quoted by Paul in Ephesians 6:2, is the fifth commandment. Because it deals with human relationships, it is often included with the last five commandments, thus dividing the Decalogue into four statements that summarize man's duty to God and six that summarize man's duty to man.

This division, however, is artificial. When the Lord Jesus summarizes the Decalogue in two statements, He gives us the true division. He says, "Thou shalt love the Lord thy God with all thy heart, and with all thy soul, and with all thy mind, and with all thy strength. ...Thou shalt love thy neighbour as thyself" (Mark 12:30-31). When we review the Decalogue, we see that this division was inherent in the law. The first five commandments are tied together by the phrase "the Lord thy God," the remaining five by the phrase "thou shalt not." This division links the command to honor thy father and thy mother with the commandments that address man's duty to God.

The distinction is important, for the fifth commandment puts the parents in the place of God over their young children. And for the rest of their lives, the children are to render honor to their mothers and fathers as the human authors of their being—as those who loved them, protected them, taught them, and sacrificed for them.

Failure to honor one's parents is an insult to the God who chose them. Rebellion against parents is high-handed rebellion against God. All sin is rebellion against God, but by grouping the fifth commandment with those that address our duties to God, the Holy Spirit makes it clear that defiance of parental authority is also sin against God Himself. (Under the Mosaic law a son who persisted in rebellion against parental authority was guaranteed a short life. He was to be publicly accused and stoned to death.)

God, however, does not want children to honor their parents

because of a threat, so he appended a promise to the fifth commandment. Paul reminded his readers of that promise when he added this to Ephesians 6:2: "Which is the first commandment with promise." That promise is the subject of the next verse.

(3) The Promise (6:3) "That it may be well with thee, and thou mayest live long on the earth."

A child who grows up to love, honor, and obey his mother and father lays the foundation for a happier, more stable, and more successful life than does a child who is rude, disrespectful, self-willed, and rebellious. A stormy path lies ahead for a disobedient child. He will drift into bad company, resent all rule and authority, and in many cases end up on the wrong side of the law. Contemporary society has produced a bumper crop of young people who are determined to "do their own thing." Many of them are enmeshed in the drug and sex scene, and are filled with restlessness and rage.

b.   The Father's Sublime Trust (6:4)

(1) A Word about Methods (6:4a) "Fathers, provoke not your children to wrath."

The Bible is a balanced book. God does not command children to obey their parents without giving an injunction to parents. Fathers (or parents, as the Greek word *pateres* can be translated) are not to provoke their children to wrath by being unreasonable in their demands, outrageous in their punishments, or inconsistent in their examples, rules, and controls.

My father often referred to children as "the little people." It was a quaint expression, yet a profoundly wise one. Children are people. They are not mindless objects to be bossed and bullied; they are people who have thoughts, feelings, hopes, fears, likes, and dislikes. As children grow older, winds of change blow over their developing bodies, minds, and personalities; life becomes more complex and decisions more significant. But children are people and must be respected as people. Because they are little people, they need constant supervision, counsel, and limits. They are growing up in a confusing world, and they encounter people whose values are quite different from those of their parents.

Parents need to study their children. The growing-up process takes every child through various phases of development. A parent ought to know about these phases and recognize when a child enters each stage.

No two children are alike. Some are strong-willed; others are passive. Some are clever; others are slow. Some are adventurous; others are timid. Some are bold; others are shy. Wise parents will study their children and make allowances. Many books on parenting are available today, but not all of them are equally good because much modern psychology leaves God out entirely. The best text-book of all remains the Bible, especially the book of Proverbs. Wise parents know the Bible, study its case histories of parents, and ponder its stories of boys and girls.

Every child needs to have a solid moral foundation on which all other Biblical instruction can be built. Parents should lay this foundation early. They should encourage their children to memorize the ten commandments, segments of the sermon on the mount, and many other Scripture passages. Psalm 119:11 says, "Thy word have I hid in mine heart, that I might not sin against thee." Parents should also teach their children to know, love, and sing good hymns and choruses with a message. In later years those ingrained truths will come back. The Holy Spirit will be able to draw on this material when confronting the boy, girl, man, or woman with the issues of time and eternity.

(2) A Word about Motives (6:4b) "Bring them up in the nurture [discipline] and admonition [instruction] of the Lord."

Spiritual education of children was a strong emphasis of Old Testament law. Israel was to keep the feast of the Passover, for instance, so children would ask, "What is meant by this feast?" Parents were required to put Bible verses on the doorposts of their homes. Children leaving the shelter of home would be confronted by those verses and would carry the haunting memory of some Word from God into their outside activities. Returning home, the children would again be faced with the verses on the doorposts. The verses would cause the children to think afresh, in the light of God's Word, of where they had been and what they had been doing and saying.

Christian parents have no greater responsibility in life than to make sure that their children are raised in the fear of God, in the knowledge of God, in the knowledge of the gospel, in reverence for God's Word, and in the presence of the Lord Jesus.

Television, that great thief of time and worldly molder of character, needs to be banished or put under severe restraint. In its place, parents must substitute good books, wholesome music, and Christian education—all bathed in godly example and fervent prayer for each child's early conversion and lifelong consecration to the will of God.

Parents neglect these responsibilities to their peril. They will pay a high price indeed if they ignore Ephesians 6:4 and fail to heed this admonition from the Lord.

---

1. See Phillips, *Exploring Genesis* (Neptune, NJ: Loizeaux, 1980).
2. See *Exploring Genesis* for a more detailed discussion of the wondrous way Genesis 22–24 foreshadows God's purpose with His earthly people (the Jews) and His heavenly people (the church).
3. It may well be in this day of much child abuse that God's will would be for an abused child to be placed in a foster home; probably the preference would be the home of a near relative. In Bible times the extended family was much more common than it is today, at least in western society.

D. In His Material Relationships (6:5-9)

1. Men and Their Masters (6:5-8)

a. The Human Master's Claims (6:5-6a)

(1) Be Obedient (6:5a) "Servants, be obedient to them that are your masters according to the flesh."

The Greek word translated "servants" here is usually translated "slave." Slavery was the blight of the age in Roman times. Vast numbers of people—including many members of the early Gentile church—were bought and sold like cattle. These slaves had no civil rights and were subject to the whims of their masters—for better or for worse. They were considered pieces of property of varying value. In danger of the scourge, the cross, or worse, they were held in the iron grip of relentless laws. The slave revolt led by Spartacus only reinforced the resolve of slave owners to keep their whips in hand.

Many slaves were highly skilled. Some were highly educated. Some enjoyed, within limits set by entrenched customs, the friendship of their masters. But all slaves lived with the peril of a change of ownership hanging over their heads. The death of a benevolent master, or his displeasure, could bring a swift change of circumstances.

Often slaves harbored deep resentments. The Holy Spirit, however, told the enslaved Christians to accept their lot in life. The time had not yet come when the shackles could be removed. As slaves they had one supreme social duty: to obey their masters.

Happily the days of slavery are gone from most of the world. Men are no longer bought and sold like so many pieces of furniture. In the workaday world, however, men sell their talents and their time, and the same principles of servanthood apply.

When we accept employment we put our skills at the disposal of our employers for so many hours a day. We expect certain remuneration for performing certain functions. To that extent, our time and talents are not our own. We have bargained them away. Thus our employers have every right to expect that we will be industrious, conscientious, and cooperative.

We live in an age of labor strife, but the Holy Spirit does not make exceptions for us. As Christians we are to be different from other people in the marketplace. We are to be obedient, cheerful, and loyal servants. We are to be the most willing and diligent people on the payroll. We are to do our best and be dutiful, polite, and dependable. That is the law of Christ. Joseph followed this law when he worked for Potipher, when he was in prison, and when he moved into the palace. God expects the same of us. Others may waste their employer's time. Others may perform their tasks in a slovenly way. Others may criticize and complain. But we Christians are to obey our masters. It is God's command.

(2) Be Subservient (6:5b) "With fear and trembling, in singleness of your heart, as unto Christ."

Subservience is not a quality we admire. Obedience yes, but not subservience. We should not have to stand in fear and trembling before anyone but God. The subservience demanded in Ephesians 6:5 is absolute yieldedness to Christ. The Christian employee must be afraid—not afraid of his superiors in the marketplace, but afraid of disobeying his Lord. If he does not show wholehearted respect to his employer, he is disobeying the Lord.

The word *singleness* in Ephesians 6:5 means wholehearted dedication to the task at hand, the determination to give it all diligence and expedition. That kind of dedication sounds like nonsense to many employees today. Today slacking on the job is considered clever, and unions will fight for a man's right to remain on the job no matter how insolent, incompetent, or indifferent he may be. He may be lazy, lie, show up late for work, and disaffect the other workers, but the union will champion him. The union has taken away his fear of man. Often he never did have any fear of God.

I was with friends in a fine restaurant in England some years ago. The waiter first asked if we wanted drinks. We declined, and thereafter we were subjected to the most insolent and careless service I have ever experienced in a restaurant. The waiter was barely civil. He practically threw things on the table and took our orders with sneering contempt. We all noticed his behavior. I said to my brother-in-law, "Should we not complain to the management?"

He replied, "It would do no good. They could not fire him. The union is too strong for that, and the labor laws here are all on his side."

A Christian employee cannot afford to project an image like that waiter. He is to be on the job for Jesus. He should do his work as though the Lord Himself were doing it. He is the only Bible some people will read. He may not fear his boss. He may find it difficult to like his boss and even more difficult to respect him. But ultimately he is not serving his boss. He is serving the Lord, and he should certainly serve Him with singleness of heart.

(3) Be Diligent (6:6a) "Not with eyeservice, as menpleasers."

We are not to do our best only when we are being watched, only when we are looking for human approval, or only when the boss is around. We should disprove that old English proverb: "When the cat's away, the mice will play." The slave was not to do his best only because he was afraid of being whipped, and we should not do good work only because we are afraid of being demoted or fired.

The Christian employee is to be diligent. He is not to call in sick when he is healthy. He is not to waste his boss's time in idle conversation or conduct personal business when he should be working. He is not to drag his feet, pad his break times, arrive late, leave early, or demand that two people do a job he could do alone. Those are the world's ways, not the Christian's.

b.   The Heavenly Master's Claims (6:6b-8)

(1) The Higher Plane (6:6b-7) "As the servants of Christ, doing the will of God from the heart; With good will doing service, as to the Lord, and not to men."

The Lord is always present. We serve Him, not men. All service is on a higher plane for believers. We are in God's will when we do "secular" work, just as much as when we do "sacred" work. The Holy Spirit in Ephesians 6:6-7 abolishes the distinction between those of us in secular employment and those of us in fulltime Christian service. All of us are in the ministry. All of us are in fulltime service—the plumber as much as the preacher, the economist as much as the evangelist, the policeman as much as the pastor, and the miner as much as the missionary.

All these vocations are in God's will, and God's will must be done from the heart. We can serve God out of a sense of *discipline*. Discipline says, "I have to"; it is motivation from a will that has been *compelled*. We can serve God out of a sense of *duty*. Duty says, "I ought to"; it is motivation from a mind that has been *convinced*. Or we can serve God out of a sense of *devotion*. Devotion says, "I want to"; it is motivation from a heart that has been *captured*.

God's will for every employee is that he serve his human master with all his heart—with wholehearted commitment to his employer's gain and advantage. His commitment should be like Joseph's when he served Potipher. The Christian employee should give the kind of selfless service the slave girl gave to Naaman's wife.

When we Christians serve our human masters, we are serving the One who loved us enough to die for us and who gave us an example of service. Mark 10:45 reads, "The Son of man came not to be ministered unto, but to minister, and to give his life a ransom for many." That kind of service took Jesus all the way to Calvary.

(2) The Heavenly Plan (6:8) "Knowing that whatsoever good thing any man doeth, the same shall he receive of the Lord, whether he be bond or free."

What a prospect! We may never receive recognition, reward, promotion, or praise down here, but we will receive it in Heaven. The Lord's payday is not at the end of the week; it is at the end of our lives. Sometimes God rewards us along the way, but these encouragements are only tokens of what is to come. Payday is at the judgment seat of Christ. Our efforts will seem worthwhile when we hear the Lord say, "Well done, thou good and faithful servant" (Matthew 25:21).

In the millennial kingdom we will rule cities, counties, provinces, countries, and continents. In eternity we might well manage worlds and galaxies in God's vast, new empires in space. We are in training for tasks of great honor in eternity as we handle mundane details down here. We may be experiencing scorn and disappointment now, but we will be crowned with glory and honor then.

2. Masters and Their Men (6:9)

a. A Word about Mutual Responsibility (6:9a) "Masters, do the same things."

Just as the master (the employer) is purring with satisfaction at the demands God puts on his slaves (his employees), the Holy Spirit turns all this heavy artillery on him. "You too," He says. "Do the same things. This is a two-way street. You have obligations and responsibilities too."

The employer expects a fair day's work; he must give a fair day's pay. The employer wants the employee to be diligent and promote the best interests of the company; the employer must be diligent and promote the welfare of the employee. Trade unions would never have formed if Ephesians 6:5-9 had been the cornerstone of all employee-management relations.

Trade unions grew out of the "dark Satanic mills" of newly industrialized Europe. The Victorians had their qualms, but largely ignored them in the interests of big business and moneymaking. The invention of joint-stock corporations made it possible for people to grow rich without pangs of conscience. A corporation with limited liability, owned by shareholders scattered up and down the countryside, had no conscience.

Friedrich Engels, seeking material for his book on the proletariat of south Lancashire, described the standing pools of refuse and sickening filth that poisoned the atmosphere of the densely populated valley of the Medlock. He wrote:

> A horde of ragged women and children swarm about, as filthy as the swine that thrive upon the garbage heaps and in the puddles. . . . The race that lives in these ruinous cottages behind broken windows mended with oilskin, sprung doors and rotten doorposts, or in dark wet cellars in measureless filth and stench . . . must really have reached the lowest stage of humanity.

Engels justifiably asked how people who were compelled to live in such pigsties and who were dependent for their water supply on a pestilential stream could live natural lives and bring up children to be anything but savages. What kind of posterity, Engels asked, was England breeding in its feverish search for wealth? The economists of his day gave him no answers. Instead, disease answered. Asiatic cholera in 1831 and typhus in 1837 and 1843 marched out of their strongholds in the industrial towns, defied every effort to halt their spread, and threatened to devastate the entire country.

There were other warnings too. A sullen, savage, and ever-increasing working class was turning against the rest of the nation's traditions and taboos. Smoldering resentment and discontent were building. Class hatred was growing. Marx and Engels began urging workers to unite. Revolution was in the air. Ever-expanding multitudes felt that this world was nothing but a dingy prison. Rebellion, rancor, and indignation were taking root. In such a soil, orators of social revolution and agitators could thrive.

The world's answer to this sick society was communism. God's answer is Christ.

b.   A Word about Managerial Restraint (6:9b-c)

(1) The Abuse of Power (6:9b) "Forbearing threatening."

The use of the whip hand to keep subordinates in line has been the problem with power from the beginning. Love, not force or fear, is the best way to encourage people to work. Force and fear, the weapons most often used by masters and employers, are counter-productive in the end because they breed resentment and rage.

Employers do have the right to use their authority to get things done. There is a legitimate use of power. All society is based on that premise. As long as sin reigns on this earth, laws must be enforced. An employee can be punished or dismissed if his behavior warrants such action. But God forbids browbeating and bullying.

Power has a tendency to erode character. Lord Acton said it well: "Power tends to corrupt, and absolute power corrupts absolutely." Those in power need to watch themselves and be careful not to abuse their power. Giving orders to people feeds the ego and inflates pride. Power is a heady draught. Power intoxicates and calls for more until people with power begin to want power for power's sake.

The almost unlimited power of slave owners led to fearful abuses. The tyranny of the Nazi concentration camps and the horrors of totalitarian governments also warn of where abuse of power leads.

Paul told us to refrain from threatening. It is contrary to Christian character and violates the law of Christ.

(2) The Abuse of Position (6:9c) "Knowing that your Master also is
     in heaven; neither is there respect of persons with him."

God is not impressed with a person's position, but He is keenly interested in what the person does in that position.

There will be abuses of position. Injustices will be done. But there is One who is watching. The Lord has His eye on what is happening, and He has His own way of squaring accounts—sometimes down here, certainly in Heaven. The day is coming when He will right wrongs and review all lives. Master or slave, it will make no difference then.

According to Ephesians 6:9, God will have the last word, and with this verse Paul ended another segment of his letter. He had one more major matter to discuss: the intrusion of the unseen world into the affairs of earth. The last segment of the letter warns Christians to beware of the dark influence that evil spirits exert.

PART IV

The Christian
and His Battles

Ephesians 6:10-20

IV. THE CHRISTIAN AND HIS BATTLES (6:10-20)

A. Assessing the Enemy (6:10-17)

1. A Word of Encouragement (6:10) "Finally, my brethren, be strong in the Lord, and in the power of his might."

As soon as Paul was saved, he threw himself wholeheartedly into the battle. Luke used the word *endunamoo* to describe Paul's activities as a new believer: "Saul increased the more in *strength,* and confounded the Jews which dwelt at Damascus, proving that this is very Christ" (Acts 9:22, italics added). Paul used the passive form of *endunamoo* when he told us to "be strong."

People who have been Christians a long time are not always strong Christians. Some remain weak in faith throughout their lives. And new Christians are not necessarily weak Christians. They may be uninformed Christians for a while, but they do not have to be weak. Being strong in the Lord has nothing to do with how long we have been saved. Our strength is derived from God, not from ourselves. We are to be strong "in the power of his might." We are to be strong in His mighty power, as in Ephesians 1:19 where Paul was referring to the mighty strength that God exhibited when He raised Christ from the dead. God makes that strength available to us.

Paul's introductory reminder to be strong was important because he was about to hurl us into battle against a mighty, tireless, and implacable foe. We must never underestimate the enemy. God doesn't.

2. A Word of Enlightenment (6:11)

a. Our Protection (6:11a) "Put on the whole armour of God."

As Paul wrote this he was chained to a Roman soldier. He had been in the company of soldiers, centurions, and tribunes for years, so he knew all about armor. No doubt his familiarity with Roman armor gave him the idea of using the imagery of Christian armor.

Roman armor was designed to protect the soldier's body from the enemy's weapons. Christian armor is designed to protect the soul. God does not throw us unprotected into the battle against Satan's empire. God has provided all that we need for complete protection of mind, heart, soul, spirit, conscience, and will. But we must put that armor on piece by piece—deliberately, thoughtfully, and intelligently.

b.   Our Protagonist (6:11b) "That ye may be able to stand against the wiles of the devil."

The evil one has many names in Scripture, the most common being *devil* and *Satan* (Revelation 20:2). As the devil, he is the *accuser*—the one who constantly assails us before God. As Satan, he is the *adversary*—the one who opposes God and constantly seeks to prevent us from entering into our birthright as children of God.

The evil one is a defeated foe, as Paul emphasized in Colossians 2:15. We stand, in Christ, on the victory side of the cross. The evil one may rage and roar, but he is powerless before a child of God who is arrayed in the armor of God, filled with the Spirit of God, and strong in the power of His might.

The Greek word translated "wiles" in Ephesians 6:11 is *methodeia*. Paul had already used the word *methodeia* in 4:14 (translated "wiles" in Revised Version). There he told the Ephesians not to be children, not to be swayed by every wind of doctrine and the craftiness of deceitful men. Satan's wiles can be seen in the deceptive strategies of the cultists who have been taught by that old liar, the devil. *Methodeia* only occurs in these two places in the New Testament.

The devil is full of evil tricks. We cannot possibly know them all, but God does. We cannot possibly guard against them all, nor can we overcome them in our own power. But God can. We are predisposed by our fallen nature to listen to Satan's lies. Through deceit he gained a foothold against the human race in the first place (Genesis 3).

The fall of the human race hinged on two pivots: deception and disobedience. Eve was deceived; Adam was disobedient. Satan is unremitting in his efforts to take full advantage of those two beachheads he has established, and with tragic success. Most of the world lies in his lap. We who have been saved are on guard against the enemy, but he still does everything in his power to deceive us and make us disobedient. So God commands us to put on the armor He has provided so that we can stand against Satan's wiles.

3.   A Word of Enablement (6:12-17)

a.   The Arena (6:12)

(1) This Is Not an Ordinary Battle (6:12a) "We wrestle not against flesh and blood."

Our enemies are not people. We must see beyond people. Satan may use people to persecute us, lie to us, cheat us, hurt us, or even kill us. But our real enemy lurks in the shadows of the unseen world, moving people as pawns on the chessboard of time. As long as we see people as enemies and wrestle against them, we will spend our strength in vain. Certainly we see wicked people, hear the evil things they say, and feel the hurts they inflict on us. People are involved, but they are not the real problem. This is not an ordinary battle. We are in a greater arena than the one we can see.

(2) This Is Now an Occult Battle (6:12b-e)

(a) We Wrestle Satan's Crowned Dignities (6:12b) "Against principalities."

Paul listed four distinct Satanic orders against whom we wrestle in our spiritual warfare: principalities, powers, the rulers of this world's darkness, and wicked spirits in high places.

Hosts of spirit beings reside in the unseen world. We cannot see them unless they choose to be seen. In the beginning they were all good and glorious. They came from God's hand, took their place around God's throne, and sang His praises. There were ranks upon ranks of angels and archangels, cherubim and seraphim. At the head of them all—the highest of all created intelligences, the supreme creature in the ranks of the angel throng—was Lucifer, son of the morning, the anointed cherub.

When Lucifer fell, the heavenly hosts divided. Many sons of light fell with Lucifer and were also cast out of Heaven. Satan is now their lord. He is given many impressive titles in the Bible, for although he is a fallen fiend, he is still powerful. Satan is called the god of this world, the prince of this world, and the prince of the power of the air. It was he who deceived Eve and used her to bring about Adam's downfall. Satan was thus able to seize the kingdom of this world to ruin it and to rule it in defiance of the living God.

The Bible does not tell us all we might like to know about the spirit world, but we do know that there are ranks in the angelic orders of Heaven who did not fall. Several angels are specifically named in Scripture. Gabriel, for instance, stands in God's presence and often appears as the herald angel. Michael the archangel is a warrior. He is the field marshal of the armies of Heaven, the defender of the nation of Israel, the one who will ultimately be God's agent to cast Satan down from the heavenlies where he roams today.

Paul mentioned thrones, dominions, principalities, and powers in Colossians 1:16. At Calvary Christ "spoiled" the principalities and powers (Colossians 2:15), which are linked in Ephesians 6:12 with Satan's fallen hosts. The thrones and dominions would seem to be unfallen angels ranking high in the hierarchy of Heaven. In Revelation 4–5 we have a hint as to who "thrones" are. There they are called "elders." They sit in the presence of God and respond to His dealings with men in wonder and worship. Scripture gives no hint as to the place of those called "dominions."

There are also ranks in Satan's spirit realm. At the head of his countless minions are the principalities—princes who share with Satan the power that he wields over other fallen angels, over evil spirits, and over this world. The word Paul used to describe these beings is *archē*, which literally means "beginning" and can be translated "chief ruler" or "magistrate." So principalities are high-ranking, governing authorities who are under Satan's control.

We learn from Daniel 10 that Satan places spirit princes over various kingdoms of men on earth. We read of "the prince of Grecia" and also of "the prince of Persia." The prince of Persia alone was powerful enough to hinder the herald angel and keep him from fulfilling his commission for three weeks. Such crowned dignities of Satan wield enormous power, but they are defeated foes for the Christian. We wrestle against them in prayer and Christian service. They strongly resent any challenge to their terrible hold on the kingdoms of men.

(b)   We Wrestle Satan's Conquering Deputies (6:12c) "Against powers."

The Greek word translated "powers" is *exousia*. It is the usual word for delegated authority, for the liberty and right to exert power.

Satan is powerful, diabolically clever, and tireless, but he is not God. He is a created being and has none of the attributes of deity. He is full of knowledge and cunning, but he is not omniscient. He does not know everything and he makes mistakes. One mistake was to attack Adam and Eve. His biggest mistake was to organize and motivate the crucifixion of Christ.

Satan has enormous power, beyond anything we can conceive. He can give people the ability to perform miracles, for instance, but he is not all-powerful. He is not omnipotent. He can be thwarted and overruled by the power of God.

> Satan trembles when he sees
> The weakest saint upon his knees.
> (William Cowper)

Christ's resurrection is a crowning example of Satan's power being broken.

Satan can move swiftly with the ease and freedom of a spirit unencumbered by a physical body. He can be here one moment, a million miles away the next, but he is not omnipresent. He cannot be everywhere at once. He can only be in one place at a time. We learn in Revelation 2:13 that Satan has a dwelling; that is, he has a throne on earth. In John's day, it was at Pergamos. The very idea of a seat or throne is associated with a single locality. We do not know where Satan has his throne on earth today, but the fact that he has one proclaims the companion truth that he is not omnipresent.

Satan seeks to compensate for his lack of omniscience, omnipotence, and omnipresence by efficiently organizing the countless clever beings who share power with him in the spirit world. Some of these beings are actually called "powers." They wield authority delegated to them by Satan. They gather information, influence events, implement Satan's schemes, inflict woe and bondage on the human race, and laugh at man's blindness in refusing to believe that such evil beings exist.

Modern man is in much the same plight as seventeenth-century man. In 1665 London was in the grip of the great plague. People were dying by the thousands—faster than they could be buried. Corpses were stacked like cordwood outside stricken houses and were carted away to hastily-dug pits on the outskirts of the city. Business came to a halt. Court disbanded. People fled London, taking the disease with them.

Nobody knew the cause of the plague. The most common notion was that the air caused it, so people sealed up their homes to keep contaminated air outside. They burned noxious material in their fireplaces to help drive out the deadly air. They buried their noses in flowers. Out of ignorance, they disregarded the most basic rules of sanitation and hygiene. Open sewers ran down the streets. Rats and vermin multiplied, and their fleas spread the plague. But people were unable to see any link between the unsanitary conditions and the spread of the plague.

If someone were to go back to 1665 and say that the plague was spread by bacteria, the people would not pay attention to him. They would not believe there could be germs so small that they could not be seen with the naked eye or that millions of germs could be found in a drop of ditch water. People knew nothing about germs or viruses. They would have laughed scornfully at anyone who tried to explain the real source of their troubles. Since germs could not be seen, smelled, touched, heard, or tasted, no one suspected that they could have caused the plague.

Likewise, most people today do not believe in evil spirits. Some may be interested in the occult, fascinated with ghosts and witches, and drawn toward what the more erudite call parapsychology. But most scorn the idea that Satan has organized and launched a diabolical plot against the human race. They scoff at the idea that evil spirits, ruthless in their hatred of mankind, are dedicated to keeping people in bondage, sin, and shame.

Why can we not halt the drug trade that is destroying countless lives and damning souls? Why has it been so hard to pass stiff laws against drunk driving? Why has sodomy become acceptable? Why is pornography such big business? Why can we not stamp out child abuse and the legalized slaughter of the unborn in abortion clinics? Why did the horrors of the Nazi prison camps, the Spanish Inquisition, and the Gulag Archipelago take place? Why can we not stop war or ban the deployment of apocalyptic weapons?

The Bible makes the answer clear: the human race is being manipulated by vast numbers of evil spirits who have great power. They encourage lust, greed, hate, fear, selfishness, and pride. People talk about making contact with extraterrestrial beings and speculate as to whether or not intelligent life exists elsewhere. But the human race has already been invaded from outer space and is held in bondage by awesome powers. People in general do not know that; they refuse to believe it when told; and they do not realize they have no hope apart from the gospel of the Lord Jesus Christ.

(c) We Wrestle Satan's Capable Deceivers (6:12d) "Against the rulers of the darkness of this world."

The Greek word *kosmokratōr* only occurs here in Scripture and means "world rulers." The beings that the Holy Spirit is exposing in this phrase are "the world rulers of this darkness."

Satan's master plan for holding the world in subjection can be summed up in a single word: deception. He keeps people in a state of spiritual, philosophical, religious, political, social, and personal blindness. He has invented every false religion and is behind every false philosophy, every false ideology, and every false theory. He keeps people in a state of darkness, and he has a legion of evil spirits whose supreme task is to fasten false ideologies like iron shackles on the souls of men.

Think of the outrageous beliefs that otherwise intelligent people hold in the name of religion. Think of the millions of people who are enslaved in various forms of idolatry. Think of the countless cults that caricature the gospel. Think of the deceptive philosophies such as communism, evolution, and humanism, which control multitudes of people. Where do all these false ideologies come from? Why are they so attractive? How can they recruit people and hold them in fanatical devotion? How can they multiply their adherents? Think of the fanaticism of Islam, the tireless zeal of the Mormons, the world goals the communists pursued, and the spread of soul-destroying, family-destroying, and society-destroying humanism.

Behind all these ideologies is more than the persuasive power of clever leaders. Behind them all are Satan's capable deceivers—the rulers of this world's darkness. Their supreme task is to blind people to the gospel.

Man's natural blindness to his lost condition and to the saving power of the gospel is so great that it takes the fulltime presence of the Holy Spirit to make it possible for any converts to be won at all.

Satan is the unsuspected god of this world. He is not afraid of us, but he is desperately afraid of the Holy Spirit. That is why we can only wage our warfare "in the power of his might" (Ephesians 6:10).

(d) We Wrestle Satan's Countless Demons (6:12e) "Against spiritual wickedness in high places."

We fight against spiritual hosts of wickedness, against wicked spirits in the heavenlies. The unseen world is swarming with demons. One poor man in Jesus' day was in bondage to a legion of them (some six thousand men comprised a Roman legion) and was beyond all human help (Mark 5:1-17). When Jesus came to earth there was an extraordinary outburst of demonic activity. There will be another outburst when the antichrist reigns. (That outburst of demon activity seems to have already begun.)

Satan has countless hordes of demons at his disposal. The word Paul used to describe these demonic hordes is *ponēria*, translated "wickedness" in the King James version of Ephesians 6:12. The decadence and depravity of our age are demon-inspired. Demons seem to be obsessed with holding people enslaved to their senses—to sexual and sensual sins. Perversion, pornography, and permissiveness are encouraged, promoted, and aided by evil spirits whose goal it is to befoul and destroy the human race.

There is considerable speculation about where demons originated. Some theologians think that they are the disembodied spirits of a pre-Adamic race. Craving to be embodied, they possess people and drive them to commit vile sins. The incident of the man possessed by a legion of demons lends credence to this view. When Jesus ordered the demons to come out of the man, those foul and fierce spirits pleaded to be allowed to enter a herd of swine. The swine instantly ran down a steep place into the sea and drowned. They preferred death to demon possession.

We are engaged in a battle with the occult. The moment we try to pray or attempt to do anything for God, these unseen but potent and organized hordes of Satan oppose us.

b.   The Armor (6:13-17)

(1)   A Demand (6:13) "Take unto you the whole armour of God, that ye may be able to withstand in the evil day, and having done all, to stand."

The least we can do is stand. We can take our stand for God, as Martin Luther did when he announced that he was going to the fateful confrontation with Rome at Worms. When facing all the power of earth and Hell, he said: "On this I take my stand. I can do no other. God help me."

We are living in "the evil day." Paul had already reminded the Ephesians that "the days are evil" (Ephesians 5:16). The days were evil then; they are evil today. We are to withstand this evil and, having done all that is possible, we are still to stand. We are to give no ground to Satan.

Perhaps the best commentary on this subject is 2 Samuel 23 where David's mighty men are listed. This review comes at the end of David's reign, just before Solomon's glorious kingdom was established. Chapter 23 is a mirror of the endtimes when at the judgment seat the Lord will review our lives prior to setting up His millennial kingdom. First and foremost in the list of David's men is Adino the Eznite "that sat in the seat, chief among the captains" (23:8). One wonders what Joab thought of that. Abishai and Asahel, brothers of Joab, were also listed, but not Joab. Love and loyalty to the king was the ultimate test, and Joab failed in both of these areas.

Similarly we look in vain for Ahithophel. His son Eliam is listed, but Ahithophel, for all his one-time professed loyalty to David, proved himself a traitor.

Nor do we find the name of Jonathan. He loved David and was loyal up to a point. But in the end he loved this present evil world and died rendering loyalty to the wrong king. He let family come between himself and David.

Much could be said about Adino, true to David in the place of danger. He faced eight hundred men. Much could be said of Eleazar who stood for God in the face of desertion. How revealing is the Holy Spirit's comment that after Eleazar's great victory "the people returned after him only to spoil" (2 Samuel 23:10).

Note what is said of Shammah, who stood for God in the place of discouragement. One might expect to see valor blaze forth in defense of a strategic pass, bridge, or gate. Shammah, however, saw value in "a piece of ground full of lentiles." He stood against the Philistines and fought over that ground. Look at how the Holy Spirit records his victory: "The people fled from the Philistines. But he stood . . . and the Lord wrought a great victory" (2 Samuel 23:11-12).

Like Shammah, we are to stand firm against the enemy. We are to stand fast against the manipulation of human life and society by principalities, powers, rulers of this world's darkness, and wicked spirits in high places. They are all the more dangerous because they are invisible.

Taking a stand may mean doing what some have already done— rolling up their sleeves and becoming active in the messy fight against perversion, pornography, abortion, drugs, alcohol, vice, error, and organized crime. Thank God for such men. Pray for them. Support them. They are fighting against the unseen spirit powers who exploit fallen human nature, fan human passions, inflame human lusts, and encourage human errors. God demands that we too "withstand in the evil day, and having done all, to stand."

(2) A Description (6:14-17)

(a) Provisions for Our Security in the Battle (6:14-17a)

i.   Protection for What We Sow (6:14a) "Stand therefore, having your loins girt about with truth."

The Roman soldier's belt or girdle held in place the armor that protected the lower part of his body—the seat of vital organs and the organs of life-creating force. We need truth's protection at the source of spiritual procreative power so that Satan cannot tamper with what we sow. Truth is vital.

We must be sure that the seed we sow is the truth of God. Often we say, "Thus saith the Lord," when we do not communicate His truth. We just express our own opinions, or we misrepresent truth because of our failure to understand it. How often have we heard well-meaning preachers proclaim erroneous teachings with all their hearts? Such men seek to persuade people to do this or experience that, but they are teaching error. Preachers and Bible teachers need to have their loins girt about with truth. They must master the principles of hermeneutics, study the Scriptures in depth, know the mind of the Lord, and be filled with the Spirit of truth. Otherwise, they may teach as God's truth what is not God's truth at all.

We all must be careful with what we sow because "that which is born of the flesh is flesh" (John 3:6). Nowhere is Satan more active than where we sow. That is why truth is the first piece of armor we must put on. The devil is the father of lies; deception is his business. He wants us to sow error sugar-coated with truth. We must be absolutely sure before God that we are wearing the truth, the whole truth, and nothing but the truth. We must not preach opinions; we must preach God's truth. We must sow His truth. Sincerity is not enough; we must also be right.

ii.   Protection for What We Show (6:14b) "The breastplate of righteousness."

The Roman soldier's breastplate protected his upper vital organs, particularly the lungs and heart. Proverbs 4:23 urges us to protect our hearts: "Keep thy heart with all diligence; for out of it are the issues of life." Matthew 15:18-19 says: "Those things which proceed out of the mouth come forth from the heart; and they defile the man. For out of the heart proceed evil thoughts, murders, adulteries, fornications, thefts, false witness, blasphemies." Satan tries to corrupt the hearts of believers so that they will display ugly passions instead of the love of Christ. Righteousness must be the guardian of our hearts.

The Greek word translated "righteousness" in Ephesians 6:14, *dikaiosunē*, occurs ninety-two times in the New Testament (including thirty times in the book of Romans). Paul's first use of *dikaiosunē* in Romans is instructive. He told us in Romans 1 that he was not ashamed of the gospel of Christ, for "therein is the righteousness of God revealed" (1:17). The theme of Romans is righteousness. Paul spoke of righteousness *revealed* (1:17), righteousness *required* (1:18; 3:10-16), righteousness *received* (4:5), and righteousness *reproduced* (6:12-23).

The Epistle to the Romans teaches us that God is righteous—He always does what is right. He does what He does because He is who He is. He does what is right because it is impossible for Him to do anything wrong. He makes no mistakes. He is not swayed by fear or favor.

Just as God does what He does because of who He is, we do what we do because of who we are. Since we are sinners by birth, by nature, by practice, and by choice, we do what is unrighteous and wrong. Sin has tainted even our most noble thoughts, our most generous deeds, and our highest aspirations.

The genius of the gospel is that God does not ask us to imitate His righteousness, for no human being could possibly do that. Instead God gives us His righteous nature by means of regeneration. He gives us His Holy Spirit to live within us and to reproduce Christ's righteousness in us and through us. Christians are to show the righteousness of God to the world. The world is waiting to see men and women behaving like Jesus.

Satan attacks the heart, so we need this breastplate. The righteousness of Christ is glorious armor for us to wear in a world of sin. When people look at us, what should catch their eyes first is the gleaming glory of Christ's righteousness. Satan has already assailed the righteousness of Christ with all the resources at his disposal and found it impenetrable. It will protect our hearts—the innermost springs of our beings—from all the unrighteousness so evident in this fallen world.

iii. Protection for Where We Go (6:15) "Your feet shod with the preparation of the gospel of peace."

We should be prepared to go, but there are some places where Christians must not go. There are some doors we must never darken unless we are encased in God's armor and our feet are protected by the gospel of peace. We should only go to these places when we are sent to save. The temptations are too great otherwise.

Everywhere we do go, we should be soldiers of the King, ambassadors for Christ. We have our marching orders in Matthew 28:19-20:

> Go ye therefore, and teach all nations, baptizing them in the name of the Father, and of the Son, and of the Holy Ghost: Teaching them to observe all things whatsoever I have commanded you: and, lo, I am with you alway, even unto the end of the world.

Millions of people still do not have even a text or two of Scripture. Lost men and women everywhere are held in the iron grip of Satan and his hosts. Surely there is someone to whom we can go with the gospel.

The oft-forgotten word in Ephesians 6:15 is *preparation*. We need to be prepared. Usually we shrink back from Christian service because we are not prepared. We should make an effort to master Scripture and learn the skills of soulwinning. Jesus spent over three years training the twelve apostles. Paul invariably had an entourage of young men he was training to become evangelists, pastors, teachers, missionaries, church planters, and soul-winners.

A man does not become a craftsman overnight. He has to learn the secrets of the trade and how to use the tools of the trade. He has to learn to read blueprints, measure accurately, and cut and join precisely. Likewise, one does not become a great Bible expositor overnight. One does not master principles of hermeneutics and homiletics in a day. One does not grasp the scope of Scripture in a week or two. Each of us needs to serve an apprenticeship, attend God's school, learn by doing, and be attentive to the Holy Spirit.

We must be prepared, and then we must be prepared to go. Where? Wherever God sends us—home or abroad. He may send us to our own family, neighbors, and friends. He may send us to a high-profile ministry or to some kind of service behind the scenes. He may send us to a delightful ministry or a dangerous ministry. Wherever God sends, we must go with our feet shod with the preparation of the gospel of peace.

iv.   Protection for What We Do (6:16) "Above all, taking the shield of faith, wherewith ye shall be able to quench all the fiery darts of the wicked."

Paul had often seen the shields Roman soldiers carried into war. The shields were made so that a row of soldiers could lock shield to shield, forming a wall of iron. Such a wall would be difficult, if not impossible, for a foe to penetrate. Each individual shield was big enough to cover the soldier's whole body. Darts and arrows hurled at the soldier hit the shield and fell harmlessly to the ground.

The wicked one (for that is the force of the words "the wicked" in Ephesians 6:16) throws many fiery darts. He has been studying human nature ever since man was created. Satan helped forge fallen human nature. He is a master psychologist. One person he assails with lusts of the flesh. He has a whole arsenal of darts that can set the senses aflame. Another person he assails with lusts of the eye; someone else with the pride of life. The lust of appetite, the love of applause, and the lure of ambition are among the host of darts Satan uses to kindle fierce fires in our souls. He knows our weaknesses and strengths. He sends his legions of evil spirits to titillate our senses, inflame our desires, corrupt our souls, weaken our wills, deceive our minds, deaden our consciences, and distort God's truth.

Satan has a thousand wiles and he never gives up. If you success-fully resist him now, he will come again later. Perhaps he will tempt you with something in a book or on television, a clever remark by a college professor, or a friend's snub or sneer. Perhaps he will arouse a sleeping lust or put an utterly lewd or corrupt thought in your mind. Perhaps he will entice you with a brilliant and seemingly flawless philosophy. (Everyone should read C. S. Lewis' classic on temptation, *The Screwtape Letters,* and his brilliant passage on temp-tation in *Perelandra.*)

We will never be out of range of Satan's fiery darts, but they can be quenched and rendered harmless by the shield of faith (literally, the faith). Satan's fiery darts cannot penetrate the shield of deter-mined, living, dynamic faith in God. That is why Satan designed the original temptation in Eden to persuade our first parents that God was not to be trusted.

The first temptation in the garden of Eden questioned *the goodness of God.* "Yea, hath God said, Ye shall not eat of every tree of the garden?" (Genesis 3:1) The implication was that the limitation was unkind; God was unkind in refusing to allow man to have something that he wanted.

The second temptation questioned *the government of God.* "Ye shall not surely die" (Genesis 3:4). Satan planted the idea that disobedi-ence to God was not really a serious matter, that it would not have the adverse result that God had said it would.

The third temptation questioned *the goals of God.* "God doth know that in the day ye eat thereof, then your eyes shall be opened, and ye shall be as gods, knowing good and evil" (Genesis 3:5). This most terrible slander of all suggested that God was selfish and jealous, that He was deliberately refusing to allow man to attain full maturity.

In this struggle in the garden of Eden, Eve threw away the only weapon she had: the Word of God. The result? She was deceived, lost her faith in God, and was pierced by Satan's fiery darts. Adam followed her into sin. His sin was more deliberate—downright disobedience—but its root was the same unbelief. He saw his beloved wife in her fallen condition and, instead of trusting God to work out her salvation, he deliberately followed her into sin. He too questioned the goodness of God, the government of God, and the goals of God.

Satan presented the same temptations to the Lord Jesus—the second man, the last Adam—in the wilderness. Satan said, "If thou be the Son of God, command that these stones be made bread"

(Matthew 4:3). The Lord had been on a forty-day fast, so He was desperately hungry. Satan was suggesting that God the Father was withholding an entitlement from Jesus and that He should take matters into His own hands and use the power inherent in His sonship to change His God-given circumstances. Satan was challenging the *goodness of God.*

The second temptation followed the same pattern. Having taken the Lord to a pinnacle of the temple, Satan urged, "Cast thyself down: for it is written, He shall give his angels charge concerning thee" (Matthew 4:6). Satan tempted Jesus to question and challenge *the government of God.* Satan was saying, "Cast Yourself down. You will not die. God would not let that happen to You. To put God to the test is no serious matter."

The third temptation, in keeping with the others, challenged *the goals of God.* Satan showed the Lord all the kingdoms of the world and offered them to Him—on Satanic terms. Satan was slanderously insinuating that God was jealous and selfishly keeping Jesus from kingdoms that were rightfully His.

The shield of faith rebuffed Satan at every point and quenched his fiery darts. To each tempting suggestion, Jesus replied with a verse of Scripture. He simply fell back on the Word of God and thereby demonstrated His unequivocal faith in God.

Our faith in God should be so alive and robust that we never question the circumstances in which we find ourselves, the limitations He has placed on us, or His right to dictate the terms of our lives. We never question the goodness of God. We never doubt His government. Because of our faith we shrink from sin because it offends Him, grieves His heart, and inevitably brings into our lives the consequences He says it will. We never question God's goals either. If He has not yet brought us into the kingdom, we believe that one day He will. The place, the process, and the time period are all in His purposes. Such faith effectively quenches Satan's darts.

v.   Protection for What We Know (6:17a) "The helmet of salvation."

Soldiers wore helmets because a blow to the head could be fatal. The head is the site of a person's intellectual powers, the faculty that sets him apart from the beasts—in his origin, his development, and his potential. Only a human being can think and express thoughts in an organized, verbal, and articulate way. Only a human being can state his thoughts in terms of music or mathematics, physics or philosophy, anthropology or astronomy. The head has to be protected at all costs.

God gives us a helmet to protect our thoughts from Satanic influence and interference. Satan usually goes after the mind. Paul told his friends at Corinth that "the god of this world hath blinded the minds of them which believe not" (2 Corinthians 4:4). The protection God gives us from Satan's deceptions, denials, and distortions is the helmet of salvation. Without this protection, our thinking—brilliant as it may be—is open to the damning influence of Satan's rulers of darkness.

Apart from God's salvation, man cannot reach correct conclusions about psychological, social, philosophical, and spiritual phenomena. He can orbit spacecraft and journey to the moon. He can split atoms and tinker with the genetic code. But sin impairs his thinking about his relationship to God and his fellows. His first sin separated him from God. His second sin separated him from man. Satan tries to ensure that he is kept in bondage and blindness in both relationships.

Satan's lies are diabolically clever. Under the influence of demonic insinuation and suggestion, man deliberately sets aside divine revelation in favor of human reasoning. Satan's deceptions appeal to the unregenerate mind. They seem to make lots of sense and they appeal to human pride. To the unsaved, the theory of evolution is more plausible than the story of creation. Communism used to seem much more practical than Christianity (especially Christianity as distorted and disseminated by Satan's dupes). A creed demanding works seems more logical than the cross. Humanism is more attractive than holiness. Psychology seems more reasonable than salvation. Satan never gives up his attacks on thought processes.

Satan would like to undermine our belief in the Bible as the inspired, inerrant, and infallible Word of God. He would like to distort our doctrines so that we base our beliefs on erroneous or inadequate hermeneutical processes. He would like us to think wrong thoughts about God the Father, the Holy Spirit, and the Lord Jesus. He would like us to be mistaken about the plan of salvation and the daily practice of Christianity. He would like us to espouse cultish absurdities. He would like us to dilute God's demands that we be like Jesus—that we be holy, loving, joyous, peaceful, patient, kind, and self-controlled. He would like us to emphasize service at the expense of worship. He would like us to be occupied with the cares of this world and the deceitfulness of riches so that we lose sight of the world to come. He would like us to lower our standards and allow the world to pour us into its mold, or go to the other extreme and mistake isolation for separation. Satan has ten thousand wiles—all aimed at influencing what we think.

God's protection for us against all these attacks on the mind is the helmet of salvation. God's salvation must encompass what we think. Paul's Epistle to the Romans gives the most complete exposition of that salvation, so Romans is one book we should master—that is, we should put it on. Actually we need to explore the whole Bible, so that our understanding of the salvation God has provided for us will be comprehensive.

As we put on the helmet of salvation and learn to appreciate its worth, we will use it to test all our thoughts. For instance, the thought that a certain movie would be good to watch or a certain book would be good to read may enter your mind. Before you translate that thought into action, you will test it with the helmet of salvation. Would watching that movie or reading that book be consistent with living a holy life, with becoming more like Jesus? Would the philosophies and ideas presented win the approval of God? We have to see or read some things in order to be stirred to holy indignation and wrath. We need to hear some arguments so that we can study them and refute them. But these subjects must be allowed to occupy our minds only with the Holy Spirit's approval.

We must always remember that the mind is Satan's domain. He goes after the mind to influence our thoughts, words, and deeds. God goes deeper; He goes after the heart. Because our minds are vulnerable, they must be protected by God's salvation. The more we wear the helmet of salvation, the more we will think about the things of God, fill our minds and memories with God's Word, and dwell on the enormous cost of our salvation and its ramifications in our lives. Therefore, the more we wear the helmet, the more we will be protected against Satan's lures and lies.

(b) Provisions for Our Success in the Battle (6:17b) "The sword of the Spirit, which is the word of God."

So far each piece of armor that the Holy Spirit has named has been for defense, not offense. Now He names the Sword that enables us to attack the enemy. Napoleon once said, "The best form of defense is attack." Neither principalities, nor powers, nor the rulers of the world's darkness, nor wicked spirits in high places, nor Satan himself, can withstand the Sword of the Spirit, which is the Word of God. The powers of earth and Hell have no defense against it.

God's Word is like a sword. Hebrews 4:12 says that it is "quick [living], and powerful, and sharper than any twoedged sword, piercing even to the dividing asunder of soul and spirit, and of the joints and marrow, and is a discerner of the thoughts and intents of the heart."

The best answer to secular humanism is the Word of God. The best answer to dialectical materialism is the Word of God. The best answer to behavioral psychology, liberal theology, cults, and false religions is the Word of God.

Because the Word of God is the Sword of the *Spirit,* it cuts through all Satan's ranks, deceptions, and devices. The devil is no match for the Holy Spirit. God's Word is the breath of God. It is the Holy Spirit's creation and partakes of His life. It is alive with His authority.

We should wield the Sword of the Spirit when we pray because it will cut through Satan's hindering hosts. We should quote it when we preach because our power does not lie in words of man's wisdom, but in words the Holy Spirit supplies. We should use the Sword of the Spirit when we face our problems, our circumstances, our needs, our temptations.

The same "almighty word / Chaos and darkness heard, / And took their flight" in the dawn of creation.[1] The word of God spoke worlds into being. The word of God rang from the lips of Jesus in magnificent authority when He cast out evil spirits, cleansed loathsome lepers, and raised the dead. The Word of God is God-breathed. The same breath made man a living soul and quickens his spirit.

Are you downhearted? The prophet said, "Thy words were found, and I did eat them; and thy word was unto me the joy and rejoicing of mine heart" (Jeremiah 15:16). Are you perplexed? The psalmist said, "Thy word is a lamp unto my feet, and a light unto my path" (Psalm 119:105). Are you tempted? The Holy Spirit says, "Wherewithal shall a young man cleanse his way? by taking heed thereto according to thy word" (Psalm 119:9). Are you in trying circumstances? Jesus quoted Deuteronomy 8:3 to the devil when He was famished with hunger: "Man shall not live by bread alone, but by every word . . . of God" (Matthew 4:4). Do you find it hard to pray? Ephesians 6:17 says, "Take . . . the sword of the Spirit, which is the word of God."

Our armor is complete. We are ready to wage war, and the next verse tells us how.

---

1. Quotation is from a hymn by John Marriott.

B.   Assailing the Enemy (6:18-20)

1.   Warring (6:18a) "Praying always with all prayer and supplication in the Spirit."

The Greek word translated "prayer" here is *proseuche*. This word is restricted in the New Testament to mean prayer to God, and it takes cognizance of God's power and sufficiency. *Proseuche* also gives prominence to the devotional side of prayer. No wonder Satan feels threatened whenever a believer prays. It is not the weak and stammering believer he fears, nor the wandering and inadequate prayer he makes. The fact that a child of God is appealing to the almighty Father is what causes Satan to fear.

Satan does not fear eloquence in prayer either. He does not fear perseverance. (Quite often prayer is the most spasmodic and disjointed of our activities.) He does not fear our understanding of the way prayer works. No, he fears the simple fact that a needy child of God is at the mighty throne of God. Satan harnesses all his minions to bar the way to the throne of God. But no demon, no angel-prince, no fallen angel can face the Spirit's flaming Sword. The Word of God clears the way to the throne of God for the child of God.

When we pray we enter three realms. First we enter *the hidden place* where we are alone with God. It may be a bedroom, a barn, a cathedral, or a car. It can be a busy street or a bus seat. The place doesn't matter, as long as we can withdraw from the restless world around us and lift our hearts to God. Jesus recommended a "closet"—a quiet place (Matthew 6:6). He often sought mountain solitudes, a garden, or the wilderness. In the hidden place, all else is shut out and we are shut in with God.

The second realm is *the heavenly place*, the sphere mentioned in Ephesians where our blessings and battles are. In the "heavenlies" evil spirits swarm to hinder, harass, distract, and discourage. This is where we need the whole armor of God. This is where we need the Spirit's mighty Sword. This is where prayer is a battle.

In prayer we battle wandering thoughts. My prayer for Aunt Susie reminds me of her cat. Thoughts of the cat remind me that Jim said there was a mouse in his office. That reminds me to get a mousetrap at the hardware store. The hardware store reminds me of the camera shop next-door and the roll of film I took in to be developed, and so on. Several minutes later I realize that I haven't been praying; I have been daydreaming. The enemy has been busy.

We also battle wicked thoughts when we pray. These come unbidden with startling suddenness. I think of a phrase from a book I should never have read, a scene from a movie I should never have watched, a voice from the past saying foul words or blaspheming. The enemy has been busy again. From the subconscious mind he dredges up filth that is lying stagnant and rotten on the ocean floor of the soul.

We battle worldly thoughts too. Our prayers focus on material things—the need to pass next week's exam, the urgent need for a raise in pay or a better job, the need for healing. It's not wrong to pray for material things, but we should not be preoccupied with them. When other tactics fail, the enemy tries to hinder our prayers by calling our attention to the concerns of time and sense. Paul's prayers barely touch on such concerns. "Give us this day our daily bread" (Matthew 6:11) is the only line in the Lord's prayer that is not otherworldly.

What can we do to win the battle? We can try praying aloud. We can try using more of God's Word in prayer. We can recognize the source of these distractions and put the enemy to rout with the Sword of the Spirit.

The third realm is *the holy place.* At last we find ourselves inside the veil. As Cleland B. McAfee put it:

> There is a place of quiet rest,
> Near to the heart of God,
> A place where sin cannot molest,
> Near to the heart of God.

There we engage in what Paul called in Ephesians 6:18 "all prayer"—prayer in all its aspects. We are absorbed in confession, adoration, petition, intercession, thanksgiving, and praise. Paul specifically mentioned the aspect of supplication. The Greek word translated "supplication" is *deesis,* which suggests a petition for a specific personal need. Such a petition would be made with the awareness of God's ability to supply that need.

There is nothing wrong with supplicating the throne for our needs, especially our spiritual needs (although "all prayer" has a much broader scope). We must not be superficially pious and ignore our needs. God's truth is wonderfully balanced. Often God allows us to have needs so that we will be moved to pray about them.

All prayer and supplication, to be effective, must be "in the Spirit." Otherwise we will not really be praying; we will merely be saying prayers. Prayer is the most purely spiritual exercise in which we can engage. Praying in the Spirit does not mean going into a trance or speaking an ecstatic utterance. The Holy Spirit does not overpower our mental faculties. He directs, but He does not dominate. He never acts despotically. "The spirits of the prophets are subject to the prophets" (1 Corinthians 14:32).

The direction of the Holy Spirit is the ultimate solution to wandering, wicked, and worldly thoughts. He gently inclines our thoughts through channels He has in mind. He brings to our minds those passages of Scripture that are most appropriate to the moment. He brings to us the gentle assurance that our prayers are heard and that He controls all the factors of space and time that are involved in the answers to our prayers.

Meeting up with the Holy Spirit, the ranks of the enemy melt away as smoke dissipates in the wind. They flee in terror, for they are desperately afraid of the Holy Spirit of God.

2.   Watching (6:18b) "Watching thereunto with all perseverance and supplication for all saints."

The Greek word *agrupneō,* translated "watching" here, literally means "lying sleepless." Many of us know firsthand what that's like. The Lord used the same word when He spoke of His coming: "Take ye heed, watch and pray: for ye know not when the time is" (Mark 13:33). In His discourse on the endtimes Jesus said, "Watch ye therefore, and pray always, that ye may be accounted worthy to escape all these things that shall come to pass" (Luke 21:36). *Agrupneō* is also used to describe the work of an elder: "Obey them that have the rule over you, and submit yourselves: for they watch for your souls, as they that must give account" (Hebrews 13:17).

We are to "lie sleepless," watching and praying. Watching sights the enemy; praying fights the enemy. Spiritual warfare is serious business. The enemy is real. He seeks to harm us and our loved ones. He wants to destroy our testimonies and hinder the work of God. We take the battle all too lightly. We would do well to have some sleepless nights over the state of our country, the woes of the world, the condition of our churches, the needs of family and friends, and our own spiritual lives.

Paul told us to persevere in our watching. We give up too soon, but Satan never gives up. He is tireless, persistent, resourceful, and desperate to delay his doom as long as possible and do as much damage as he can in the meantime. When God sends sleepless nights, let us pray. Let us seize insomnia as a gift from God so that "with all perseverance and supplication for all saints" we can turn the quiet night hours into golden moments of communion with God.

3.   Witnessing (6:19-20)

a.   Sharing in a Brother's Opportunity (6:19) "And for me, that utterance may be given unto me, that I may open my mouth boldly, to make known the mystery of the gospel."

This is an example of how to employ supplication as a means of smiting the enemy. We can offer supplication for brothers near or far away. Prayer *annihilates distance.* Paul was under arrest in Rome and his readers were scattered throughout Asia Minor, but prayer takes no account of distance.

Prayer *annihilates dread.* Paul was chained to a guard, charged with treason, and expecting to be arraigned before Nero. Yet the prayers of God's people could help him overcome his fears and cautiousness and enable him to speak boldly.

Prayer *annihilates difficulty.* There are inherent difficulties in communicating the "mystery" of the gospel. Paul wanted to proclaim this mystery, and man's dullness of hearing and his inability to comprehend had to be overcome. That, Paul knew, was the work of the Holy Spirit, but before the Spirit of God could do His work, the human messenger needed his mind to be flooded with divine light and his tongue to be touched with God's eloquence. Paul also needed hearers whose ears and hearts had been made receptive. These needs could be met through prayer.

Paul realized that his situation in Rome was a golden opportunity. He could win members of the imperial guard to Christ and make converts in caesar's household. Possibly he would have the privilege of witnessing to Nero and members of the Roman court. There were Christians and churches all over Rome that he could encourage to be bold by being bold himself.

Paul asked his brothers in Christ to share in his opportunities by means of prayer. Their prayers could strengthen his spirit and batter the unseen enemy. Their prayers could smite the foe, render him powerless to hinder the witness, and break his hold on the minds, hearts, wills, and consciences of those Paul was seeking to win for Christ. His brothers could share in Paul's witnessing, even though some of them were hundreds of miles away. Distance, a purely human factor, means nothing to God.

b.   Sharing in a Brother's Opposition (6:20) "I am an ambassador in bonds: that therein I may speak boldly, as I ought to speak."

One of the most important officials in the Roman world was the imperial legate. As one of the emperor's personal representatives, a legate lived in an outpost of the empire and enforced imperial policy. He was directly accountable to the emperor, and lesser officials were responsible to the legate. He was an ambassador. The word translated "ambassador" in Ephesians 6:20 is *presbeuō,* which means "the emperor's legate."

Paul was Christ's legate. As Christ's ambassador Paul had already magnificently represented the throne of Heaven in province after province and city after city throughout the empire. In Athens, Antioch, Paphos, Philippi, Corinth, and Crete, God had used Paul to shake Satan's kingdom to its very foundations. Now Satan had him in chains, but Paul was dauntless. He was still Christ's ambassador; Satan could not change that. Paul was an ambassador in bonds.

Every time Paul moved his arm, his chain rattled, making him aware of the enemy's opposition. Through prayer his fellow believers could help him face that opposition to the gospel. They could help bear his chains. They could lighten his load and buoy up his spirits.

We do not understand how prayer works. How a brother praying for me in southern California can lift my spirits as I minister in northern Canada is beyond my understanding. How my prayers in Chicago can bring a fresh surge of victory to a believer in China, I cannot say. You and I only know that when God considers all the aspects of a situation and all the forces that govern the universe, prayer is one of the key factors He takes into account. We know prayer works because God says it does.

PART V

Conclusion
Ephesians 6:21-24

V. CONCLUSION (6:21-24)

A. Paul's Fellow Worker (6:21-22)

1. His Titles (6:21a) "That ye also may know my affairs, and how I do, Tychicus, a beloved brother and faithful minister in the Lord."

Intelligent prayer is based on information. It is hard to pray in the abstract. Tychicus brought information about Paul to the Christians at Ephesus who were praying for him.

Tychicus is mentioned in the companion letter to the Colossians. He was a native of Asia Minor (Acts 20:4) and possibly of Ephesus. He and Onesimus carried the Epistle to the Ephesians, the Epistle to the Colossians, and possibly a letter to the Laodiceans (Colossians 4:16) to the churches of Asia. Tychicus was one of the men chosen to accompany Paul when he took a financial gift from the Gentile churches to Jerusalem. On occasion Paul used Tychicus as a messenger (2 Timothy 4:12; Titus 3:12).

Paul called Tychicus "a beloved brother." The family of God makes brothers and sisters of all who love the Lord. Some become *beloved* brothers, often nearer to us than our natural siblings. Tychicus had the privilege of being a beloved brother to the great apostle Paul.

Tychicus was also a "faithful minister." The word translated "minister" in Ephesians 6:21, *diakonos,* means "an active servant." Tychicus was willing to devote himself to the service of God; he was a helper to Paul and an active worker for the cause of Christ. Paul had chains on his arms; Tychicus had them on his heart. His sole ambition was to be useful in relieving Paul's restrictions and furthering the kingdom of God. People like Tychicus are invaluable in the Lord's work. *A beloved brother* and *a faithful minister* are titles of nobility in the kingdom of God. We should covet them for ourselves.

2. His Task (6:21b-22)

(a) To Minister Tidings to Them (6:21b-22a) "Shall make known to you all things: Whom I have sent unto you for the same purpose, that ye might know our affairs."

Tychicus would bring information about Paul's health, for instance. Paul was not a well man. He had not completely recovered from the ill-treatment and maulings he had suffered in championing the cause of Christ.

There would also be information about Paul's finances. Paul had no regular income as far as we know. He lived by faith. God's people helped him. Although Paul never mentioned his financial needs, he did say on one occasion that he had learned how to have plenty and how to do without.

The Christians at Ephesus were probably wondering whether Paul had prospects of a speedy or late trial. Tychicus would be able to bring the saints up to date on the details of Paul's approaching legal battle. The mills of justice were evidently moving slowly.

Tychicus would also report on Paul's psychological condition. In Scripture Paul nearly always appears as a victorious Christian, on top of his circumstances. But 2 Corinthians implies that he experienced depression too.

There would be stories about soldiers won to Christ, news of Paul's latest Epistles, a description of the house where Paul lived, the remarkable account of a vital Christian ministry being carried on despite chains, tales of visitors coming to Rome from all over the world. Tychicus would have to relay all this information. It would be grist for the mill of prayer.

(b) To Minister Tenderness to Them (6:22b) "That he might comfort your hearts."

Paul did not forget for a moment the tender love of so many in the Ephesian church. He remembered his last farewell to the Ephesian elders at Miletus when "they all wept sore, and fell on Paul's neck, and kissed him, Sorrowing most of all for the words which he spake, that they should see his face no more" (Acts 20:37-38). Tychicus would bring them comforting news because Paul was optimistic about the outcome of his impending trial.

Paul had a feeling that his work was not yet done, and he had ambitious plans to evangelize the rest of the world, starting with Spain. Beyond Spain were Huns, Goths, and Vandals to be reached with the gospel. Yonder too were the islands of Britain. Even if his optimism were unfounded and he should be executed, Paul was anticipating a triumphant exodus. He was not afraid of death.

Although Paul was separated from the Ephesians by miles and circumstances, he harnessed himself in the whole armor of God and sallied forth to do battle on their behalf daily. He loved them all. The proof was a letter ablaze with the love that many waters cannot quench—an Epistle for them that was God-breathed and deathless as God's throne.

B. Paul's Final Word (6:23-24) "Peace be to the brethren, and love with faith, from God the Father and the Lord Jesus Christ. Grace be with all them that love our Lord Jesus Christ in sincerity. Amen."

Peace—the Hebrew salutation. *Grace*—the Gentile salutation. *Love with faith*—the Christian salutation.

Peace! Grace! Love! Faith! These words will ring on the chimes of time until at last earth's shores recede and we stand amid the scenes of glory and lay our armor down . . . until grace gives way to glory . . . until faith gives way to sight . . . until love's vast ocean fills all horizons and bathes our souls in bliss.

"Peace be to the brethren." In this world we are in a battle. Satan's dogs of war will bark at our heels and hound us right down to the river. But we are not at war with the brethren. We may not agree with some of our brothers and sisters in Christ. We may dislike and dispute some of their doctrines, but we are not at war with them. If we are, we are fighting the wrong battle.

"Love with faith." Love is the source and faith is the force. Love reaches down; faith reaches up. Love is the alpha and omega, the beginning and the end; faith lies in between. Love reaches out the hand of God; faith takes hold of it. Love provides all we need; faith appropriates it.

"Grace." Thus Paul began this letter (Ephesians 1:2). Thus he ended it. It is God's unmerited, unlimited favor that shines upon us all the time along all the way. It is grace that set our feet on the highway to Heaven. It is grace that keeps us company all the journey through. It is grace that will see us safely home at last.

Peace, love, faith, and grace come from God the Father and the Lord Jesus Christ, who are coeternal and coequal. How wonderful that God, in the supreme and crowning revelation of Himself, is a Father. Here Paul did not emphasize God as Judge, though He is a Judge; nor did he emphasize God as the Creator, though He is the Creator; nor did he emphasize God as a holy God, though He is holy beyond all we could imagine. Instead, he emphasized that wonderful word *Father!* God is the Father, made known to us as such by the Son, *"the* Lord Jesus Christ" (Ephesians 6:23, italics added), who is *"our* Lord Jesus Christ" (6:24, italics added).

Paul added a safeguard to his benediction. Our love for Christ is not to be sentimental. It is wrong to use sentimental terms of endearment such as "dear Jesus" when addressing our Lord. In His title *Lord Jesus Christ,* the human name *Jesus* is flanked by titles of dignity and power. He is Master and Mediator, Lord and Christ. Paul emphasized the dignity of the title in his last word: "Grace be with all them that love our Lord Jesus Christ in *sincerity*" (italics added). Sincerity, not sentiment, should characterize our love.

The word translated "sincerity" in Ephesians 6:24 is *aphtharsia,* which literally means "without corruption." Our love should be incorruptible. It should be a deathless unfading love that takes on the nature of immortality (see 1 Corinthians 15:42). With his final word, Paul left us face to face with our Lord Jesus Christ, contemplating a love relationship that reaches into eternity.